# ELDERLY PUNJABIS IN INDIAN DIASPORA

# ELDERLY PUNJABIS IN INDIAN DIASPORA: A COMPARATIVE STUDY OF PUNJAB AND UK

Rahul Kumar

KALPAZ

First Published, 2019

*Published by*

Kalpaz Publications
C-30, Satyawati Nagar,
Delhi – 110052
Ph.: 011-47034999, 9811692060
www.kalpazpublications.com
E-mail: kalpaz@hotmail.com

*Printed at:* G. Print Process, Delhi

**Cataloging in Publication Data—DK**
Courtesy: D.K. Agencies (P) Ltd. <docinfo@dkagencies.com>

**Kumar, Rahul,** *Dr.*, **author.**
Elderly Punjabis in Indian Diaspora: A Comparative Study of Punjab and UK / Dr. Rahul Kumar.
pages cm
Includes bibliographical references.
ISBN 9789353240776

1. Panjabis (South Asian people)—England—Migrations. 2. Older people—Services for—India—Punjab. 3. Older people—Services for—England. 4. Well-being—India—Punjab. 5. Well-being—England. 6. India—Emigration and immigration. 7. England—Emigration and immigration. I. Title.

LCC DS432.P232K86 2019 | DDC 304.842054552 23

*Dedicated*

*to*

*My Parents*

# Contents

# Foreword

Diaspora studies have now acquired an independent status of discipline with their multidisciplinary and interdisciplinary approach of knowledge production. They have changed the meanings of a number of disciplines and concepts. Few new concepts were also propounded during the development of this discipline. As far as seeds of 'Indian Diaspora' are concerned, they were sown during 1838 when the slavery was abolished from the British Colonies throughout the world.In this context the British needed labourers from its shores were taken to various parts of the world. Soon the indentured labourers found it difficult to return home; and kept on nursing their hope that 'one day they will return back to their homeland'. But for many it could never happen and this gradually transformed into 'Old Indian Diaspora'. The whole process of migration, adaptation and change among Indians gave birth to a debate between Hugh Tinker, who called this migration of Indian labourers as 'another system of slavery' and others who explained and analyzed the migration as emancipatory.

It was after the independence of India in 1947 a new wave of Indians migrating to the first world countries like UK, USA, Canada, etc. started. During this period many educated Indians migrated to these countries in search of business and lucrative jobs. This phenomena was further intensified during 1960 and 1970 when a number of pass out from IITs and other regional engineering college started migrating to US and UK. Number pass out from IITs and doctors follow the suits. This process gave birth to what is called today as 'New Indian Diaspora'. The new Indian Diaspora was further developed after 1990s with the emergence of the process of globalization and information revolution which gave them new opportunities in Silicon Valley and many other MNCs. Today, it is said that approximately 25 to 30 million strong Indian Diaspora lives in most parts of the world. However, when we try to locate this book in the larger rubric of Indian Diaspora, this opens a new chapter. The book by Dr. Rahul Kumar, an alumnus of Centre of the Study of Social Systems, School of Social Sciences, covers totally new area of research in the discipline of 'Diaspora Studies'. Dr. Rahul's book "Elderly Punjabis in Indian Diaspora: a comparative study of Punjab and UK" opens new vistas for research. This pioneering study on the elderly in Indian Diaspora by Dr. Rahul Kumar has expanded the scope of Indian Diasporic Studies. We are aware that a number of scholars have covered socio-economic, political, cultured aspects of Indian Diaspora. Specifically, brain-drain, the question of caste, gender, conflict between Indian and adopted country's identity, generation conflict etc. a host of topics have been covered in Indian Diaspora. Even the depiction of Indians in films have been covered. But the status of Indian Elderly in Diaspora was a neglected area. Dr. Rahul Kumar has covered this area with academic honest and commitment. The book 'Elderly Punjabis in Indian Diaspora' covers two frames in comparative perspective. The frame of reference are the UK society and the treatment given to the elderly. Indian Society which although respects the elderly but the treatment given to them while they are in need of medical help is lot to be desired. The book reveals untold facts of the Punjabi Diaspora in UK and the elderly left behind in India. 'Elderly in Indian Diaspora' by Dr. Rahul very insightfully probes the family structure, generational relationship, neighborhood, role of occupation of Indians in Diaspora. This is vast canvas which the study has covered. Secondly, it also covers the role of CSOs and the government's health policy in the lives of the Elderly Indians in UK.

What is more significant of the book 'Elderly Punjabis in Indian Diaspora' is that it is based on field-work data conducted both in England(UK) and Punjab (India) which is rare in Indian scholars doing their Ph.D. This book has made use of narratives of the elderly living in UK and India for investigating their plight and their lived experiences. The book also captures the fact that why elderly face hardships in UK. They suffer from generational conflict, neighborhood exclusion, language handicap and ill-treatment by their sons and daughters and even then they want to live in London. Hence, on the basis of pioneering nature of the study, that is, 'Elderly Punjabis in Indian Diaspora' and the high quality nature of primary data collected from Punjab and UK, I am of the opinion this book has enriched the discipline of 'Diaspora Studies'. Secondly, this book has policy implication as well because it has revealed and topped an undiscovered area in the Indian Academia. I am confident that this book will become the basis of number of researches in the near future. I hope the students, researchers, policy makers in the sphere of 'Diasporic Studies' will take full benefit of the data and framework contained in the book.

I wish Dr. Rahul and his book all the success. I congratulate him for serving the profession of Sociology and Diaspora Studies by producing such a book. I am confident that he will continue to produce this type of exceptional academic material in future as well.

With best wishes,

01 July, 2019

**Professor Vivek Kumar**
Chairperson
Center for the Study of Social Systems
School of Social Sciences
Jawaharlal Nehru University
New Delhi (India)-110067

# Acknowledgements

I would like to express my deepest heartfelt thanks to my immensely learned and highly intellectual supervisor Professor Vivek Kumar who has encouraged me to tread on this journey. Professor Vivek Kumar, a recipient of Fulbright Teaching fellowship coined the term "Dalit Diaspora". He is a human right activist and prolific writer. His supervision and enthusiastic inputs towards the end result of my research project is beyond imagination. My supervisor is an academic mentor to me. I found him a committed teacher and generous scholar. He taught me there is always more to know and more to learn. Almost on every page of this book when it was in the form of a thesis, he scribbled handwritten copious notes recommending relevant articles, books, and scholars.

My special thanks to Dr. Gurram. Srinivas, Dr. Sadanand Sahoo who spared their valuable time and energy to read my thesis. I am grateful to Dr Ratheesh Kumar. He gave his suggestions during PhD progress seminar.

Their comments and suggestions really helped me to complete this gigantic work. I would like to thank Prof. Paramjit Singh Judge, Prof. Surinder Singh Jodhka, Prof. Avijit Pathak, Prof. Maitrayee Chaudhuri, Prof. Nilika Mehrotra, Dr Tanweer Fazal, Dr Divya Vaid and for their assistance.

Since childhood, I found inspiration from the wise words of my respected and great father Sh. L.R.Balley. My reverent and worshipful mother (Late) Mrs. Ajit Kaur Balley always taught me to choose a right path in life and helps those who need the most.

My wife Dr. Saroj Rani, currently teaching Economics at the Department of Economic, Maitryei College, University of Delhi stood by me day and night to complete this monumental work. She is an inspiration to me. My elder son Vishaw Gaurav and younger son Sheel Saurabh stepped in when family support was needed. Vishaw Gaurav helped me in Proofreading. Their practical support over the years enabled me to start out on this academic journey. This acknowledgment will be incomplete if I do not express my profound thanks to my respected sisters- Shakuntala, Sunita, and Sujata. My brother Mr. Anand Balley, from Canada, a social and human rights activist always stood by me whenever I need his help. I could not have reached my destination without them all.

In Punjab during my Interview Schedule, Mr. B.R. Bhardwaj, Mr. Charan Dass Sandhu, Mr. Kamalsheel extended a helping hand in locating Punjabi left behind elderly and immigrant families in Jalandhar, Kapurthala, and Hoshiarpur. I am grateful to them for their unconditional support.

My gratitude to Mr. Gautam Charkraborthy, Secretary General of Dr. Ambedkar Centre, Southall and Bhante Abhiparsano, Dr. Ambedkar Memorial Committee of Great Britain, Wolverhampton for providing me accommodation to stay in England. I am thankful to Mr. Khushwinder from Wolverhampton who took me despite shivering cold and unpredictable rain to various Buddhist, Sikh, Ravidassi, Valmiki temples and Gurdwaras for meeting the elderly Punjabis. I am grateful to my classmate Rakesh Ranjan and Akhilesh for their unswerving help. I would like to thank my maid Mrs Pushpa.

Last but by no means least, my sincere gratitude goes to the librarian, the staff of Jawaharlal Nehru University, Nehru Memorial Library, Bhai Vir Singh Sahitya Sadan, New Delhi, Guru Nanak Dev University, Amritsar, and Punjab University Chandigarh. Federation of Indian Chambers of Commerce and Industry, Indian Council of World Affairs, New Delhi, Southall Public Library, Norwood. I am grateful to Sh. Ramjot Singh for typing the questionnaire in Punjabi language. Without all their help and support this journey would have been unimaginable. Thank you all!

**Rahul Kumar**

# List of Tables

# List of Maps

# Abbreviations

| | | |
|---|---|---|
| ADL | : | Activities of Daily Living. |
| BKPAI | : | Building Knowledge Base on Population Ageing in India. |
| ESHG | : | Elderly Self-Help Groups. |
| ICMR | : | Indian Council of Medical Research. |
| IPOP | : | Integrated Programme for Older Persons. |
| MOSJE | : | Ministry of Social Justice and Empowerment. |
| NPHCE | : | National Programme for Health Care of Elderly. |
| NGO | : | Non -Governmental Organization. |
| RSBY | : | Rashtriya Swasthya Bima Yojana. |
| UN | : | United Nations. |
| UNFPA | : | United Nations Population Fund. |
| WHO | : | World Health Organization. |

# I

# Introduction

This chapter introduces the study on migration and well-being of Punjabi elderly. It will examine the history of Punjabi migration before and after British rule from India to various parts of the world. Apart from this, the introductory part will also list the objectives of the study. This study will try to analyze and understand the migration of the elderly Punjabis from Doaba (Punjab) to England (UK). This study will examine the socio-economic conditions of the left behind elderly in Punjab. This study will also examine the socio-economic conditions of the elderly Punjabis living with their children in the UK. This study will also probe the healthcare service available to the older persons in both that is Punjab and UK. The remittances are important for the elderly Punjabi hence this study will try to understand the role of remittances in the life of the left behind elderly. Pension and social security as a welfare schemes available for the older persons will also be examined. The left behind parents rely heavily on the remittance sent by their children from abroad. However, the elderly Punjabis living in England with their children receive social security, free healthcare services from the government of the United Kingdom. According to Amartya Sen and Jean Dreze (1999:5), "the basic idea of social security is to use social means to prevent deprivation and vulnerability to deprivation". The universe of the study is selected districts Jalandhar, Kapurthala and Hoshiarpur in Punjab and districts Southall, Wolverhampton, and Birmingham in UK.

## Understanding Migration and its Patterns

Migration is a world phenomenon. Many Europeans, Portuguese and Spanish undertook maritime travels and explored the Americas, Africa, Asia, and Oceania between 15th and $17^{th}$ century. 'Many living species have migrated from one part of the earth to another. Today, human life on every continent in nearly every one of the world`s climate landscapes, altitudes' (Bodvarsson and Berg, 2013:10). Stalker argues that many contemporary movements have antecedents in the migration associated with colonialism (Tyagi, 2017: 37). In Preface of his book entitled: *Migration: A World History*, Fischer (2014: Xii) wrote: "We are all the descendants of migrants and we virtually all migrate during the course of our own lives. From the origin of our *Homo Sapiens* species about 200,000 BCE until today, we have expanded our range over the entire planet. We have emigrated to seek new opportunities, often driven out of determining social and physical environments. As the earth`s climate has changed and our societies have developed, migration has enabled us to better our lives and those of our children".

A recent book on international migration proffers the following definition: "Migration is a spatial phenomenon. People move from one place to another, alone or together with others, for a short visit or for a long period of time," (Talbot and Thandi, 2004:97). There are opportunities as well as challenges in the path of migration in the sending as well receiving countries. From ancient to the contemporary period, an attempt to understand the movement of people from India to the rest of the world is known to be a fascinating story of migration.

Migration of Punjabis from Punjab to Britain, Europe, America, Canada, Australia, Hong Kong, and Singapore has historical background. Punjab region was annexed by the East India Company in 1849. Before annexation, Punjab was ruled by a Sikh ruler, Maharaja Ranjit Singh (1780- 1839). The British Raj designated certain ethnic-groups as martial races. (Banerjee, 2005:31) argues that in the post-1857 recruitment for the India army the British became attracted to the sturdy peasant inhabitant of Punjab. Maharaja Ranjit Singh, the famous Sikh leader had particularly impressed the British army commanders with his military acumen. She further explains that Sikh and some Punjabis embodied some of the raw material-strength, bravery, loyalty consequently; a Punjabization of the Indian army took place wherein seventy-five percent of the troops were recruited from this region.

Mitra (2012:2) states three prominent ways through which emigration of the Punjabis to the British Colonies took place. "First, exposure to North America by the Punjabis as soldiers in the British army created appetite for emigration. They were able to conceive going outside of the Punjab to fulfil their social and economic desires. Second, Punjabis Sikh were actively recruited as laborers by British steamship companies. Third, the development of *Canal Colonies* by the British colonial government after the annexation of Punjab created conditions for departure from the state, especially for the *Jat Sikh*". (Helweg, 1979:146) describes that the socio-economic crisis of the post-partition India after the great upheavals of 1947 was what many Punjabis wanted to escape.

Scholars working on migration and Diaspora issues observe that the British colonial government was heavily responsible for making up the mind of the Punjabis to emigrate. There are different patterns of migration of the Punjabis to different parts of the world. Singh and Tatla demonstrate "the first wave of migration began between the 1860s and 1890s when the favored position of Sikh in the Indian army attracted them to foreign lands. The second phase of migration began in the 1890s and lasted beyond the Second World War. They further stated that Operation Blue Star in 1984, several Sikh youths sought political asylum in Britain" (Singh and Tatla, 2008:33).

After the Second World War, British economy began to expand and boom. Such boom offered an opportunity to the Sikh already settled in Britain to sponsor their family members. The Migration was facilitated by the British Nationality Act of 1948. The provision of the British National Act, 1948, were perceived by large numbers of the community as offering an opportunity to all of India's Anglo-Indians to attempt to re-locate to Great Britain (Almeida, 2015:3).

Push factor such as huge demand for laborers in the western countries and pull factors such as the impact of the partition of 1947 and recently political instability and collapse of the rural economy in the state of Punjab worked in tandem. *Doaba, Majha,* and *Malwa* are the regions in the state of Punjab from where the most of the immigration takes place. Since centuries, Doaba region in Punjab has been a location for international out-migration. According to (UNODC, 2009:5) report, "Every year more than 20,000 youths from Punjab attempt irregular migration. Irregular migration to the UK from Jalandhar district of Punjab noted. Data shows that in Punjab, the district Jalandhar reported about 26 percent, 17 percent and 18 percent of cases of irregular migration cases in 2005, 2006, and 2007 respectively".

Today, migration from Punjab to the developed countries has become a culture of migration. (Rahman and Yong, 2015) found that Punjabis moved in huge number to the west, among which migration to the United Kingdom is longstanding and still vibrant. Judge (2012:46) also argues that Culture is self-perpetuating in Punjab. According to them, 45 percent of the 1.2 million strong Indian communities in the United Kingdom is estimated to be Punjabis. Southall, Birmingham, and Wolverhampton are the oldest and most famous settlements of Punjabis in England. Southall is also famous as '*Mini India*'. (Hundt and Sharma, 2014:221) state that since the mid-20$^{th}$ century, Southall is still considered the historic heart of the Punjabi and in particular Sikh community. For understanding Punjabi diaspora it is important and significant to know historical dimensions of migration from India to Britain.

## Migration from India to England: A Historical Background

Shirras G. Findlay has divided the history of Indian migration into three periods: "From the abolition of slavery and the recruiting of unskilled labor under the indenture to the consolidation of the laws regarding the migration of such labor. This period extends over the 75 years, 1833-1908; the dawn of a national policy, 1908-1922. In this period of 14 years indentured labor was stopped and the law of 1922 removed many of the evils of `Coolieism`;The execution of a national policy in regard to emigration. This period extends from 1922 to the present" (Shirras, 1931:595). "The relationship between the Indian subcontinent and the United Kingdom can be traced back over four centuries with the rise and fall of trading relationships, colonial dominance and independence of the Indian subcontinent in 1947"(Somerville and Dhudwar, 2010:42).The phases which occurred in the process of migration are discussed below:

### Pre-Colonial

According to World Economic and Social Survey, United Nations (2004:34) report indicates that the process of migration in the sixteenth century during the age of European expansion from Punjab to British Empire gained momentum in the overseas colonies. During this period, migration was driven by Europe's mercantile needs and centered on the establishment of plantations for the large-scale cultivation of sugar, cotton, coffee, and tobacco.

"The year from 1400 to 1600, saw the rise of several new empires and the destruction of as many previous empires. Since the early 1600s, there has been a small but significant current of voyagers, migrants and visitors. The first arrival of British sailors, merchants, soldiers and businessmen and later joined by missionaries and clerks, teachers and bureaucrats of the British Empire to India offered an opportunity to Indians to establish social, economic connections with Britain. As early as the 17th century, the recruitment of lascars (East Indian seamen) and domestic (such as ayahs or nannies)". (Visram, 2002:77).

Manning and Trimmer study demonstrate "Asian empire arose among peoples who had previously been in contact to remake the map from the Mediterranean to the Pacific. Those empires caused migration. Arab, Portuguese, Indian Migrants arrived in the East African city of Mombasa joining and forming the families. The British Empire created, in earlier centuries expanded significantly from 1870 to 1905. By 1920s, a larger portion of the world was governed by empires than any previous period of time in history" (Manning and Trimmer, 2013:117).

British abolished slavery in 1833 and with this demand for labor proliferated to work in the empire's various colonies. Appiah and Gates writes, "after the British Imperial Eats African company was granted its royal charter in 1988, it encouraged Indian immigration to Eats Africa, primarily to provide indentured labour for railways" (Appiah and Gates, 2004:291). According to historian, Brij V. Lal more, than1.5 million Indian had been shipped to colonies in the Caribbean, Africa, Asia, and Oceania. (as quoted in Devesh Kapur, 2010). In his article` *Punjabi Diaspora and Homeland*` Shinder Thandi (2006) states, "Punjabi migration commenced during the final quarter of the 19th century. The majority of these migrants were Sikhs who originated mainly from the rural areas of Punjab and many went abroad either through military postings, police service or other economic operations. The first quarter of the 20th century saw further expansion of this migration, especially to East Africa, associated with construction of railways and the new trading and business opportunities".

It is estimated that close to 28 million Indians emigrated between 1846 and 1932 to work as free or contract laborers (Narayan, 2005:6). Gillion explains, "the first Indian traders in Fiji for instance, were two jewelers, originally from Kathiawar, who in 1906 went from Natal to that far-off south pacific isle, which they had first heard of from Indians who had been there as indentured laborers" (as quoted in Rao, 1986:176). Jain describes, "In the Pacific, migration to Fiji started in the 1870s and more recently, mid-twentieth century labor migration to the Gulf continues to this day. As contrasted with the old diaspora, the `new` diaspora dates back from the 1950s and 1960s to the United Kingdom" (Jain, 2018:47). The Komagata Maru incident is well known in the history of Sikh Migration. (Ray, 2018) states that 'On 4th 1914, a Japanese ship named '*Komagatu Maru*' chartered by Gurdit Singh, a Singapore entrepreneur carried 376 passengers to Vancouver who were denied entry to Canada. This organization of this historical incident was against the Canadian and British authorities for justice to foreground issues of race, ethnicity, nation, empire, sovereignty, subject-hood and citizenship.

According to Desai, "Indians are no strangers to the United Kingdom". Desai writes, "almost from the beginning of India `s contact with the English, Indians have come to the United Kingdom in increasing numbers, mainly as sailors, students, professional men, businessmen"(Desai, 1963:2). In the same context, Ballard also described their pre-War immigration into Britain. While describing the history of immigration of Sikhs in England, he writes that, "There has been migration from India to Britain for a very long time: even before the First World War. By 1939 almost every large city seemed to have had a small number of Sikh residents" (Ballard, 1972:12).

A large number of Sikh soldiers who had served in the British army also began to look for alternatives to colonial services or subsistence farming. The recovery of British industry following the Second World War brought Indian immigrants to London. Shukla hold, "a small amount of chain migration occurred, especially during the inter-war period where a number of Punjabis worked as peddlers" (Shukla, 2003:15). Ballard explains, "South Asian migration to post-war Britain has seen a number of significant waves initially; the post-war economic boom in Britain saw large numbers of Caribbean, then South Asian men, specifically from Punjab, Gujarat, and Kashmir. Secondly, the wives and families of these men came to join them" (Ballard, 2002:16).

Given the increased presence of Indians in Britain, the British state also fixated on the possibilities of large-scale migrations from India to the west, without the natural inhibition and control that the imperial relationship had once provided. During these years, "the British government kept detailed files on the movement for naturalized citizenship in the United States of America. And Britain continued to monitor closely the number of Indians who actually went to the United States of America. The British government installed a quota of only one hundred immigrants from India per year" (Shukla, 2003: 21).

## Colonial

East India Company annexed Punjab region in 1849. During this period, the Punjab underwent dramatic changes that were to leave a permanent imprint on the successor provinces. (Singh and Tatla, 2008). Before annexation, Punjab was ruled by a Sikh ruler, Maharaja Ranjit Singh (1780-1839). The British Raj designated certain ethnic-groups as martial races. Singh and Tatla opines that Sikhs became the ideal subaltern community and their loyalty rewarded by mass recruitment into the Indian Army (Singh and Tatla, 2008:3). Bhachu writes, "East African Asian known as 'Twice Migrants' arrived from Tanzania, Kenya, and Uganda in the UK also settled permanently" (Bhachu, 1985:105). Ballard argues that those who came from these British colonies settled permanently and are of Punjabi ancestry (as quoted in Somerville and Dhudwar, 2010:42). During the 18th and early 19th centuries, thousands of Indian soldiers termed *Sepoys,* fought in British wars in China, Southeast Asia, Africa, West Asia, and Europe. British also forcibly transported thousands of Indian prisoners through its empire in Asia, both removing them from their homes, societies and using them as cheap labour in other colonies (Fisher, 2014:81).

## Post-colonial

In 1947, the departing British partitioned their largest colony into the new nations of Pakistan and India on the basis of religious identity. At least twelve million people immigrated: Muslim moved to Islamic West and East Pakistan; Hindu and Sikhs to secular India. Up to two million emigrants died en route (Fisher, 2014:112). The oil boom of the early and mid-1970s provided the next major demand led Sikh migration. Singh and Tatla hold that "precise figures for Sikh migration are unavailable but it is estimated that currently there are 60,000 to 175,000 Sikhs in the Gulf States" (Singh and Tatla, 2008:35). The number of those who have been in the Gulf States at any time since the 1970s is considerably higher, for the average period of the contract varies from several months to few years. In Britain, Thatcherism destroyed the manufacturing economy, the mainstay of Sikh employment while imposing strict controls that all but curtailed primary immigration. Singh and Tatla explains, "As a result Sikh migrants from Punjab increasingly made North America and other countries their main destination" (Singh and Tatla, 2008:35). "On the 4th of August 1972 General Idi Amin, President of Uganda, declared that Ugandan Asian be forcibly expelled from the country. Britain allowed 27,000 Ugandan Asian refugees (54% of the total) to enter the United Kingdom between 18th September and 8th November 1972" (Khamis, 1996).

## Understanding Ageing in India

"Ageing as a process of physiologic deterioration that gradually impairs the capacity of people to function socially constitutes a continuum that requires multiple development responses" (Rob Vos et al., 2008:3). "Gerontology is the study of old age and ageing. Ageing could be said simply to be the process of growing older" (Ian Stuart- Hamilton et. al., 2011:1). According to Janet and Kenneth (2013:4) "Age, as a concept, is synonymous with time, and time in itself cannot affect living function; it does not have physical dimensionality to impinge upon the senior human. Time is a crude index of many events and experiences, and it is these indexed events, which are causal". There are different connotations to old age. In some country, they are called *older people, elderly, senior citizens*. The word 'Ageism' is said to have first been used by Robert Butler MD in 1969.

The World Health Organization (WHO, 2008) define 'old' noted that although the "ageing process is, of course, a biological reality which has its own dynamic, largely beyond human control", however, "it is also subject to the constructions by which each society makes sense of old age". The perception of old age differs in the developed and the developing countries.

It is significant to understand the definition of the term *Elderly*, both from India and UK perspective. As per, Ministry of Health and Family Welfare (MOHFW), Indian man lives beyond 67 years and women about 70 years. (Census, 2011). As per report of United Nations, "the current world population of 7.6 billion is expected to reach 8.6 billion in 2030, 9.8 billion in 2050 and 11.2 billion in 2100"(United Nations, 2017).

By this time, the population of the old age is likely to outnumber the proportion of the young age people (0-14 years) all over the world. Surveys indicate that the oldest segment of the age group (80 years and above) has been growing rapidly. The present, as well as the future, is therefore filled with the ageing of the aged. On the contrary, European societies, especially the western side has been undergoing demographic transition since there is a fall in fertility, as women prefer to have fewer or no child "Old age is associated with declining of mental and physical faculties, which varies culturally and historically, however, in terms of economic benefits, people beyond 60 years are considered elderly" (NHRC, 2011). "In older age, mortality among people belonging to the lower economic group has therefore been reported to be higher than among those who have a higher economic group" (Huisman, 2004:464). "In India, family still plays an important role in supporting the elders. Institutional care in the case of India do not prefer by the members of the family as the case in most developed countries. Following the traditional culture, family satisfies the needs of the elder's in regard to food, clothing, and shelter" (Vermani et al., 2004:159). Phillipson et al, argue, "the experience of growing older is not shaped solely by family and kinship groups but also encompasses wider social relationship such as friends and neighbors" (as cited in Christina, 2005:161).

International Year of Older Persons was declared in 1999 by the United Nations which was followed by the Government of India while approving the National Policy for Older Persons for hastening welfare measures. India is a welfare state; its welfare programme for the elderly is not sound enough. The Old age pension amount that is given is woefully inadequate to meet even the bare minimum of the elderly people. (Vermani et al.2004:163) state that elders have very low socio-economic conditions in India, and while some well-off elderly lives on pensions and land holdings, most of the elders have basically no means to depend on. Elders with better socio-economic conditions have better economic support in their old age. Until recently, elders in India, however, did not have such issues with regard to their socio-economic living until their death, since they lived together with their children in joint families. But the process of modernization has broken down this joint family unit into a nuclear family making younger Indian generation to change.

## Understanding Ageing in UK

In the United Kingdom, age between 60 to 65years is considered the age of retirement. "Here it is important to note that in 1875, the Friendly Societies Act in Britain, enacted the definition of old age as, "any age after 50", yet pension schemes mostly used age 60 or 65 years for eligibility" (Roebuck, 1979). "In chronological order of old age in the United Kingdom, however, starts from 60 for women and 65 for men, i.e. the age of retirement" (Department of Health UK, 2001).

Laslett argues that the nuclear family is probably the norm even in pre-industrial Britain because of the high mortality and fertility rates (as quoted in Christina, 2005:165) In UK, there is a strong preference towards such institutionalized setup, and most elderly people are subjected to the treatment of the institution. Khaw argues that this retirement homes, however, speak immensely of the socio-economic conditions of the old people, in a sense that privileged people have the tendency to have better facilities than the ones who are poor (as quoted in Christina, 2005:167). "In addition to the retirement homes, the country also provides pensions benefit schemes to the elderly" (Digby, 2001). "However, studies show that many of the Asians living in the UK are unaware of the social services provided by the state. Among these Asians, the Punjabis in Southall suburbs are also included. Even when they are aware of the social schemes, they also suffer from language problems that deprive them of claiming the social services" (Donaldson, 1986). Without proper information, the elderly often end up without having the access to these facilities and services in the UK. In an alien society in general, Khoo (2012:126) states, "Iimmigrant's experience difficulties with the language of the country of settlement may be less integrated into the community and more dependent on their relatives for social and economic support rather than government services".

## Statement of the Problem

Migration has been taking place from Punjab since time immemorial. However, it picked up during and after the colonial period. Some migrants from Doaba region of Punjab take their elderly parents along with them and some leave them behind. Migrated as well left behind parents face physical, psychological, emotional and health challenges. With this backdrop, this chapter will try to understand and analyze socio-economic and emotional problems faced by the elderly Punjabis in Doaba region of Punjab. In this background this chapter I has undertaken review of literature related to the subject, accordingly, we have found that Darshan Singh Tatla (2008), Verne. A Dusenbery (1989), Paramjit Singh Judge(1994), Manjit Singh(2013), Swarn Singh Kalhon(2016), Steve Taylor(2015) have conducted studies on Sikh Migration, Sikh Diaspora, and Sikh Diaspora Philanthropy, Sikh Diaspora Politics. Oberio (1980), Waltron-Roberts(2004), Supriya Singh(2016) have conducted studies regarding Indian diaspora. Further, we have also found that, Satwanti Kapoor(2004) and BKPAI(2011) have done study on the Elderly in Punjab. Similarly, in England a few studies by Amarjit Singh (2014) and Sarah Lamb (2009) have been conducted but they are few.

## Objectives of the Study

The specific objectives of the study include the followings:

- To assess patterns of migration of Punjabis from Doaba to England.
- To analyze the socio-economic condition of elderly Punjabis migrant families in Doaba and England.
- To examine the family structure of Punjabi migrants in Doaba and England.
- To inquire into ageing conditions of elderly Punjabis left behind in Doaba and those who have migrated from Doaba and settled in England.

## Research Questions

The secondary sources such as books, journals, articles, government reports and census data illustrate rapid growth of elderly population in India and UK. In order to explore the socioeconomic condition of the elderly Punjabis and ascertain structural changes taking place in those families of elderly Punjabis living in Doaba and in England primary data will be collected and analyzed. For that purpose, the following questions from two different sets of respondents-one in three districts of Doaba and three districts in England (UK) will be interviewed through an open-ended questionnaire. I shall use a snowball sampling techniques to meet research subjects.

- What are the causes and patterns of Punjabi migration from Doaba to England?
- Whether the socio-economic conditions in Punjab influence migration.
- When and how the Punjabis take their parents after their settlement in England.
- What similarities and differences exist in the socio-economic conditions of elderly Punjabis living in England and left behind in Doaba?

- Whether the socio-economic status of migrant Punjabis impact their family structure in England and in Doaba.
- Who takes care of elderly Punjabis left behind in Doaba? Is the amount of remittance sent by their children from England is sufficient to lead a healthy and stable life?
- Whether elderly Punjabis living in Doaba and England feel neglected by their family members.

## Methodology

### Universe of the Study

The rationale for the chocies of this study is that Punjbais have migrated to England(UK) from Doaba region of Punjab. In Punjab Doaba region, we have slected Jalandhar, Hoshiarpur and Kapurthala and in England(UK) we have slected Southall, Wolverhampton and Birmingham for the study of area. Through the secondary sources, we have come to know that a substantiak number of immigrants from Doaba region of Punjab live in England. The universe of the research is three districts of Punjab and three provinces of England(UK). The porcess of migration from Punjab to England has lied to a situation in which a vast number of elderly Punjabis have been left behind. Some of the migrants have taken their older parents along with themto the both the places. However, in both the places elderly have been suffering socio-economic and emotional problems. Althorugh there have been studies on problems of the edelry in India and England(UK). However, the problems of elderly Punjabis in Punjaba and England(UK) have not been dealt. Therefore, this study has chosen Punjab and England(UK) to understand the problems of ageing and well-being of the elderly Punjabis in a comparative perspective.

### Sampling

After rationally choosing the universe of the study the next step was to choose the respondents. Therefore, the researcher tried to have an assessment of the density of the migrant and immigrant population in Punjab and England(UK) respectively. The researcher has found that there exists a big population of the elderly Punjabis in both the places of the study. In such circumstnaces, in-depth interviews from selected cases of elderly people was considred to be the best way to select a respresentative sample.For this the researcher has applied purposive and snow ball technique. On the basis of this in Punjab, 50 elderly Punjabi families respondents were selected from three district of Doaba region of Punjab. In Jalandhar, 20 Hoshiarpur, 20 and 10 respondent families in Kapurthala respectively. Similarly, 25 respondent families were seclected from three districts in England(UK). In Southall, 15 Wolverhampton, 05 and Birmingham,05 respectively. For the information of the readers, it is informed that Google shows these places in England(UK) districts but the natives call it province. Most of the respondents were head of the family member belonging to 60-80 years of age.

## Tools of Data Collection

The primary data was collected through mixed methods. The data was extracted in an infromal interview with the help of interview guide. The first part of the interview guide included the information about the demograhpic profile of the respondetns. Second part included the health status and third and the last inculded in-depth anlayse of socio-economic, family and health status of the elderly Punjabis. The interviews guide is attached in Interview Guide. Most of the conversations with the elderly Punjabis in both the places were held in Punjabi as the elderly Punjabis were not conversant with English. In addition to this, focused group discussions were held in the field. Last but not the least, the researcher also substantiated the data colllected through his observation.

**Table I.I: Socio-Economic Profile of Elderly Punjabis in Punjab and England(UK)**

| Particulars |
|---|
| Age 60-80 years |
| Income |
| Remittances (a) |
| Government Pension and petty business (b) |
| Both (a+b) |
| Visit/Staying |
| Visit (social occasions) |
| (a) Stay |
| (1) Do not want to stay because of harsh weather and English language barriers in the host society |
| (2) Want to stay because they want to avail dual citizenship benefits |
| Awareness |
| Not aware of old age pension benefits |
| Not aware of public transport concession |
| Health |
| Health Problems |
| Government and Private hospital services |
| Mentally depressed and isolated in the absence of loved ones |
| Dependent on immediate relatives during health problems |
| Expenditure (50 families) |
| Food and Medical |

| Other Expenses |
|---|
| (a) Extend financial help to relatives and friends |
| (b) Donations to the Sikh religious organization. |

*Source:* Field Work.

Table I.I shows age, income, health and expenditure variables are taken into consideration to understand the socio-economic status of elderly Punjabis in Doaba (Punjab) and England (UK).

## Qualitative Methods

"Qualitative research refers to methods and techniques of observing, analyzing and interpreting attributes, patterns, and characteristics and meanings of specific, contextual or gestalt features of phenomena under study"( Leininger,1985:12). "The use of qualitative research methods in this study is appropriate for a number of reasons. The first reason qualitative research techniques are well suited to the study is that they allow us to get inside the lived experience of the participants, thereby revealing the more subjective aspects of everyday life"(Denzin,1989:27). Corbin writes, "Drawing from behaviors of daily living organized patterns of behavior to generate theory, qualitative techniques ground a study in the natural environment in which people move and live".( Strauss and Corbin,1998:12). Interviews Guide was conducted with the help of an open-ended questionnaire in Doaba (Punjab) and England (UK).

## Scope of the Study

The significance of this study and its contribution to knowledge is to enhance the well-being of the elderly people. Survey conducted in the past indicate a rapid decline in the joint and extended family system. The support from the communities to the elderly people is lacking. The elderly people are more vulnerable to isolation and loneliness, as a result, their health condition deteriorate sometimes leading to disability. In such situations, the elderly live a life under psychological distress. Elderly abuse is common in the families in all societies. The scope of this study is to enhance awareness among the children, family members, and society at large to cultivate a sensitive attitude towards the elderly people in their old age. The aim of this study is also to recommend a stable mechanism to assist older persons in order to fight loneliness and depression so that these elderly people can live happily ever after.

## Limitations of the Study

There are, of course, certain limitations in this study which might alter the outcomes. One is that the primary investigator did not have control over the participants chosen for the interviews. The participants were chosen randomly through the help of the intermediates in order to gain primary knowledge about their family, migration status. In the initial stage, the investigator faced a tremendous problem in making the elderly and their family members understand to explain the nature of this study. They were told this study is academic and nothing to do with government or any private agency to collect their personal information. The limitation is perceived as strength of the study since the investigator finally won the confidence of the family members of the elderly to sit and talk about their life histories. A potential bias within the study was identified as those participants who were less interested to share their personal information. Likewise, those who happily participated during the field survey may have done so because it was an avenue to talk to someone which also served as a form of biases. The use of lengthy interview schedule which might have tired the elderly people in between the interviews. This study is constrained by financial resource. A final limitation is that the study has two different countries that too in a larger population. Well-being and settlement process are an integral part of elderly Punjabi immigrants. Further research that particularly addresses the interactions between immigrant parents and their children and the activities in which they participate is recommended.

## Why Compare India and UK

This study tries to compare the socio-economic status of the left behind Elderly Punjabis and those who have migrated to England (UK). This study also examines the impacts of remittances on the life of the elderly people who are left behind in Punjab. This study tries to understand the problems related to isolation and loneliness. This study in a comparative perspective tries to understand how the elderly Punjabis at both the destinations spend their time and in what activities they get themselves engaged. This study looks into the effects of abuse on physical and emotional health of the elderly people in both the destinations. This study also tries to understand the well-being of the Elderly Punjabis in both the countries. This study tries to compare the health policies and schemes available in Doaba (Punjab) and England (UK). This study also looks into integration and caste aspects at both the destinations. This study tries to compare the pension and social security benefits available for the older persons in Punjab and England(UK).

## Conclusion

In this chapter, we have introduced of the study. We have looked into migration and ageing in Punjab and England (UK). This chapter has also discussed the patterns of migration of elderly Punjabis from Punjab to England (UK). The Punjabis have been migrating to England (UK) since colonial times. During pre-colonial period, migration was driven by Europe's mercantile needs and centered on the establishment of plantations for the large-scale cultivation of sugar, cotton, coffee, and tobacco. British abolished slavery in 1833(Slavery Abolition Act, 1833, British Parliament, UK) and subsequently turned to indentured labor to respond to labor demands in the empire colonies. Punjabis also migrated when Punjab was experiencing drought and famines and the employment opportunities consequently declined. Punjabis also were taken as indentured labor to work in British colonies particularly in British African colonies. It was the handy work of the British government. Some of the Punjabis were recruited by the British Army and sent to different parts of the world. We have found that a majority of the Punjabis migrated during colonial times did not return back to the homeland. Many of them settled permanently in British colonies and formed families. Therefore, today we have members of extended family out of these Punjabi families.

Different patterns of migrations during post-colonial period took place. Migration during this time was not out of financial requirement but it became a culture among the Punjabis(Singh and Tatla, 2008). After the liberation of immigration policies by the developed nations, immigration was made easy and simple. While taking advantages of the liberalized immigration policies, the majority of the Punjabis applied for immigrant as well family visa. Immigrated daughters or sons after obtaining British citizenship started sponsoring their older parents. Similarly, older parents who were already settled in England (UK) started sponsoring their left behind children. Last but not the least, a regular streams of students also went to UK. This study has observed that many students who came to UK, did not go back to India. It is these process of migration of Punjabis to UK in both during colonial and post- colonial period has formed a big diaspora in UK.

It is in this socio-economic background that we have located in this chapter the concept of ageing in India and England (UK). We have observed that older persons have been experiencing social and emotional problems in both the countries. In India, we have found that despite several welfare policies and schemes for the older persons, the elderly people have been experiencing problems in availing the benefits of the policies and schemes on two accounts, one is because of inadequate awareness about the welfare policies and schemes and second is corrupt bureaucracy. In India, we have also found that the elderly people suffer more. Along with lack of awareness about welfare policies and schemes and corrupt bureaucracy, there are inadequate healthcare services and shortage of doctors and nurses, especially in government hospitals. In England (UK) we have observed that the older persons are treated carefully. The healthcare services are free of cost for the older citizens. We have also found that doctors and nurses are very sensitive to the treatment of the elderly people. We have also found that the hospitals run by the government provide home delivery of services to the older persons in England (UK).

This chapter also included statement of problem. Here we have argued that migration has been taking place from Punjab since time immemorial. However, it picked up during and after the colonial period. Some migrants from Doaba region of Punjabi also took their elderly parents along with them and some left them behind. Migrated as well left behind parents face physical, psychological, emotional, health challenges. We have found that although there have been a number of studies which have studied the status of migrant Punjabis, there have been studies which have given account of elderly within in India and Punjab. However, there have been not studies which compare the elderly in India and Punjab.

In this chapter, we have included the objectives of the study**.** The specific objectives of the study includes the followings: To assess patterns of migration of Punjabis from Doaba to England; To analyze the socioeconomic condition of elderly Punjabis migrant families in Doaba and England; To examine the family structure of Punjabi migrants in Doaba and England; To inquire into ageing conditions of elderly Punjabis left behind in Doaba and those who have migrated from Doaba and settled in England. Along with this, this chapter also includes research questions. Next we have discussed the methodology of this study. To begin with we have tried to give a rational of choice of the universe. As far as, universe is concerned. Punjab state of India and UK are the two places where this study would be conducted. Within Punjab we have selected Jalandhar, Hoshiarpur and Kapurthala in Doaba. In England (UK) we have selected Southall, Wolverhampton and Birmingham as the universe of this study of area. The rationale of the choice of the universe was that through the secondary sources, we have come to know that a substantial number of people have migrated from these districts of Punjab. As far as the rational of choice of the universe of the study in the UK is concerned we have come to know that most of the migrated Punjabis live in these three areas viz Southall, Birmingham and Wolverhampton of England (UK).

In this chapter, we also included the methods of selectións of respondents. The rational of choice of the universe of the study. Therefore, the researcher tried to have an assessment of the density of the population of migrant and immigrant population in Punjab and England (UK) respectively. The researcher has found that there exists a vast population of the elderly people in both the places. In such circumstnaces, in-depth interviews from selected cases of elderly people was considred to be the best way to select a respresentative sampling for this study. Accordingly, the researcher has applied purposive and snow ball sampling technique. On the basis of this, 50 elderly Punjabi families respondents were selected in three district of Doaba region of Punjab. In Jalandhar 20, Hoshiarpur 20 and Kapurthala 10 respondent families were selected respectively. Similarly, In England(UK) 25 elderly respondent families were selected. In Southall 15, Wolverhampton 05 and Birmingham 05 respectively. For the information of the readers, it is told that Google shows these places in England(UK) as districts but the natives call it province. Most of the respondents were head of the family beloging to 60-80 years of age.

Tools of Data Collection, the primary data was collected through mixed methods. The data was extracted in an infromal interview with the help of interview guide. The first part of the interview guide included the information about the demograhic information. Second part included the health status of the respondents and third and the last inculded in-depth anlayse of socio-economic, family and health status of the elderly Punjabis. The interviews guide is attached in Interview Guide. Most of the conversations with the elderly Punjabis at the both the places were held in Punjabi language as the elderly Punjabis were not conversant with English. In addition to this, discussion were held with the younger population in both the destination of the universe and relevant data was collected. Last but not the least, this chapter has also included chapterisation of the study. Accordingly, this study has been divided into eight chapters including introduction and conclusion.

## Description of the Book

Various aspects of elderly in Punjab and UK have been contextualised and discerned in the logical and sequence in the following pages

### Chapter I

Chapter I introduces the study on migration and well-being of the elderly Punjabis and provides insights on various migration trajectories followed by the Punjabis to migrate to the developed countries. It throws light on the history of Punjabi migration before and after British rule in India. It also talks about ageing from Indian and England (UK) perspective respectively. Besides this, the introductory part also lists the statement of the problem, objectives of the study, research questions, methodology, sampling tools of data collection. It also tries to understand the study in a comparative perspective between Punjab and England (UK).

### Chapter II

Chapter II discusses about the research settings. This chapter tries to examine the demographic profile of the research area that is Jalandhar,

Hoshiarpur and Kapurthala in Punjab and Southall, Wolverhampton and Birmingham in England (UK). This chapter attempts to understand the causes of migration of Punjabis to England (UK). This chapter also looks into the caste factor among the Punjabi families in Punjab and England (UK).

## Chapter III

Chapter III attempts to understand the existing literature survey on migration and ageing of the elderly. This chapter tries to know how theories on migration and ageing had evolved over time. This chapter tries to explore the findings of the previous studies conducted on migration and ageing from a comparative perspective. This chapter attempts to examine the gaps in the existing literature on migration and ageing in relation to the older persons. This chapter also looks into theories on migration, diaspora and remittances. This chapter also tries to understand loneliness, isolation and elderly abuse in Doaba (Punjab) and England (UK).

## Chapter IV

Chapter IV examines central and state government policies on older persons in India and England (UK). This chapter also attempts to understand formal and informal institutions existing for the welfare of older persons in India and England (UK). This chapter also attempts to understand constitutional provisions for the welfare of the older persons in Punjab and England (UK).

## Chapter V

Chapter V attempts to explore the family structure and socioeconomic status of elderly Punjabis in Punjab. This chapter tries to understand various forms of family including joint, nuclear and extended family. This chapter attempts to look into isolation and loneliness among the Punjabi elderly. This chapter also looks into social exclusion and elderly abuse in Punjab. This chapter discusses about the engagements of the elderly Punjabis in Punjab. This chapter also examine the healthcare system in Punjab. This chapter tries to examine the impact of migration of children on the left behind elderly Punjabis. This chapter also assesses the role of remittance in the life of the left behind parents in the state of Punjab.

## Chapter VI

Chapter VI attempts to explore the family structure and socioeconomic status of elderly Punjabis in England (UK). This chapter tries to understand various forms of family including joint, nuclear and extended family. This chapter attempts to look into isolation and loneliness among the Punjabi elderly in England (UK). This chapter also looks into social exclusion and elderly abuse in England (UK). This chapter discusses about the engagements of the elderly Punjabis in England (UK). This chapter also examine the healthcare system in England (UK).

## Chapter VII

Chapter VII tries to understand socio economic status, social exclusion, elderly abuse, isolation and loneliness of the elderly Punjabis in a comparative perspective. This chapter discusses social cultural and economic challenges experienced by the elderly Punjabis in Punjab and England (UK) with or without children. This chapter also examines the integration experiences of the elderly in British society in England (UK).

## Chapter VIII

Chapter VIII discusses the broader findings of the study. This chapter also discusses constraints of this study. This chapter also deliberates on the contribution of knowledge of this study. This chapter presents summary of this study followed by a detailed bibliography.

## References

Almeida, Rochelle. (2015). Immigrants, Refugees, or Both? Migration Theory and the Anglo Indian Exodus to Great Britain, *International Journal of Anglo-Indian Studies*, 15(2): 2-24.

Amartya Sen and Jean, Dreze. (1995). Public Action for Social Security in E.Ahmed Jean Dreze, John Hills and Amartyasen (Eds). *Social Secuirty in Developing Contries*, Oxford University Press.

Anjali Gera Ray. (2018). *Imperialism and Sikh Migration: The Komagata Maru Incident*: New York, Routledge.

Ballard, Roger. (1972). Family Organization among the Sikhs in Britain, *New Community*, 2, 12-24.

———— (2002). The South Asian Presence in Britain and its Transnational Connections in Singh, H., and Vertovec S (Eds), Culture and Economy in the Indian Diaspora, London, Routledge.

Banerjee, Sikata. (2005). Make Me a Man! *Masculinity, Hinduism, and Nationalism in India*, Albany, State University of New York Press.

Bhachu, P. (1985). *Twice Migrants: East African Sikh Settlers in Britain*. London: Tavistock.

Bodvarsson, Orin.B, and Berg, H.V.Den. (2013).The Economics of Immigration: *Theory and Policy*, New York, Springer.

Christina, Victor (2005).The Social Context of Ageing*: A Textbook of Geronotology*, London and New York, Routledge.

Devesh, Kapur. (2010). *Diaspora Development and Democracy*: The Domestic Impact of International Migration from India, United Kingdom, and Princeton University Press.

Denzin, N. K. (1989). Interpretive interactionism. CA: Sage Publications, Inc.

Digby,B.(2001).*Global Challenges. Student's Book. Per Le Scuole Superiori*, Oxford, Heinemann.

Donaldson, L.J. (1986). Health and Social Conditions of Elderly Asians/: A Community Survey. *British Medical Journal*, 293(October),1079–1082.

Fisher, Michael H.(2014). *Migration: A World History*. Oxford University Press.

Helweg, Arthur. W. (1979).Sikh in England: *The Development of a Migrant Community*, New Delhi, Oxford University Press.

Huisman, M. (2004) Socio-economic inequalities in mortality among elderly people in 11 European populations. *Journal of Epidemiology and Community Health*, 58(6),468–475.

Ian Stuart-Hamilton (Eds). (2011).*An Introduction to Gerontology,* Cambridge, Cambridge University Press.

Jain, Ravindra K.(2018). *Innovative Departures: Anthropology and the Indian Diaspora*, London, Routledge.

Janet M. wilmoth and Kenneth F. Ferraro(2013). Gerontology: Perspective and Issues, New York, Springer Publishing Company.

Judge, Paramjit Singh. (2012). "Mapping the Social Background of Punjabi Diaspora", in Sahai et al (eds.), *Indian Diaspora: Migration and Development with Focus on the State of Punjab, Chandigarh*: Centre for Research in Rural and Industrial Development (CRRID).

Khoo, Siew-Ean. (2012). Ethnic disparities in social and economic well -being of the immigrant aged in Australia, *Journal of Population Research*, 29(.2), 122-123.

Kumar, Sampath. S., Sirijakumari, S., and Brindia.V. (2015). Understanding Elderly abuse – A Special Reference to Elderly in Urban, *International Journal of Scientific and Research Publications*,5(6),470-835.

Leininger, M. M. (Ed.). (1985). Qualitative research methods in nursing. Orlando, FL: Harcourt Brace Jovanovich.

Mitra, Diditi. (2012). Punjabi Immigrant Mobility in the United States: *Adaptation through Race and Class*, New York, Palgrave Macmillan.

Narayan, K.L. (2005). *Indian Diaspora: A Demographic Perspective*. Occasional Paper 3, Centre for the Study of Indian Diaspora, University of Hyderabad. Retrieved on 16 Oct, 2017 from http://www.uohyd.ernet.in.

Manning and Trimmer.(2013).*Migration in World History* (Second edition), London, Routledge.

Rahman, Md Mizanur, and Tong, Tan Tai. (2015).*International Migration and Development in South Asia*, London, Routledge.

Rao, M.S.A (1986). Studies in Migration: Internal and International Migration in India, New Delhi: Manohar Publications.

Rob Vos, Jose Antonio Ocampo and Ana Luiza Cortez. (2008). *Ageing and Development*, London and New York, Zed Books.

Singh, Gurharpal and Tatla D.S. (2008).Sikhs in Britain: *The Making of a Community*, London, Zed Books Ltd.

Shinder, Thandi. (2006).*Punjabi Diaspora and Homeland Relations*, available at http://www.india-seminar.com/2006/567/567 shinder s thandi.htm,retreived 23 April 2016.

Shukla Sandhya (2003).India Abroad: *Diasporic Cultures of Postwar America and England*, Princeton University Press, Princeton and Oxford.

Strauss, A., & Corbin, J. (1998). *Basics of Qualitative Research*: Techniques and procedures for developing grounded theory. Thousand Oaks, CA: Sage Publications.

Talbot, Ian and Shinder Thandi (Eds). (2004). *People on the Move: Punjab Colonial, and Post-Colonial Migration*, Karachi: Oxford University Press.

Sodhi, Ram. (1989). *Indian Immigrants in Britain*, Bradford, England, Inter-India Publications.

Somerville, will and Dhudwar. (2010). Indian Immigration to the United Kingdom, Working Paper 21, available at http://lib.jnu.ac.in/sites/default/files/pdf/ imds p/IMDS Mar 2010 WP 21.pdf.

Tyagi, Madhu. (2017). Theory of Indian Diaspora: *Dynamics of Global Migration, Horizon Book* (A Division of ignited Minds Edutech Pvt Ltd).

UNODC.(2009). Smuggling of Migrants from India to Europe and in particular to UK: *A Study on Panjab and Haryana*, United Nations Office on Drug and Crime and Institute of Social Sciences.

United Nations. (2004).*World Economic and Social Survey*, International Migration, Department of Economic and Social Affairs, United Nations, United Nations Publications.

Vermani, S., Madhu and Darshan, S. (2004). Economic Support of Family to Elders in Rural Haryana. In A. K. Kapoor and S. Kapoor( eds). *India's Elderly: A Multidisciplinary Dimension*. New Delhi: Mittal Publications.

Visram, Rozina. (2002). Asian in Britain: *400 Years of History*, Pluto Press.

WHO.(2008). Definition of an older or elderly person. *World Health Organization*. Available at: http://www.who.int/healthinfo/survey/ageingdefnolder/en/ [Accessed March 9, 2016].

# II

# Research Settings

## Introduction

This chapter will explore a brief historical background of Punjab. This chapter very briefly will explore the socio-economic profile of Punjab and England (UK). In Punjab, This chapter will discuss three districts Jalandhar, Hoshiarpur and Kapurthala. This chapter will also see population and literacy rate in Punjab. Similarly, this will explore three districts in England (UK) Southall, Birmingham and Wolverhampton. In England (UK), this chapter explore the demographic profile of these places of the universe of the study. This chapter will discuss the causes of migration from Punjab to England (UK). Further, this chapter will also discuss the caste system which is part of the social structure among Punjabis of both the countries.

## Historical Background of Punjab

"The word Punjab consists of two persion words:'Punj' and 'ab' means water or 'river'. The land in the north-west of the vast Indo Pakistan Sub-continent is known as the Punjab because therein flow five tributaries of the Indus River- the Jhelum, the Chenab, the Ravi, the Beas and the Sutlej. At present, however, this 'Land of Five' Rivers or the Punjab is not held by one single state. In 1947, the predominantly Muslim areas of this land were given to Pakistan – a newly created state and the eastern portion of this land remained a part of India. In the days of Maharaja Ranjit Singh, the Punjab or the 'Lahore Kingdom' as it was called, extended right up to the Khyber in the west and upto to the Sutlej in the east. After the mutiny, when the British finally took over the administration of the Punjab, the added the Haryana Prant(Including) Hissar, and Delhi to the Punjab. Under the British rule, it came to be called, 'The province of the Punjab' and after independence, as mentioned above, the Indian portion of the Punjab got the name 'East Punjab'. In the new constitution of India, it is called 'The Punjab State'(Narang, 1969:1 and 2).

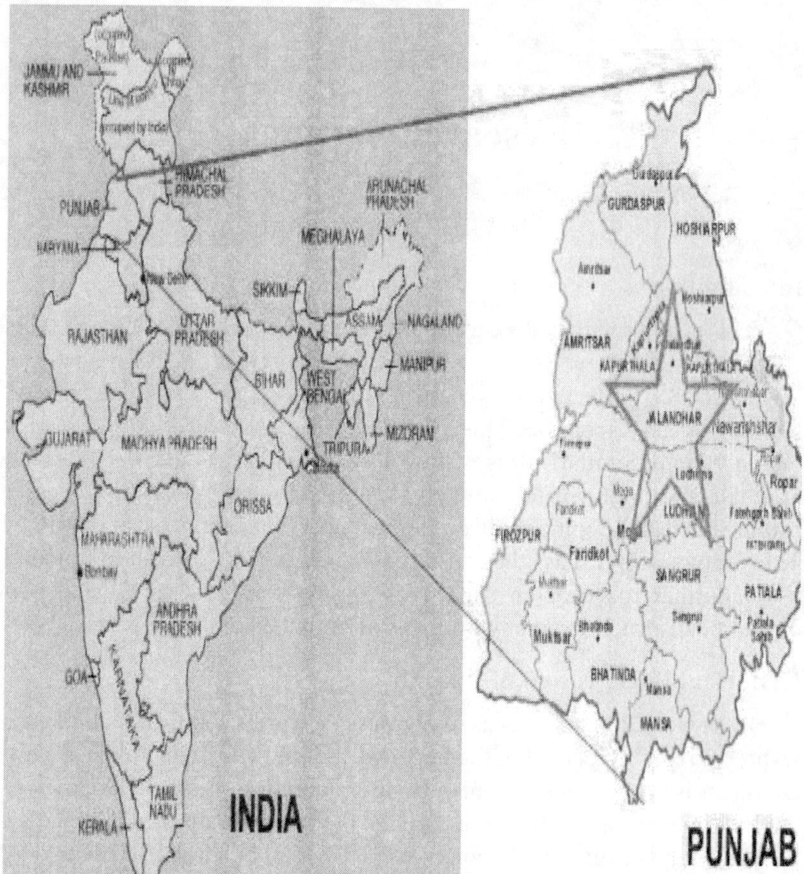


***Map 1: Political Map of Doaba (Punjab) showing districts Jalandhar, Kapurthala and Hoshiarpur***

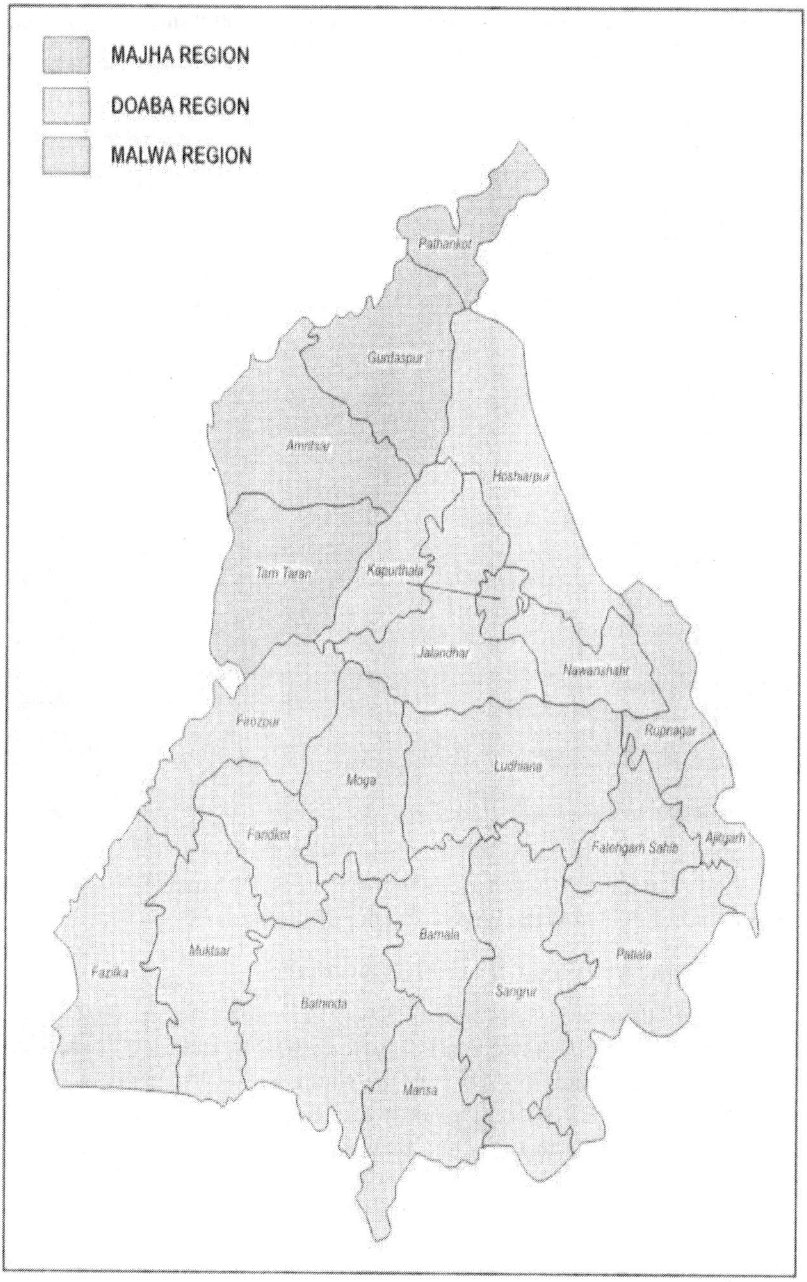


***Map2: Political Map of Punjab showing 22 Districts***

**Table 2.1 : Demographic Profile of Districts of Punjab**

| *No.* | *District Name* | *Population (Census 2011)* | *Area (Sq km)* | *Region* |
|---|---|---|---|---|
| 1 | Amritsar | 2,490,656 | 2647 | Majha |
| 2 | Barnala | 595,527 | 1410 | Malwa |
| 3 | Bathinda | 1,388,525 | 3385 | Malwa |
| 4 | Faridkot | 617,508 | 1469 | Malwa |
| 5 | Fatehgarh Sahib | 600,163 | 1180 | Malwa |
| 6 | Fazilka | 1,063,737 | 3113 | Malwa |
| 7 | Firozpur | 965,337 | 2190 | Malwa |
| 8 | Gurdaspur | 1,621,725 | 2635 | Majha |
| 9 | Hoshiapur | 1,586,625 | 3365 | Doaba |
| 10 | Jalandhar | 2,193,590 | 2632 | Doaba |
| 11 | Kapurthala | 815,168 | 1632 | Doaba |
| 12 | Ludhiana | 3,498,739 | 3767 | Malwa |
| 13 | Mansa | 769,751 | 2171 | Malwa |
| 14 | Moga | 995,746 | 2216 | Malwa |
| 15 | Pathankot | 676,598 | 929 | Majha |
| 16 | Patiala | 1,895,686 | 3218 | Malwa |
| 17 | Rup Nagar | 684,627 | 1369 | Malwa |
| 18 | Ajitgarh (Mohali) | 994,628 | 1093 | Malwa |
| 19 | Sangrur | 1,655,169 | 3610 | Malwa |
| 20 | Shaheed Bhagat | 612,310 | 1267 | Doaba |
| | Singh Nagar | | | |
| 21 | Shri Muktsar Sahib | 901,896 | 2615 | Malwa |
| 22 | Tarn Taran | 1,119,627 | 2449 | Majha |

*Source:* Census 2011, Government of India.

Table 2.1 shows there are 22 districts in Punjab with 27,704,236 inhabitants as per the 2011 census. In terms of areas, Pathankot is the smallest district and Ludhiana is the largest district of Punjab.

## Demographic Profile of District Jalandhar

District Jalandhar is a prominent district in Doaba region of the Punjab. Jalandhar division lies between north latitude 30 -58' and 31 -37' and east longitude 75 - 08' and 76 - 18'. On the south, Sutlej River flows which separates it from Firozpur, on the northwest, Kapurthala district intervenes between the Jalandhar territory and Beas River, and on the north-east, and it shares boundaries with Hoshiarpur district, broken by area of Phagwara tehsil of Kapurthala district, which extended out into Jalandhar territory. For the administrative purposes, the district is a part of Jalandhar division. The district is the basic unit of administration. For the purposes of general and revenue set up, five tehsils Shahkot, Nakodar, Phillaur Jalandhar-I and. Jalandhar II are set up. All of them have sub divisional status. District has been divided in 10 zones that is Jalandhar East, Jalandhar West, Bhogpur,

Adampur, Nakodar, Shahkot, Phillaur, Nurmahal, Lohian Khas and Rurka Kalan. As per Census 2011 Jalandhar district comprises of 941 out of which 19 are uninhabited villages.

## Demographic Profile of District Kapurthala

Kapurthala is the smallest district in Punjab population and areawise. Some prominent districts such as Hoshiarpur, Gurdaspur and Amritsar are established on the north side. Amritsar and TarnTaran on the west side. Jalandhar division is the main division for administrative purpose. The district is the basic unit of administration. For the purposes of general and revenue set up the district is divided into four Tehsils- Bhulath, Kapurthala, Sultanpur Lodhi and Phagwara. All of them have sub divisional status. The district is comprises of 688 villages out of which 76 villages are uninhabited. It has 9 towns comprising of 6 statutory towns and 3 Census towns.

## Demographic Profile of District Hoshiarpur

Hoshiarpur district was functioning since pre independence. The district takes its name from the district headquarters town, known as Hoshiarpur. For the administrative purposes, Hoshiarpur is a part of Jalandhar Division. Some of the prominent villages of Hoshiarpur are Adamwal, Begumpur, Badowal, Bari Khad and Bassi Ballo.

**Table 2.2: Literacy Rate in Punjab by Education Level**

| *Education Level* | *No. of Persons (In Lakhs)* | *Literacy Rate (in %)* |
|---|---|---|
| Total Literates | 187 | 75.84 |
| Without Education | 5.66 | 2.30 |
| Below Primary | 22.28 | 9.03 |
| Primary | 42.88 | 17.38 |
| Middle | 30.66 | 12.43 |
| Matric | 41.86 | 16.97 |
| Senior Secondary | 23.10 | 9.37 |
| Non-Technical Diploma | 0.24 | 0.10 |
| Technical Diploma | 2.34 | 0;95 |
| Graduate or above | 17.60 | 7.14 |
| Unclassified | 0.42 | 0.17 |

Source: www.Punjabdata.com-literacyrate.

Table 2.2 shows Punjab total literacy rate 75.84percent. 5.66 lakhs are without getting any education from any formal education. 22.28Lakhs are below the primary level. 42.88 lakhs are the people who got education at the primary level. 30.66 Lakhs are the people who obtained middle level education.41.86 lakhs got education at the Matric level.23.10 lakhs got education at the senior secondary level.0.24 lakhs got non-technical diploma and 2.34 lakhs technical diploma. 17.60 lakhs graduate or above and 0.42 lakhs comes under unclassified. Literacy profile shows that the level of education is quite depressing. Data also shows that the majority of the youngster's aims to go to a foreign country hence they do not take serious interest in studies.

**Table 2.3: Migration Rate in Punjab**

| *State* | *Population (1991)* | *Out-Migrants (2001)* | *Migration Rate (per 100) 1991-2001* |
|---|---|---|---|
| Punjab | 20,281,969 | 501,285 | 1.7 |

Source: www.Punjabdata.com-literacyrate

Table 2.3 shows that the migration rate from Punjab to foreign countries is 1.7 percent. The migration data also indicate that the youngsters prefer to go to a foreign country rather than getting education in Punjab.

**Table 2.4: Population Rate in three Districts of Punjab**

| *Districts* | *Kapurthala* | *Jalandhar* | *Hoshiarpur* |
|---|---|---|---|
| Population | 754,521 | 1,962,700 | 1,480,734 |
| Growth Ratio Population (1991-2001) | 16.68 | 18.96 | 14.02 |
| Ratio of SC Population to Total Population | 29% | 37% | 37% |
| Sex Ratio | 888 | 887 | 935 |
| Literacy Rate | 73.5% | 77.9% | 81.4% |
| Total work participation ratio | 35% | 34.5% | 34.7% |
| Below Poverty Line ratio | 3.0 | 9.1 | 2.9 |
| Life Expectancy | 64.5 | 64.2 | 64.5 |
| Punjab Human Development Index | 7 | 6 | 5 |

Source: Rani, Anita (2011), Poverty in Punjab: A District Level Study, available at http://hdl.handle.net/10603/10225, retrieved on 15 July 2017.

Table 2.4 shows that growth ratio of population in Kapurthala 16.68percent, Jalandhar 18.96 and Hoshiarpur 14.2percent. From this population, the ratio of SC population is 29percent, 37percent and 37percent respectively. Sex ration has been observed in Kapurthala 888, Jalandhar 887 and Hoshiarpur 935. Literacy rate in Kapurthala 73.5 percent, Jalandhar 77.9percent and Hoshiarpur 81.4percent respectively. Total work participation in Kapurthala 35percent, Jalandhar 34.5percent and Hoshiarpur

34.07percent respectively. Below poverty line in Kapurthala 3.0percent, Jalandhar 9.1percent and Hoshiarpur 2.9 percent. Life expectancy has been observed as 64percent on an average in three districts. Human Development Index 7percent in Kapurthala, Jalandhar 6percent and Hoshiarpur 5percent has been observed. This data shows that where there is higher literacy rate the work participation and human development index is greater.

***Map 3: Political Map of England (United Kingdom) showing Southall, Birmingham and Wolverhampton***

## A brief Historical Background of England

"At the battle of Hastings, the Normans (powerful northern Frenchmen) defeated the English and started a century long conquest of England. William (Duke of Normandy) crowned himself the ruler of England in 1066. Elizabeth first Queen of England, after the defeat of the French in both America at Quebec in 1795. England is a part of the United Kingdom and shares borders with Scotland and Wales. On Northwest lies Irish Sea and Celtic Sea lies on the Southwest. The country covers five-eighths of the island of Great Britain. The name Britain stems from Brythonic, one of the two dialects spoken by Celtic people of the Isles: Brythonic was the language of England and wales, Goidelic the tongue of Scotland and Ireland. England is 50,000 square miles. Great Britain is the legal political entity that came into being when England and Scotland were formally united in 1707, and the UK was created in 1801"(Lacey,2007:3 and 5).

## Demographic Profile of District Birmingham

"Birmingham is a dynamic city for an international comparison because it is large, very diverse and active in the field of ethnic politics while retaining an essentially English "provincial" aspect that makes it typical of many other British cities" (Garbaye 2001). Birmingham is a happening city. The city is located in the West Midlands. Since industrial revolution, the city is a house to metal and engineering industry. The population of Birmingham 1,111,307. Asian population is around 26.6 percent (Census UK, 2011).

## Demographic Profile of District Southall

The birth of Southall took place after the cutting in 1796 of the Grand Junction (now Grand Union) Canal and the opening of Southall station in 1839. Southall is house to ethnic communities. Sikhs are the main ethnic sub-groups. Southall is also inhabited by Muslims and Hindus. Muslims from Pakistan constitutes a sizeable number in Southall. On the Broadway and South Road, people from Asian origin run shopping areas in Southall. Southall predominantly populated by Punjabis. India culture and languages especially Punjabi dominate the area's large number of groceries, cinema and video shops, newspapers and magazines as well as temples and Gurdwaras. Dhanjal states, "the early core of the post- 1945 South Asian settlement in Southall, West London was made of migrants from Punjab mainly from the districts of Hoshiarpur and Jalandhar". Socially and culturally, Southall is a diversified town. Southall is well known by the name of 'Little India'. "The population of Southall Broadway was 13,439 and is made up of approximately 47percent females and 53percent males" (Dhanjal, 2010:109).

## Demographic Profile of District Wolverhampton

The population of Wolverhampton was 249,470. There were approximately 51percent females and 49percent males. Wolverhampton is rated 259 out of 380 districts on industrial structure. This indicates that Wolverhmapton is a knowledge economy that perform in the bottom 40percent of districts nationally (Census UK, 2011).

**Table 2.5: Twenty most reported main languages other than English in England(UK), 2011.**

| *Rank* | *Language* | *Number* | *% of population aged 3+* |
|---|---|---|---|
| 1 | Urdu | 29,403 | 2.9 |
| 2 | Punjabi | 21,166 | 2.1 |
| 3 | Bengali | 14,718 | 1.4 |
| 4 | Pakistani Pahari | 10,827 | 1.1 |
| 5 | Polish | 8,952 | 0.9 |
| 6 | Somali | 8,139 | 0.8 |
| 7 | Chinese/Cantonese | 7,807 | |
| 8 | Arabic | 6,921 | 0.7 |
| 9 | Pashto | 6,123 | 0.6 |
| 10 | Gujarati | 4,871 | 0.5 |
| 11 | Persian/Farsi | 3,031 | 0.3 |
| 12 | Kurdish | 2,716 | 0.3 |
| 13 | French | 2,558 | 0.2 |
| 14 | Hindi | 1,540 | 0.2 |
| 15 | Romanian | 1,233 | 0.1 |
| 16 | Tagalong | 1,186 | 0.1 |
| 17 | Portuguese | 1,127 | 0.1 |
| 18 | Tigrinya | 1,074 | 0.1 |
| 19 | German | 1,009 | 0.1 |
| 20 | Tamil | 999 | 0.1 |

Source: 2011 Census, Crown Copyright, 2013.

Table 2.5 shows 2.1percent people speak Punjabi language in UK. This data shows that from India many Hindi, Gujarati and Tamil speaking people have migrated to England. The percentage of Punjabi speaking people are much higher than other languages which shows that majority is the Punjabi people migrated to England (UK).

## Causes of Migration

According to a number of social scientists have argued that colonialism provided the objective conditions for the emigration of the Punjabis, but the subjective conditions emerged much latter and in the form of the marginalization of the soldiers within the family and the village community. In the migration trajectories, push and pull factors play a significant role. The pull factor is a matter of individual choice and the push factor can be associated with poverty, political persecution and riots. However, it was the Doaba region (Jalandhar, Hoshiarpur and Kapurthala districts at that time) from where the migration occurred. Both Mayo Singh and Kapur Singh were from Hoshiarpur district belonging to the neighboring villages of Paldi and Kharaudi respectively, who owned the lumber mill in British Columbia. (Judge, 2012:41). Lintner opines, "The economic push and pull requirements have given rise to a new-fangled class of criminal people called 'human traffickers" (Lintner, 2007:18).

"There were an estimated 15,000 Punjabi youth detained in various prisons across the world for staying illegally" (India Today, 2011). As per United Nations Office on Drugs and Crime, "Every year nearly 0.02 million Punjabi youths try to illegally migrate to European Union (EU) countries in pursuit of greener pastures. A majority of these irregular migrants from Punjab go to Britain" (Saha et al., 2009). "Punjab has become the hub of the 12,000 crore rupees human trafficking racket. It is estimated that 10,000 to 20,000 Punjabis contribute to this flourishing business each year by paying anything between Rs. 2.5 lakh to Rs. 10 lakh each on being promised greener pastures abroad. The preferred destinations are mainly the USA, Canada, Australia, England, Italy and Greece. In Punjabi language, human trafficking is termed as *'kabootarbaazi'*, traffickers as *'kabootarbaaz'* and victims as *kabootars*" (Dogra, 2007:3).

Singh describes, "The Sikh diaspora is stated to have begun after the fall of the Sikh kingdom in 1849, which led to the annexation of the last emperor, Maharajah Duleep Singh. After being exiled from India by the British Raj aged 15, Maharaja Dulep Singh arrived in the UK as the first Punjabi Sikh settle in the UK" (Singh, 2011). As estimated, 420,000 Punjabis Sikhs are currently living in the UK; of which 240,000 are British born (Census UK, 2011).

## Existence of Caste System among Punjabi Diaspora

A substantial body of literature is available on the caste and community characteristics of the Punjabi diaspora. Two Punjabi communities that is Bhatras and Jats arrived UK. Their settlement is recorded during the First and Second World Wars. Some Punjabi community known as Ramgarhia Sikhs arrived UK from East Africa. This comes under the category of secondary migration. The Sikh community is divided into several sects. For example Radha Soami, Narankari. Other caste groups Ravidassi and Valmiki community people also migrated to the UK. Separate religious institutions by Sikhs, Buddhists, Valmiki and Ravidassi, Radha Soamis and Valmikis are established. Such religious institutions are the avenues for meetings and solemnizing marriage (Chanda, 2012).

Sabarwal found the Ad-dharmi as the most mobile Dalit caste. Mango Ram, Ad-dharmi left his native village in Hoshiarpur district for the USA" (Sabarwal, 1990:107). Judge argues that at the present the caste background of the Punjabi diaspora in the English speaking countries has not undergone any change except for the fact that over a period of time. Most of the caste groups could be found in these countries. Despite the fact that there is a noticeable number of inter marriages taking place, the specter of caste weighs heavily on the minds of the first generation Punjabis. A typical Jat is not worried about his daughter marrying a white man, but he is horrified to think or of his daughter marrying a black or a Dalit man (Judge, 2012:48).

## Conclusion

In this chapter, we have explored the demographic profile of Punjab and England (UK). In Punjab, we have discussed three districts Jalandhar, Hoshiarpur and Kapurthala and found that literacy rate is high in Punjab. Similarly, we have tried to understand three districts in England (UK) Southall, Birmingham and Wolverhampton. In England (UK) we have explored the demographic profile of these places to substantiate the universe of the study. We have also discussed the causes of migration from Punjab to England (UK) and found that migration is dynamic in Punjab. In the past decades, people from Punjab migrated to the developed nations for better economic opportunities but currently, it has been observed that the people from Punjab have been migrating to the developed countries for various other reasons such as marriage, family reunification and for the purpose of study. We have observed that the caste system is prevalent in Punjab and England (UK). The people belonging to the marginalized sections of the society are excluded from the mainstream society in Punjab and England (UK). This study found that caste has travelled from India to England (UK) through Indians.

## References

Chanda, Rupa. (2012). The Punjabi Diaspora in the UK: An overview of characteristics and contributions to India, Indian Institute of Management, Bangalore, Working Paper No; 380.

Dhanjal, Beryl. (2010). Sikh Women in Southall (Some impressions), *New Community*, 5(1-2), 109-114.

Dogra, Chander Suta. (2007). 'This Bird Has Flown: Flawed Flight', World Prout Assembly, May, *Journal of Sikh Studies*, 9(6), 1-12.

Garbaye, R. (2001).*City template Birmingham: Basic information on ethnic minorities and their participation.* Worcester College, Oxford University, Oxford. Prepared for UNESCO-MOST Multicultural Policies and Modes of Citizenship in European Cities (MPMC) project. http://www.unesco.org/most/p97city.htm.

Judge, Paramjit S. (2012).Mapping the Social Background of Punjabi Diaspora. In *Indian Diaspora: Migration and Development with focus on the State of Punjab* (Eds), Centre for Research in Rural and Industrial Development (CRRID), Chandigarh.

Lacey Baldwin Smith. (2007). English History made brief, irreverent, and Pleasurable, Chicago, Academy Chicago Publishers.

Lintner, Bertil. (2003), *'Illegal Migration in The 21st Century'*, Yale Global, 10 January (online edition).

Narang,K.S.(1969). History of Punjab 1500-1858, New Delhi, U.C. Kapur and Sons.

Sabarwal, Satish. (1990).*Mobile Men: Limits to Social Change in Urban Punjab*, Shimla, Indian Institute of Advanced Study in association with Manohar Publications, New Delhi.

# III

# Conceptual Clarifications and Literature Survey

## Introduction

This chapter attempts to understand the existing literature survey on migration and ageing of the elderly. This chapter tries to know how theories on migration and ageing had evolved over time. This chapter tries to explore the findings of the previous studies conducted on migration and ageing from a comparative perspective. This chapter attempts to examine the gaps in the existing literature on migration and ageing in relation to the older persons. This chapter also looks into theories on migration, ageing, diaspora and remittances. This chapter also tries to understand loneliness, isolation and elderly abuse in Punjab and England (UK).

## Operational Definitions and Terms

- Health: means mental and physical fitness and social well-being.
- Elderly in the present study are treated as those aged 60+. They are also referred to as 'aged'.
- Ageing refers to deterioration in the functional capacity of an individual resulting from the advancement in age.
- International Migrant means a person who has crossed domestic territory beyond 6 months.
- Care means attentive assistance or treatment to those in need.
- Well–being is a satisfied state of being happy, healthy and prosperous.
- Remittance means transfers of money by a foreign worker to his or her home country. However, remittance do not include NRI deposits.

- Left behind Elderly means those elderly who are not co-residing with their children as children are international migrants.

## Understanding Ageing in India

Demographic transition in the 21st century in terms of longevity based on improved medicine and economy has made 'ageing' population to occupy prominent position all across the world (Subaiya and Bansod, 2011). In this context, Thakur explains, "Ageing of the human population is one of the major demographic transitions of the last hundred years or so" (Thakur, 2012).

According to Akanksha et.al (2011:509), "Socio-economic changes such as increased urbanization and modernization, increasing participation of women in economic activities, mobility of the younger generation and the growth of individualism are leading to breakdown of the joint family structure, which used to be the primary support for the elderly in India". They further argue that modern changes can be seen among the Indian youths becoming more individualistic, utilitarian, and indifferent towards the elders. In conjunction to this, the younger generation has come to regard older generation as a burden and a liability. Challenges among elderly after migration is not new concept for Indian society only but prevalent in other countries too.

According to the study conducted by King and Vullnetari describes, "Massive internal and international out-migration from rural Albania since 1990 has disrupted traditional social and kinship systems and has made elderly people particularly vulnerable. Although remittances cushion their social isolation, the loss of children and grandchildren through emigration has undermined elderly people's self-respect and raison d'être in Albanian family life. One of their coping mechanisms has been to follow their children abroad to care for the grandchildren, enabling both parents of the children to engage in paid work".(King and Vullnetari 2006:783).

According to Amarjit Singh, "seniors and grandparents themselves need and want to be listened to, and to share their experiences and wisdom with others. This process of listening to their life stories based on their long-term memories is extremely rewarding for their well-being and that of the listener" (Singh, 2013:19). However, various studies emphasize that the joint family is a symbol of unity and solidarity. The most important advantage of the joint family is that it provides social, economic and emotional security to its members. Elderly have to endure economic vulnerability while they live alone. Older people are often perceived as lonely, hopeless, and sad. Emotional needs among the elderly require an active participation in the society and in that the role of the relatives and children becomes all the necessary.

Poverty and cultural factors also contributed to immigrant' poor health. In the Indian context, "Today an average Indian man lives beyond 67 years and women about 70 years"(Census,2011).The United Nations has projected the increase in the number of older persons and it is expected to reach two billion by 2050(United Nations, 2017). By this time, the population of the old age will outnumber the proportion of the young age people (0-14 years) all over the world. It is also estimated that the oldest segment of the age group (80 years and above) has been growing rapidly, and by 2050, around 20% of the global old age group is expected to come within this range. The present, as well as the future, is therefore filled with ageing of the aged.

On the contrary, European societies, especially the western side have been undergoing demographic transition since there is a fall in fertility as women prefer to have fewer or no children (Digby, 2001). "Segregates the old age into 'early elderly' i.e. individuals falling within the age group of 65-74 and 'late elderly' that is who are over 75 years of age" (Orimo et al., 2006). "India's perspective of old age is associated with declining of mental and physical facilities, which varies culturally and historically, however, in terms of economic benefits, people beyond 60 years are considered elderly" (NHRC, 2011). In older age, mortality among people belonging to the lower economic group has therefore been reported to be higher than among those who have a higher economic group (Huisman, 2004:472).

"The elderly abuse has serious consequences on the health and well-being of older people and can be of various forms: physical, verbal, psychological/emotional, sexual and financial. Elderly Abuse has been reportedly experienced by more than one fifth of the elderly with the most common forms experienced being disrespect and neglect". (WHO, 2008). "Most of the elderly are experiencing it almost daily. The most common form of abuse nationally experienced by elderly was disrespect 79percent followed by verbal abuse 76percent and neglect 69percent and a disturbing 39percent elderly faced beating or slapping" (Help Age India Report, 2013:4).

Raju argues, "the older individuals suffering from depression, poor health or physical impairments were more at risk of being abused than those of similar age and normal health status". Brill conducted study in Australia and found, "The most frequent form of reported or suspected abuse of elderly people is financial abuse and the adult daughter or son are most likely to be the abusers".(as quoted in Yatish and Bhargava, 2014:3).

Reddy states, "in the recent years, indignity, disgracefulness, embarrassment, dishonor, disheartening, disregard, indifference, injustice, lack of care, psychological torture and host of negative behaviors and attitudes are reflected in the society towards elderly. Millions of elderly are suffering emotionally from the growing phenomena of gross indifference, profit motive, selfishness and decay in the family system. Although family ties in India are still strong and an overwhelming majority of the old still live with their family members, the position of an increasing number of order persons is becoming vulnerable. In the present scenario, they cannot take it for granted that their children will be able to look after them when they need care in their old age; keeping in view the longer life span which implies an extended period of dependency" (Khan, 2004:174) Ramamurthy argue, "in most countries of the world the older persons do not enjoy a decent status in society. This is all the more so in developing countries such as India which are economically poor and have been subjected to the ravages of demographic transition, migration, modernization, dwindling joint family, market economy, poor public health and hygiene and low social and income security"( as cited in Khan, 2004:174).

"Henry found that social disengagement occurs during old age. The marital dissolution of the senior citizens also has a strong bearing on their socioeconomic well-being. It is frequently reported that married persons tend to enjoy higher social participation compared with unmarried ones and widows or widowers" (Henry, 1994). Shrut says institutionalized elderly had stronger fear of death compared 36 to others who live in families. Moreover, it was unmarried and widows, who were more in institutions. Again, majority of the aged derived satisfaction only when they were with their family and, therefore, institutionalization was not beneficial to the elderly" (Shrut, 1958).

Ramamurthi (1968) observed, "The status of the elderly depends upon their socio-economic status. The higher income group people are better adjusted than the lower income group people". Rao (1990:90) studied "psychiatric illness of the aged in the context of different living arrangements". The study revealed that living with the family does not ensure a healthy integration. Soodan conducted a study on ageing in India, pertaining to the aged in the city of Lucknow. "In this study, he compared the educational level, the number of years of migration to the city and their economic dependence. It was found that majority of the aged spent their free time doing odd jobs connected with household work, looking after their grandchildren, and 'doing nothing'. Free time of men was solitary in nature while women spent free time in interpersonal activities" (Soodan, 1972:50).

"An important variable frequently associated with the adjustment of the elderly is religiosity" (Cherian, 1999). "It is believed that religions become increasingly important with the onset of later life. For many elderly people, spiritual well-being can relate to basic life and death questions that may become more frequent and urgent in the later years" (Thorson, 1983:10). "Both Western, as well as Indian studies, have reported that religiosity is a salient feature in the lives of the elderly, despite the lack of organized religious participation" (Ramamurti and Jamuna, 1993:60). "Older people give more importance to rituals and church worship, dogmas and observances" (Gangarade, 1988). "The reason for this can be viewed from two angles, namely, the desire to experience the fullness of life in a socially acceptable manner in the later years, and to seek more social and communal support, when the physical strength is getting degenerated" (Palmore, 1969:86).

"Retirement is a major and personally important life transition. New patterns of personal involvement must be developed in the context of changing roles and life styles in retirement" (Schlossberg, 2004:45). "Adjustment to retirement may often be difficult for individuals, as it requires adopting a new life style, characterized by decreased income and activity and increased free time" (Streib and Schreider, 1971), "Retirement causes extreme stress in males because a significant part of their identity lies with their job. Sometimes, with the loss of the job retirement with meagre economic sources older persons feel stressed and depressed".

"Adjustment during retirement involves two conditions. First the individual attempts to meet the demands of environment; second the individual perceives and experience a sense of general well-being in relation to the environment. Factors such as satisfactory health, married life, good family relationship, friendship, feeling of security, social status equal to what they had previously and plan for the future, religiosity and belief in rebirth to be positively associated with good adjustment in old age" (George, 1980). "Adjustment is a process involving both mental and behavioral responses by which an individual strives to cope with inner needs, tensions, frustrations and conflicts and to bring harmony between these inner demands and those imposed upon him by the world in which he lives, if the conflicts are solved to satisfy the individual needs with in tenets approved by the society" (Kotwal and Prabhakar, 2009:118).

Punia and Punia conducted, "a study on personal problems of retired elderly in Haryana. The survey was conducted on total number of 240 elderly (120 men and 120 women) from urban areas. Age of the sample ranged between 58 to 67 years. Results revealed that 57.5 percent faced severe adjustment problems followed by moderate level (35.8%) of adjustment problems. Findings showed that 65.5 percent of females encountered severe adjustment problems against 53.6 percent of males. Both male and female equally faced moderate level of adjustment problems" (Punia and Punia, 2003:93).

## Understanding Ageing in UK

"The population is also becoming older and more ethnically diverse" (Butt and Neil, 2014). According to Census (2011), "the number of people living alone in the United Kingdom aged 65-74 has risen just slightly and the number aged 75 and over living alone has remained much the same". Kannan conducted a study of cultural adaptation of young people and their parents of Asian immigrants of Britain and found that cultural integration existed among the first generation immigrants; cultural assimilation in the case of second-generation immigrants and their child but complete neglect of their tradition and culture in the case of third generation immigrants and the younger people. Thus, according to him, migration leads to cultural assimilation" (Kannan, 1978:102). In UK, "There is a strong preference towards institutionalized setup for the elderly people. This retirement homes, however, speak immensely of the socio-economic conditions of the old people, in a sense that privileged people have the tendency to have better facilities than the ones who are poorer" (Khaw, 1999). "In addition to the retirement homes, the country also provides pensions and benefit schemes to the elderly"(Digby, 2001).

However, studies show that many of the Asians living in the UK are unaware of the social services provided by the state. .Among these Asians, the Punjabis in Southall suburbs are also included. Even when they are aware of the social schemes, they also suffer from language problems that deprive them in claiming the social services" (Donaldson, 1986). Without proper information, the elderly often end up without having the access to these facilities and services in the UK.

In an alien society in general, Khoo (2012) states, "immigrant's experience difficulties with the language of the country of settlement may be less integrated into the community and more dependent on their relatives for social and economic support rather than government services". People over 60 years, they pointed, have various benefits like free prescriptions, eye tests, and other minor health benefits. Health services are administered through various ways like rationing products, resource allocation, budget management, etc. The study further shows that in UK, there were only few Asians who were aware of social services given by the state. They also suffer from language problems that make them relegate in claiming social services.

British Sikh Report (2013) demonstrates, "68percent of older Sikh have a language barrier problem, due to Punjabi being their main language spoken. If older Sikh within an area which does not have a Punjabi speaking population, they will find it difficult to access help without any assistance". "Without proper information, they often do not have access to facilities and services. Norman argues that the elders of ethnic minorities face a potential triple jeopardy- at risk through old age, through discrimination and through lack of access to health and social services"(as quoted in Amanda, 1998).

Jutlla explores, "The impact of migration experiences and migration identities on these ethnic minority individuals` particular experiences of both the formal statuary services and of caring for a family member with dementia. Through her analysis of her Sikh research participants` personal histories and experiences of caring for their older family member with demoniac, she illustrates how the actual barriers to service use for her research participants are much more external to the Sikh community than is generally recognized, existing in the form of the perceived and actual racism and structural inequalities experienced by these ethnic minority people in their capacity as immigrants, as opposed to simply being linked with issues of `community` and `culture` in a straightforward way. Furthermore, the social and cultural heterogeneity exiting ethnicity this otherwise ethnically defined community means that there is also a diversity of experiences in relation to how the inequalities are experienced by members of the this community, with some members being better equipped than others to negotiate access to the required services"((Jutlla,2014:1045).

## Understanding Socio-Economic Status and its Relationship with Well-being

The longevity of older people are increasing due to better health care facilities and invention of new medicines by science to fight out chronic diseases. Hoffman (2008) reveals, "old age is often characterized by pain, and when expectation increases, their pain, and situation becomes dire and complex in nature. The older people gets, the easier it becomes to lose the ability to adapt. He concludes there are multicultural attitudes to old age in different countries. Such attitudes involve all socio-economic aspects like manageing resources, health management, health services, and cultural inhibition, among others. These aspects have varied effects on the elderly people, irrespective of place of residents".

In broad understanding, it is emphasized that economic development in terms of high Gross Domestic Development (GDD) are necessary for initiating new economic development. In fact, they exerted many other factors that condition the socio-economic conditions such as health, education, technology, life expectancy, sensitivity, civic engagement, technology, income, work-life balance, housing, education, jobs, environment and safety in the community, etc. Jaffe (1998) looks into the transition from traditional-to-modern changes in all social aspects starting from education, health, culture, and all other elements that are a part of larger social process. According to the elderly, high income does not necessarily condition happier and more satisfactory socio-economic well-being than those who come under low-income earners. He further stated that the health and sensitivity factor constitute as the major indicator of their well-being and socio-economic conditions".

For the elderly, the social reasons become more apparent, and happiness and well-being of socio-economic conditions tends to become psychologically subjective, in a sense that their happiness can depend on the mind, personality, demography, and culture. Well-being living atmosphere conditioned by these factors can make a person intrinsically happier. "This reinforces the view that happiness and self –fulfillment in later life are dependent on the moral responsibility of individuals to reconstruct a youthful body, identity, and social life. Self-empowerment in this account is a technique of the self-based on individual willingness to access resources and participate in society" (Foucault, 1980).

Cooke (2008) elaborates, "socio-economic conditions influence the situation of old people immensely. It affects their adaptation in the society and personal situation any people experience loneliness and depression in old age, either as a result of living alone or due to lack of close family ties and reduced connections with their culture of origin. Socio-economic conditions of an individual have a strong correlation with health". Lynch et. al. (1997) point out that elderly people with disproportionately low income are exposed to various social and psychological conditions. Such exposure affects their health either directly through inadequacy in housing and sanitation or indirectly by socially disrupted neighbors and their projection of behavior and psychosocial features, thereby proving deleterious to health. Phillipson et al (2005) assert, "the experience of growing older is not shaped solely by family and kinship groups but also encompasses wider social relationship such as friends and neighbors".

## Understanding Socio-Economic Status in Punjab

"Disability in older people such as, cognitive impairment, morbidity, depression, increase or decrease of body mass, low frequency of social contacts, poor self-perceived health, vision impairment. Withdrawal, anxiety, lack of motivation and sadness complements depression and loneliness."

(Stuck et al., 1999). Bowling (2005) reveals, "that in socio-economic groups reflects poor health scenario and shorter lives in comparison to higher income groups. He asserts that socio-economic factors lead to high rate of morbidity and mortality among individuals". Bagga and Dayabati (2006:41) while exploring, socio-economic factors and deteriorating health conditions in mental health of the elderly, "they concluded that socio-cultural factors such widowhood reduced or no income, educational level, death or migration of children and living arrangement adversely affected the mental health of elderly women".

Widows exhibit strong adverse consequences as it is linked with high rates of mortality, morbidity, and self-reported ill health. Studies on Punjab show that elderly widows suffer from neglect at home owing to economic dependence. Goyal and Kajal (2014) observe that socio-economic factors have grave *emotional* risk in the elderly. Kaur and others conducted in district Faridkot of Punjab that in the absence of caregiver's older people face numerous challenges related to health. Similarly, the study in the municipal corporation of Kapurthala, Punjab on the socio-economic condition of the elderly found that socio-demographic variables, lifestyle, employment conditions and psychological conditions of the geriatric population of Kapurthala have resulted in chronic diseases like depression, insomnia, hypertension, anemia, lung diseases, and hyperlipidemia among others. They further observed that such chronic disease causes disability among the elderly (Kaur et. al., 2014:82).

A study conducted under the project of United Nations Population Fund –India by (Alam et. al.,2013) reveal, "due to poverty and low bases among the elderly in Punjab particularly those who belong to the lower socio-economic groups (owing to disintegration of families, absence of caregivers, etc.) engage themselves in less remunerative, informal employment. Employment is an issue concerning the elderly".

Marya explains that most of the elder respondents of Patiala, Hoshiarpur and Mansa, Punjab have left their job after attaining the age of 60plus. Therefore, their economic conditions have to some extent deteriorated and are mostly dependent on pension or children. She further states that in the absence of economic sources there is a danger in losing authority as head of the family" (Marya, 2013:75).

Zelizer explains, "money is a medium of care, support and filial relationship across countries. She demonstrates that remittances maintain long-distance household ties between the emigrants and people back home. Remittance plays an important part in alleviating poverty and meeting day to day expenses. Remittances sent by children back to their parents are utilized for various needs" (as cited in Babacan and Singh, 2010:87) Similarly, Walton-Roberts (2004:84) opines, "remittance works like an oxygen for the families left behind, especially for the unemployed or retired elderly people. In her study, she found that Punjab has been receiving huge remittances from overseas Punjabis and the large percentage of remittances has been spent for consumption purposes. She also observed India is currently the single largest overseas remittances receiving country in the world, partly because of the privileged economic and legal status accorded to non-resident Indians(NRIs) by Indian states and central government as an incentive for overseas Indian to play a role in the country`s economic development". In the same vein, Ghuman elaborates, "that in modern days, however, the practice of sending remittances through town and village associations has become very popular, which gained momentum specifically over the past 10-15 years. He further emphasized that the community or individual remittances have been largely helpful in bringing socio-economic changes across Punjab in terms of ushering in new infrastructure, income-generating programs, helping the old and the aged"(Ghuman,2012:98).

## Understanding Socio-economic Status in UK

"The British evidence suggests that personal care need is exclusively provided by the family while professional services may provide help with some tasks such as bathing. This research confirms that the so-called informal sector or second welfare state is the main provider of help to older people in the community. Formal care services are much more likely to be provided to those who live alone and have no family members who live near them, or those whose available relatives do not have the necessary capacity and skills" (Phillipson, 2001). "The problems of divided families, caused by restrictive immigration rules, resulting in many elderly people having no family support in the UK" (Ahmed and Walker, 1997:145).

As per Census (2011), "Sikhs in Scotland account for just 2.2 percent of British Sikhs". Szirmai (2005:72) notes that a country overcome such socio-economic challenges and fulfills the needs of the people, and then their socio-economic conditions can be considered as being taken care off. Population's well-being can help in understanding its socio-economic conditions which differs from developed to non-developed countries, from one society to another, and from culture to another, in its own capacities and in its own variations. From economic perspective. Kuate argues that per capita income, and other economy -related services" (Kaute, 2006).

## Theoretical Perspective on Migration

International migration has become an integral and inevitable feature of globalization and it has become a structural and permanent element of societies and economies (United Nation, 2007). Ravenstein (1885:218) has suggested that all migration emanates from low productivity areas and proceeds towards high productivity areas. Migrants from the rural areas frequently move first to nearby towns, if any, and then to large towns and cities. He observes that between the rural and urban people, the latter are less migratory than the former and migration is positively related to the growth of trade and industry. Similarly, Sjaastad, (1962:88) writes, that people will migrate when the benefits arising out of migration outweigh the costs involved in the process.

Military service in the Second World War again offered many young Sikh men the opportunity to immigrate to the UK. Ballard states, "a fair proportion of the Sikhs now resident in Britain have come by way of East Africa, but the majority have come here directly from India. There has been migration from India to Britain for a very long time even before the First World War, a few hardy individuals came to Britain to peddle clothes and ribbons in the villages. By 1939, almost every large city seemed to have had a small number of Sikh residents, for the most part, engaged in selling clothes in the markets. At the end of the war numbers slowly started rising and large contingents began to arrive, particularly in the late 1950s and early 1960s" (Ballard, 1972:17).

"During the 1950s and the 1960s, a substantial proportion of those who migrated to the UK and, to some extent, to Canada, were unskilled or semi-skilled. During the 1970s and the 1980s, skilled and educated emigrates with professional expertise moved. The technical qualifications opened up doors for white-collar workers. International migration wielded considerable impacts on demographic structures, expenditure patterns, social structures and poverty levels. Impacts include reducing population growth; enhancing the dependency burden within households; increasing consumption expenditures and reducing poverty levels. Remittances generate a considerable impact on regional economies" (Sasikumar and Hussain, 2008:27).

The partition of Indian sub-continent, as noted by the author, made many of the Sikhs caught in the partition to further the process of migration. "Many emigrants were from the Jalandhar district, a densely populated area in which the respondents of the universe of the study situated. People in Jalandhar suffered from shortage of land and therefore the means of self-support" (Marsh, 1967:23). Sikh community is well established in Britain. Writing about the Sikhs of Gravesend (Kent) Helweg (1986:5) summarizes, "the turban and beard of the [Sikh] man, along with the Salwar-kameez of the woman, make them noticeable". "These distinctions, plus their banding together in communities where their rural culture is transplanted, make them appear more numerous than they actually may be" (BSR, 2015).

"People migrated from Indian sub-continent are called 'Asian' in Britain. "Until accurate and suitable terminology is used in the literature, much research on members of ethnic communities will remain confusing, conflicting and perplexing" (Ahdieh and Hahn, 1996:97). "Social class defines by occupation and does not always reflects economic status but rather is a better reflection of education. The British social classification cannot reflect the status of South Asians as it does not take into account their original status or overall living standards" (Marmot, 1984:1456).

"In England people from India, Pakistan and Bangladesh including people arrived from East Africa are known as 'South Asians'. The Asians are a homogenous group of people who share a common culture and heritage. This assumption could be further from the truth" (Bhopal et al., 1991:244). As per British Sikh Report (2013), "95 percent are proud of their `Britishness`. British Sikhs with their sheer hard work took up top-level jobs. Sikhs have been contributing to the British economy. According to the British Sikh Report (2014), 87 percent British Sikhs own their homes".

Punjabis through marriage alliance also migrate to UK. In this context, Judge argues, "emigration has started taking place from all regions of Punjab, but Doaba still continues to lead in sending the largest number of emigrants" (as quoted in Sahai, and Lum, 2013:6). "The first Punjabi settlers in the UK were members of trading castes and later Sikh soldiers, who remained in the UK after fighting in France during the First World War" (Ballard, 1990:222).

Some study have concluded that diaspora and a higher rate of international migration as well as migration from rural to urban areas among the youths have hastened this process more rapidly. (Irudaya et. al., 1999:20) demonstrate, "while the increasing number of the elderly is attributed to demographic transition. Their deteriorating condition is considered as the end result of the fast eroding traditional family system in the wake of rapid migration resulted into urbanization and modernization".

Diasporic structure as noted by Thandi(2013:49) assessed that within the structure of diaspora, overseas Punjabis considers themselves as the one upholding their traditions since there is a rapid dying out of family structure, culture, and tradition at home (native Punjab). Among the first generation Punjabi diaspora, according to him, parents making their children to have Indian spouse has become the means in maintaining link with the Indian culture, tradition, and homeland. This culture, however, is now slowly changing among the second and the third generation parents, and they now look for more compatible partner than stick with tradition and culture. Most of the Punjabis continue to maintain diaspora-based kinship, but it has been slowly dying out making it more difficult to maintain kinship and tradition.

According to (Vertovec,2008; Singh and Tatla, 2008) Southall, "a large suburb in West London have therefore emerged as dominant place for discourse on diaspora in everyday lives, not only for the Sikh but even for many other Asians, who migrated considerably since partition" Burholt et al. state that apart from Southall in United Kingdom, many elders Sikh are found in Lozells and Handsworth, both suburban areas in Birmingham. The place easily identifies with culture-community where many ethnicities and cultures interplay their own parts. They further noted that research of South Asian diaspora in England and the study of the Punjabi Diaspora is not a new phenomenon; since many scholarly works have been done on this topic"(Burholt et al.,2002:54).

However, the study of elderly Punjabi remains neglected to a large extent. Various earlier studies conducted in the UK on the elderly substantiate that elderly abuses are common practices in household and public places. Saber Khan presents a poignant case of an elderly Punjabis man who spends his days in the park to avoid a family dependent on one's daughter's wage in which the children are 'out of control' (Philip and Elisabeth, 2005).

Migration involves the movement of people from one place to another in search of better employment opportunities and thereby raising the standard of living. Migration of young and old from the state of Punjab is not a new phenomenon. Migration from Punjab started during the British colonial government which recruited Punjabis in the British Army to work in the British colonies in different parts of the world. Different scholars and researchers from the diverse field have dealt with the subject of migration. Different migration theories have been propounded from time to time. Massey et al. (1993:437) opines, "remains mired in nineteenth-century concepts, models, and assumptions…a full understanding of contemporary migration processes will not be achieved by relying on the tools of one discipline alone, or by focusing on a single level of analysis. Rather, their complex, multifaceted nature requires a sophisticated theory that incorporates a variety of perspectives. Levels, and assumptions". From time to time, scholars from the diverse field of study attempted to describe migration in terms of various theories. In order to explain international migration, no single theory of migration could receive consent from different scholars. International migration has been divided into prominent two groups –one is classical migration and other is perpetuation theory of international migration. Major migration theories relevant to this study are discussed below:

## Classical Theory of Migration

From antiquity to modern times, people have been migrating in search of better economic opportunities. It is also termed as labor migration. According to "Adam Smith known as the father of economics, argues that labor migration is due to the imbalance in the labor market at different locations". According to Ravenstein`s, "Laws of migration is the concept of the search of opportunity as the main motive for migration" (Ravenstein, 1889).

## The Neo-Classical Theory

Hicks(1932) has propounded the Neo-classical theory of migration based on micro and macro aspects of migration. According to him, "Migration of labour is due to the difference in the real wages between the countries and migration of labour brings equilibrium in the international labour market which wipes away the wage differences between the countries". "The Neoclassical model works as a magnet to lure peasants into urban areas. The people are attracted toward bright lights of the city. The migration under this model occurs due to differences in wages. The wage differences can be bridged by finding an urban job. The people tend to migrate for better opportunities available in the developed nations. People always look for better remunerations. The aim is to uplift standard of livings" (Harris and Todaro, 1970:128). World Migration Report reported that rich people prefer to migrate than poor because poor people cannot bear the cost of migration (2003:36).

## Push and Pull Theory of Migration

Push and Pull theory of migration was propounded by Lee (1966). According to him, "The push-pull factors are the most important factor in migration. Decision and process of migration are determined by factors associated with the area of origin, destination, intervening factors, personal factors and fluctuation in the economy".

## The World System Theory

According to this theory of migration, Wallerstein (1974) tried to link "the development process of the countries with international migration. Due to the existence of unequal development between the central developed countries and the peripheral agricultural countries, the migration takes place. He argues, "migration is the natural consequences of globalization and market penetration across national boundaries" Joly notes, globalization, cheap air transportation, and growth of multinational companies etc. lead to the enhancement of migration" (Joly, 2000:35).

## The Dual Labour Market Theory

This theory indicates differentiation in wages between the skilled worker those falls under the category of primary segment and unskilled workers those falls under the category of secondary segment. This disparity in wages pushes labor shortages. On the other hand, the employers desire to preserve wage differentials in order to serve the local workers. "The labor shortage at the bottom of the job hierarchy, employers are compelled to recruit the unskilled foreign workers, who do not plan to stay permanently, but accept the secondary job more easily since it pays them more income"( Piore, 1979).

## Liberal Choice and Structural Theory

"Migration widens wage and income disparities as a result of the differences in the economic and political situations of countries. This theory also asserted that movement of labor is caused by economic factors and two models of migration have been presented. These models are classical theories (liberal choice) and core –periphery conflict (structural) theories. According to classical theories, workers move from low wage countries to high wage countries and this result in the efficient use of labor and narrows down the inter-country wage gaps". (Ghosh, 1996:85).

## Dual Economy Model of Development

According to this theory, "migration decision by an individual is to raise income. Labor migration plays a crucial role in the economic development of a country. The flow of migration over a long period of time is due to the prolonged disequilibrium that exists between the countries" (Lewis, 1953:480).

## Perpetuation Theory of Migration

Till and Brown emphasize, "The interpersonal ties connect migrants, former migrants, and non-migrants in origin and destination that encourage circular migration and reduce migration risk" (Till and Brown, 1967:142).

## The Migration Networks Theory

"The networks helps immensely the migrants to move. With the assistance of close friends and family members already migrated and settled in the host country, the new migrants find it easy to settle and find a job, house and also maintain cultural continuity. "This networks helped migrants to maintain continued relations with their community members back in the homeland" (Glick-Schiller et al., 1992). It happens due to improved means of transportation and communication technologies. According to Massey et al., (1993), "Migrant networks are sets of interpersonal ties that connect migrants, former migrants, and non-migrants in origin and destination areas through ties of kinship, friendship, shared community origin. They increase the likelihood of international migration movement because they lower the costs and risks of movement and increase the net returns to migration". International Organization on Migration reports, "the interaction facilitates migration by reducing the costs and risks. It further reported that migration through illegal means by friends and relatives result in hardships and sometimes these illegal migrants become victims of violence and exploitation"(IOM,2003:185).

## The Cumulative Causation Theory of Migration

Massey (1990) has propounded this theory. According to this, "continuance of migration is due to the intermingling of migrants with other persons of the origin. It is asserted by this theory that migration is sustained itself by creating more migration". According to historical-structural views as propounded by Papademetrio, "migration does not mean it would resolve, or substantially ameliorate the structural conditions that were believed to cause migration. He also argues, "migration is essentially interpreted as a negative "flight from misery" which contributes little to development. According to him, migration would contribute to the evolution into an uncontrolled depletion of their already meager supplies of skilled manpower-and the most healthy, dynamic, and productive member of the populations" (Papademetrio, 1985:212).

## Understanding Diaspora

Cohen explains, "diaspora means dispersal from an original homeland, often traumatically, to two or more foreign regions. Alternatively or additionally, the expansion from a homeland in search of work, in pursuit of trade or to further colonial ambitions. A collective memory and myth about the homeland, including its location, history, suffering and achievements. An idealization of the real or imagined ancestral home and a collective commitment to its maintenance, restoration, safety and prosperity, even to its creation. The frequent development of a return movement to the homeland that gains collective approbation even if many in the group are satisfied with only a vicarious relationship or intermittent visits to the homeland. A strong ethnic group consciousness sustained over a long time and based on a sense of distinctiveness, a common history, the transmission of a common cultural and religious heritage and the belief in a common fate. A troubled relationship with host societies, suggesting a lack of acceptance or the possibility that another calamity might befall the group. A sense of empathy and co-responsibility with co-ethnic members in other countries of settlement even where home has become more vestigial. The possibility of a distinctive creative, enriching life in host countries with a tolerance for pluralism" (Cohen, 2008:16).

## Sociological Theories of Family

Sociological theories of the family have for long time have been dominated by functionalism. Many have concentrated on the supposed relation between industrialisation and the changing 'functions' of the family seeing the family as a wholly dependable variable. "Industrialisation is considered to have changed the family from an 'extended' family to 'nuclear' unit, losing its productive and man of its educational functions in the process" (Gittins, 1982:72). According to Parsons (1964), the primary function of the family is social cohesion. Durkheimian perspective illustrates the family is universal. Parsons and Bales (1956) discuss the division of labor within the family in terms of 'natural differentiation and performance ascribing to women. Goode (1969) emphasises on the importance of inheritance as a determinant of family organisation and attitudes to children. He argues that parents among the lower strata did have less power over their children than those in the upper strata. Bott (1968:34) stresses on power as essential a dimension to the family structure as it is to society itself.

## Conceptual Meaning of Social Isolation

Nicholson defines "Social Isolation as a state in which the individual lacks a sense of belonging socially, lacks engagement with others, has a minimal number of social contacts and is deficient in fulfilling and quality relationship"( as quoted in Yuchun and Chang,2011:4). Social isolation among the elderly migrants is notably predictable. Duffy states, "due to arrival in unfamiliar social environment, poverty, poor health, and communication problems, it is difficult for them to participate effectively in the economic, social, political, and cultural life. As a result, they become alienated and isolated from the mainstream society" (Duffy, 1995:32). Maiter states, "a sense of loneliness and social isolation reinforces among the elderly people when they feel difficulties in understanding media news reports, reading newspapers and magazines or making use of public transportation to visit friends or shop" (as cited in Hossen, 2012:1). Felce and Perry argue that social isolation as "living alone, lacking instrumental support and being unable to share life expectations with a confidant". According to them, the social isolation is related to confidents. People who are socially isolated will be reluctant or unwilling to share the personal feeling with their own confidants" (as cited in Yuchun and Chang, 2011:8).

Loneliness, anxiety, and stress are generally caused by social isolation. Sometimes, extreme social isolation leads to cognitive decline, impairment, and dementia and depression. Social isolation puts stress on mental and physical health in later life. Several studies indicate that older people with weak social ties have fifty percent higher risk of mortality than those who are socially connected. According British Medical Council, "one million older people in England report not speaking in over one month. Older people are more likely to be fuel poor as they spend longer in their homes and require more heating through the winter months and are also often on lower incomes than other age groups. Older people are also more vulnerable to colder temperatures, cardiovascular disease, trips and falls and respiratory illness during the winter months. Therefore older people living in a cold home have higher levels of morality and morbidly than those in warm homes. In 2014-15 there were 36,300 excess winter deaths amongst people over the age of 75, while not all these will relate to poor housing and cold homes, cold housing has been estimated to cause approximately 20 percent of excess winter deaths"[1].

Laura et al., describe, "migrants to England and Wales from the Indian subcontinent show greater variation in patterns of morality. Proportional mortality ratio for cancer was lower for Hindu groups than for Moslems and was lowest for Punjabis, while significantly more Punjabis males die from cerebrovascular disease and cirrhosis of the liver. Morality due to ischemic heart disease (IHD) was high in all groups, but highest in Moslems and diabetes was commonest among Guajaratis" (Laura et al., 2013).

## Conceptual Meaning of Loneliness

"Loneliness is a common problem" (Weiss, 1973). According to Eliopoulous, in the ageing process, "hearing and speech deficit and language differences, which present communication barriers can foster loneliness" (as cited in Yuchun and Chang, 2011:1). "Loneliness also has been defined as a significant risk for health" (Savikko, 2008:14). Russel et al., states that "loneliness is an emotionally unpleasant experience. In particular, loneliness has been linked with feelings of general dissatisfaction, unhappiness, depression, anxiety, emptiness, boredom, restlessness, and marginality" (as quoted in Cook and Wilson, 1979:102). It has been argued that several forms of loneliness might exit due to various physical and social environments. Some studies indicate that older people experience social isolation and loneliness particularly in an alien culture where they find themselves not fully integrated. This case is prominent in European countries. Older people residing in the United Kingdom may experience loneliness due to several reasons. Some prominent reasons can be cited as a racial and ethnic milieu, religion, harsh weather conditions, language barrier, and loss of autonomy, feeling of loss, distress, separation, and isolation, the departure of one's children, retirement, unemployment and sometimes perpetual conflict in the family. Institutional residence aggravates loneliness among the older people. Such adverse environmental conditions affect physical and mental vivacity. Fromm- Reichmann believes, "Loneliness decreases motivation" (as quoted in Cook and Wilson, 1979:103).

Some studies demonstrate, "Loneliness is linked with gender, marital status, income, and age. Although it may only reflect greater willingness to reveal their feelings, more women than men report feeling lonely" (Donson and Georges, 1967; Weiss, 1973). "Loneliness is lower among married people than unmarried" (Weiss, 1973). "The unmarried group is further subdivided, loneliness is higher among widowed and divorced people than among singles, who do not differ from married" (Gubrium, 1974). According to (Weiss, 1973), "loneliness is higher among the poor". Dyer and Fidler argue "loneliness can occur at any age, it may be more common at particular points in the life cycle, especially late adolescence and perhaps in old age" (Dyer, 1974 and Fidler, 1976). Schulz found that "who could choose and predict when their visitors would come reported less loneliness than patients whose visitors just dropped in, even though the total interaction time in both conditions was identical"(Schulz,1976).

## Conceptual Meaning of Well-being

### *Definition of Well-Being*

"It is a known fact that health status and personality are the most important predictors of well-being. The well-being is a broad category of a phenomenon that includes people emotional responses domain satisfactions a global judgment of life satisfaction. It has been further argued that subjective well-being is the only ingredient of a good life" (Pelletier as quoted in Diener, et al., 1999:285). Ingeroll- Daytson el al. enumerated the following interpersonal and intrapersonal components having conducted a study on Thai elder's well-being. "These are *Harmony* means happy and harmonious relations with others. *Interdependence* means mutual support. *Respect* means respect other`s wisdom and advice. *Acceptance* means disregard negative thoughts and ready to face adverse situations. *Enjoyment* means enjoy life and participate in society recreational activities to gain modest pleasure" (as quoted in Susanne and Tim, 2014:8).

"Well-being can refer to a positive state of being. It often refers to a person's overall sense of health and wellness; it can also refer to a person's feelings of happiness or general satisfaction with his/her quality of life; it also points to the experience of contentment and fulfillment with one's life circumstances. Well-being is said to be experienced when a person's individual, relational, and collective needs are fulfilled" (Geoffrey and Prilleltensky, 2010:323).

"Well- being is an ` individually judged`, yet socially experienced, state of happiness freedom, safety and capability, shaped by interrelations with social -cultural (and natural) environments" (Hall, 2010:279). "Social network and social resources are important factors in reducing stress among the population, especially among older ages, being more sociable uplifts the depression and boots the psychological aspects it is an important indicator of social capital; it is an array of social contacts that gives access to social, emotional and practical support" (Gray, 2009:22).

## Elderly Abuse and its Types

Almost all countries of the world are facing the menace of elderly abuse. To combat this menace governments have been adopting new methods and processes to prevent elderly abuse. Some, for example, Argentina, Canada, Sweden, Turkey, the UK and the US have included coverage of abuse of the elderly under their legal systems and have created systems for reporting and treating cases of abuse; but many other do not have specific programmes designed to protect older persons from abuse" (Rob Vos et al., 2008:67). The National Centre for Elder Abuse, USA reports types of elder abuse "physical abuse means to inflict bodily injury, physical pain or impairment. Emotional or psychological abuse includes verbal and non-verbal infliction. Financial or material exploitation is referred as the illegal or improper use of an elder`s funds, property or assets. Neglect means the refusal or failure to fulfill any part of a person`s obligations or duties to an elder" (Adult Protective Services, National Center on Elder Abuse, 2004).

## Sub-types of Elderly People

"Multiple sub-types of older adults have emerged in research on ageism. Three elderly subtypes emerged; the *grandmotherly* type, described as helpful, kindly, serene, and trustworthy; *the elderly statesman*, described as intelligent, competitive, aggressive, and intolerant; and *the senior citizens* described as lonely, old-fashioned, weak, and worried" (Nelson, 2004:7). "The supposed inability of older individuals to cope with change is reflected in stereotypical beliefs that older people are inflexible, rigid, cautious, resistant to apply new methods, careful, critical, and cranky, and unadaptable" (Neussel, 1982; Shea, 1991). "Younger people`s perceptions of older people as communicatively close-minded, out of touch, and focused on the past" (Williams at el., 1997).

## Conceptual Meaning of Remittances

According to IMF, "remittances can help improve the country`s development prospects, maintain macroeconomic stability, mitigate the impact of adverse shock and reduced poverty". With the help of Remittances, families can retain or increase expenditures on basic consumption, businesses, housing and education. Mostly, families left behind use remittances for covering their basic consumption needs(2005). Faist argues, "the flow of money, knowledge and universal ideas called remittances can have a positive effect on what is called development in the countries of emigration" (Faist, 2008:21).

"As remittances are inherent in relations between those that migrate and those that stay, they have more or less explicitly been addressed in numerous studies on international migration, transnationalism, development, and social transformation" (Magdalena and Vojin, 2016:2). "Remittances are integral to migration because one of the basic motives for migrating is to remit a portion of earning to the communities of origin, especially under conditions of temporary labor migration" (Rahman et al., 2014). In recent times, "migrant worker`s remittances have also become an important source of funding to a number of developing countries" (Opong, 2012:12).

Comte explained, "the motivation that underlies a migrant`s decision to remit. According to him, this behavior is termed as altruistic behaviors on the part of a remitter. According to this theory, migrants will be willing to transmit resources to make up for the income shortfall of family members for either their consumption or investment. It further suggests that a migrant will willingly sacrifice his or her own well-being or interest for the sake of the welfare of relations due to the love and concern they may have for their relation's welfare. Comte believed that individuals are morally obligated to renounce self–interest and live for others" (Comte,1852).

Cligget argues, "migrants remit more than money; they send objects, exchange information, transfer ideas and values, among other things. It is also well documented that money has a symbolic value for people involved in the exchange" (as quoted in Magdalena and Vojin, 2016:4). Chant et al. opine, "migrant mothers who leave their families behind are expected to willingly practice self-denial and self-sacrifice in the name of their families and especially their children, while social norms have made it less reprehensible, if not more acceptable, for migrant fathers to neglect the support of their children"(as quoted in Lan and Brenda,2015:6).

## Monetary Remittances

Knerr states that a portion of earning sent by an international worker to the families left behind in the homeland. In a similar vein, Van Doorn observes that it is cash transfer by a migrant worker back to their families and community (as quoted in Izhar, 2007:8).

## Social Remittances

Levitt coined the word social remittances means distribution to economic remittances. Levitt categorized them into three domains: "(1)normative structures(ideas, values, beliefs that include norms of behavior, the notion of family responsibility, principals of neighborliness, community participation, aspiration for social mobility); (2) systems of practices(actions shaped by normative structures such as organizational practices: recruiting and socializing new members, goal setting and strategizing, establishing leadership roles, and forming interagency ties; including how individuals delegate household task and how much they participate in political, religious and civic groups(acts, actions, rituals);(3) social capital based on values and norms which form the resource for collective actions and facilitates the circulations of norms and values" (Levitt,1988:938).

## Cultural Remittances

"Social relations are always cultural in nature" (Levitt and Lamba-Nieve,1998). Boccagni and Decimo argue, "objects and money carry emotional meanings for those involved in this social relationship" (as quoted in Magdalena and Vojin, 2016:5).

## Conceptual Meaning of Social Exclusion

According to Xu, "the term of social exclusion was first utilized in France to refer to the plight of those who fell through the net of social protection" (as quoted in Wenmeng Feng, 2010). This term became prevalent since 1980s in the United Kingdom (UK) and Europe. Migrants face gender and racial inequality in western countries. Commins states, "social exclusion' refers to the separation of individuals and groups from mainstream society" (Commins, 2004:1). According to Silver, "social exclusion is a multidimensional process of progressive social rupture, detaching groups and individuals from social relations and institutions and preventing them from full participation in the normal, normatively prescribed activities of the society in which they live" (as quoted in Kieran Walsh, 2017:81) Sen argues, "in developed nations, the local people see a threat in migrants to their jobs. The natives feel as if the immigrants are snatching their jobs. Native people who are unable to find jobs often criticize the migrants. It also feeds the politics of racism and intolerance" (as quoted in Wisman, 2010:16).

## Conclusion

In this chapter, we have tried to understand the health and well-being and other concepts in general meaning as well specific meanings in which they have been used in this chapter. Indian and Punjabi diaspora in European, American and African countries, in particular, have drawn attention of the scholars of history, sociology, demography, economics, and of course, literature. Their attention towards Indians settled in European countries, America and Africa is understandable as they remit a great amount of foreign exchange and wield considerable influence in shaping policies of the governments of the countries of their domicile and India and vice versa.

This study has examined the elderly Punjabi migrants and left behind in a comparative perspective between two diverse geographical regions that is Doaba (Punjab) and England (UK). Since the 19th century, the members of Punjabi families have been migrating to the developed countries. Our findings demonstrate that during the First World War, young, single and poor tend to migrate to the British colonies to pay off agricultural debt. Some young Punjabis joined British Indian army and migrated to several British Colonies to assist the British Army. The majority of the members of such Punjabi families belonged to the Sikh community. However, Dalits (Ad-Dharmi) also migrated to various western countries. In the early phase of migration, the push factor such as poverty, political persecution and riots pushed the Punjabis to migrate but later on pull factors such as individual choice have become the norm of the day. In this context, we can safely say that economically well-off families started migrating to the Western world to set up business. The Punjabis who went on Immigration Visa become citizen legally in UK hence they started the process to invite their left behind members such as spouse, children and elderly parents. This study found that the migration of Punjabis followed different trajectories. Some Punjabis arrived in the United Kingdom from African British colonies after expulsion from Uganda in 1972 and some directly migrated from India. This migration resulted in building the extended family. Family reunification under the liberal immigration policies of the United Kingdom gave impetus to bulk migration of Punjabis. In recent times, a lot of students from Punjab took admission in various UK universities to study. The Punjabi Diaspora in the United Kingdom is dynamic and vibrant.

## References

Adieh, L. and Hahn, R.A. (1996). Use of the terms 'race', 'ethnicity', and 'national origins': a review of articles in the American Journal of Public Health, 1980-1989. *Ethnicity and Health* 1, pp. 95-98.

Ahmad, W.I.U and Walker, R. (1997). Asian Older people: Housing, health, and Access to services, *Ageing and Society,* 17(2): 141-165.

Akanksha, Srivastava, Sanjay, K Mohanty. (2011). Poverty among Elderly in India, *Social Integration Research,* 109(3): 493-514.

Alam, M.et al. (2013). *The Conditions of Elderly in Punjab, 2011*, Chandigarh. Available at: http://countryoffice.unfpa.org/india/drive/BKPAI Punjab Book 20th Dec 2013. pdf [Accessed: January 11, 2016].

Amanda J. Squires. (1998). Rehabilitation of Older People: *A Handbook for the multidisciplinary team*, California, Singular Publishing Group Inc.

Amarjit Singh(Eds). (2013).India Diaspora: *Voices of Grandparents and Grandparenting*, Rotterdam, Sense Publishers.

August Comte. (1852).Catechism of Positivism, trans. R. Congreve, (London: Kegan Paul, 1891) Rapoport, H, and Docquier, F (2005) 'The Economics of Migrants' Remittances, Discussion Paper no 1531, Institute for the study of Labor (IZA), Bonn.

Babacan, Alperhan and Singh, Supriya. (2010). Migration, Belonging and the Nation State, United Kingdom, Cambridge Scholars Publishing.

Ballard, R. (1972). Family Organization among the Sikhs in Britain, *New Community*, 2, 12-24.

————(1990) Migration and Kinship: The Different Effect of marriage Rules on the Processes of Punjabi Migration to Britain. In C. Clarke and C. Peach, (Eds) *South Asians Overseas: Migration and Ethnicity*. Cambridge: Cambridge University Press.

Bagga, A., and Dayabati, S.(2006). Ageing in women: *A Study in North-East India*, New Delhi, Mittal Publications.

Bhopal, R.S. Phillimore, P and Kohli, H.S. (1991). Inappropriate use of the Term (Asian): An obstacle to ethnicity and Health research, *Journal of Public Health Medicine*, 13,244-246.

Bowling, A (2005).*Measuring Health: A Review of Quality of Life Measurement Scales*, England, and Open University press.

Bott, E. (1968).*Family and Social Networks*, London: Tavistock.

British Sikh Report. (2013). BSR 2013. Retrieved from: http://www.britishsikhreport.org/british-sikh-report download.

British Sikh Report. (2014). *An insight into the British Sikh Community*, London, UK. Available at:http://www.britishsikhreport.org/wp-content/uploads/2014/04/British-Sikh-Report-2014.pdf [Accessed:March 9, 2016].

Burholt, V., Wenger, G.C. and Shah, Z.(2002). *Families and Migration/: Older People from South Asia (Older Punjabi Immigrants in Birmingham)*, Birmingham.

Butt and A O'Neil (2014).'Let's Move On': *Black and minority ethnic older people's views on research findings.* Joseph Rowntree Foundation, Retrieved from www.jrf.org.uk/publications/black-and-minority-ethnic-older-peoples-views-research-findings.

Commins, P. (2004). Poverty and Social Exclusion in rural areas: Characteristics, processes and research issues, *Sociol Ruralis*, 44:60-75.

Cohen, Robin. (2008). *Global Diaspora: An Introduction*, London, and Routledge.

Cooke, M. (2008). Relating Socio-Economic Issues to Older People and Pain: Independence, Dignity, and Choice. In P. Schofield, ed. *The Management of Pain in Older People*. West Sussex: John Wiley and Sons.

Cox, H.G. (2006).Later Life the Realities of ageing. Upper Saddle Rivers, NJ Pearson's, Allyn and Baco Russell, D., Peplau, L. A. and Ferguson, M. L. Developing a measure of loneliness. Journal of Personality Assessment.

Diener, E., Eunkook, M.S., Richard, E.L. and Heidi, L.S. (1999). Subjective Well-Being: Three Decades of Progress. *Psychological Bulletin*, 125(2), 276-302.

Digby, B.(2001).*Global Challenges. Student's Book. Per Le Scuole Superiori*, Oxford, Heinemann.

Duffy, K. (1995). Social Exclusion and Human Dignity in Europe. Council of Europe: Background Report for the Proposed Initiatives by the Council of Europe.

Faist, Thomas. (2008). ' Transnationalisation and Development: Toward an Alternative agenda', *Social Analysis*, 53(3), 38-59.

Foucault, Michel. (1980). Power/Knoweldege: *Selected Interviews and Other Writings, 1972-1977*, Pantheon Books.

Gangrade, K.D (1988). Crisis of Values: A sociological study of the old and the young. In A. B. Bose and K.D. Gangrade (Eds.). *Ageing In India: Problems and potentials*. New Delhi: Abhinav Publications.

Geoffrey, Nelson and Prilleltensky, Isaac. (2010). Community Psychology: In Pursuit of Liberation and Well-being, London, Palgrave Macmillan.

George, L.K. (1980). *Role transition in later life*. Monterey, California: Brooks Cole.

Gittin, Diana. (1982). *Fair Sex, Family Size and Structure in Britain, 1900-39,* London, St. Martin's Press.

Glick Schiller N, Basch L, Blanc-Szanton C. (1992). *Towards a transnational perspective on migration: Race, Class, Ethnicity and Nationalism Reconsidered*. New York, Academy of Sciences.

Goyal, A. and Kajal, K.S. (2014). Prevalence of depression in elderly population in the southern part of punjab. *Journal of family medicine and primary care*, 3(4), pp.359–61. Available at:http://www.pubmedcentral.nih.gov/articlerender. fcgi? artid = 4311342 and tool = p mcentrezandrendertype=abstract [Accessed January 11, 2016].

Ghosh.B, (1996) "Theories on Labour Migration", *in* Julien Vanden Broeck (ed.) *The Economics of Labour Migration*, pp.77-113.

Ghuman, R.S. (2012). The Sikh Community in Indian Punjab/: Some Socio-Economic Challenges. *Journal of Punjab Studies*, 19(1), 87–109.

Goode, W.J. (1969*). Changes in Family Patterns*, London: Routledge and Kegan Paul.

Gray, A.(2009). The Social Capital of Older People, *Ageing and Society*,29,(5),5-31.

Hall, E.(2010) "Spaces of Wellbeing for people with Learning Disabilities"Scottish, *Geographical Journal*,126,275-284.

Harris JR, Todaro MP. (1970). Migration, unemployment, and development: A two-sector analysis. *American Economic Review* 60,126-42.

Help Age India. (2013). *Elders Abuse in India*, https://www.helpageindia.org/images/pdf /Elder Abuse India 13.pdf [Accessed: December, 21.1 2017].

Helweg, A. (1986). *Sikhs in England*, Delhi, Oxford University Press.

Hoffmann, R.(2008). Description of Social Inequality. In R. Hoffmann, ed. *Socioeconomic Differences in Old Age Mortality*. Rostock: Springer Science and Business Media.

Hossen,Abul.(2012). Social Isolation and Loneliness among Elderly Immigrants: The Case of South Asian Elderly Living in Canada,*Journal of International Social Sciences*,1(1),1-10.

Huisman, M. (2004) Socioeconomic inequalities in mortality among elderly people in 11 European populations. *Journal of Epidemiology and Community Health*, 58(6),468–475.

Hussain, S. and Kaur, J. (1995).*Manual for Shamshad-Jasbir old-age adjustment Inventory*, Tiwari Koti, Agra.

Irudaya, S. Rajan, V.S Mishra, P. Sankara Sharma, (1999). India's Elderly: *Burden or Challenge*, New Delhi, Sage Publications.

IOM. (2003). An Overview of International Migration, available at https://publications.iom. int/system/files/pdf/wmr 2003 1.pdf.

Izhar Ahmed Khan Azhar. (2007). Overseas Migration and Its Socio-Economic Impacts on the Families Left Behind in Pakistan: A Case Study in the Province Punjab, Pakistan, Kassel University Press.

Janet M. Wilmoth, Kennath F. Ferraro.(2013). Geronotology: *Perspectives and Issues*, New York, Springer Publishing Company.

Jaffee, D.( 1998). *Levels of Socio-economic Development Theory*, Greenwood Publishing Group.

Joly. (2000). "Some Structural Effects of Migration on Receiving and Sending Countries", *International Migration*, 38 (5), 25-40.

Jutlla, Karan. (2014).The impact of migration experiences and migration identities on the experiences of services and caring for a family member with dementia for Sikhs living in Wolverhampton, UK, *Ageing and Society*,35(5),1032-1054.

Kannan, C.T. (1978). *Cultural Adaptation of Asian Migrants, First and Second Generations*, Middle Sex, England, Dillon University.

Kaur, J., Singh, S., and Kaur, K. (2014). Impact of Age on the Prevalence of Chronic Diseases in Geriatric Population, *International Research Journal of Biological Sciences*, 3(9), 79-85.

Khan, A.M. (2004). Decay in the Family Dynamics of Interaction, Relation and Communication as Determinants of Growing Vulnerability among Elderly, *Indian Journal of Gerontology*, 18(2), 173-186.

Kotwal, N. and Prabhakar, B. (2009). Physical needs and adjustments made by the elderly. *Stud HomeComm. Sci*., 3(2): 115-121.

King, R. and J. Vullnetari. (2006). "Orphan pensioners and migrating grandparents: The impact of mass migration on older people in rural Albania." *Ageing and Society*, 26, 783–816.

Kuate-Defo, B.(2006). Interactions Between Socio-economic Conditions and Living Arrangements in Predicting Gender-Specific Health Conditions Among the Elderly in Cameroon. Available at: http://www.ncbi.nlm.nih.gov/books/NBK20313/ [Accessed: March 3, 2016].

Lan A.N.H. Hoang and Brenda, S.A. Yeoh. (2015). Transnational Labour Migration, Remittances and the Changing Family in Asia, New York, Palgrave Macmillan.

Lebhart, (2005). *Migration Theories, Hypotheses, and Paradigms: An Overview, International Migration and Its Regulation*, http:// www. imscoe. org/ publications/ working papers/documents/international migration.pdf.

Lee S.E. (1966). "Theory of Migration", *Demography*, Vol.3, pp.47-87.International Organization for Migration (IOM), (2003): World Migration 2003: *Manageing Migration Challenges and Responses for People on the Move*, Geneva (2).

Levitt, P. (1998).Social remittances: Migration driven local-level forms of cultural diffusion. *International Migration Review*, 32 (4): 926–948.

Lewis. W.A. (1953). "Economic Development with Unlimited Suppliers of Labour", reprinted *in* Agarwal. A.N and Singh S.P. (eds.), *The Economics of Underdevelopment*, Oxford University Press, New York, pp.400-491.

Lynch, J.W., Kaplan, G.A. and Shema, S.J.(1997). Cumulative Impact of Sustained Economic Hardship on Physical, Cognitive, Psychological, and Social Functioning. *N Engl J Med*, 337, pp.1889–1895. Available at: http://www.nejm.org/doi/full/10.1056/ nejm 199712253372606 [Accessed: January 11, 2016].

Md Mizanur Rahman, Tan Tai Yong and AKM Ahsan Ullah.(2014). Migrant Remittances in South Asia*: Social, Economic and Political Implications*, Palgrave Macmillan.

Magdalena, Nowicka and Vojin, Serbedzila.(2016). Migration and Social Remittances in a Global Europe, Germany, Palgrave Macmillan.

Massey DS, Arango J, Hugo G, Kouaouci A, Pellegrino A, Taylor JE. (1993).Theories of international migration: A review and appraisal. *Population and Development Review* (19), .431-66.

Mark Cook and Glenn Wilson. (1979). Love and Attraction: An International Conference, Oxford, and Pergamum Press.

Marsh, P. (1967). *Anatomy of a strike:* Union, employers and Punjabi workers in a Southall factory. International Race Relations, London.

Marmot, M.G., Adeisten, a.M.and Bulusu, L.(1984). Lessons from the study of immigrant mortality, *Lancet*1(8392), pp. 1455-1457.

Marya, Nisha.(2013). Socio-Economic and Health Conditions of elderly in Punjab Anlaysis, PhD Thesis, Punjabi University, Patiala.

Nelson, Todd D.(2004). Ageism: Sterotyping and Prejudice against Older Persons, London, England, A Brand Ford Books.

Nicholson, Jr., (2008). Social isolation in older adults: an evolutionary concept analysis. *Journal of Advanced Nursing*, 65(6): 1342-1352.

Novak, M. (2009).*Issues in ageing*. Upper Saddle Rivers, NJ Pearson's, Allyn and Baco. Nuessel, F. (1982). The Language of ageism, *Gerontologist, 22*, 273-276.

Opong, Kwaku K. (2012). Prospect Theory and Migrant Remittances Decision Making, pp.1-33, available at file:///C:/Users/ss/Downloads/SSRN-id2127615%20 (1).pdf.

Orimo, H. et al. (2006).Reviewing the definition of "elderly." *Geriatrics and Gerontology International*, 6(3),149–158. Available at: http://doi.wiley.com/10.1111/j.1447.

Palmore, E. (1969). Trends in the relative status of the aged.*Social Forces*, 50, 84 – 91. Papademetriou DG. (1985). Illusions and Reality in International Migration: Migration and Development in post World War II Greece. *International Migration* XXIII: 211-23.

Pelletier, C.L., (2004). The effect of music on decreasing arousal due to stress: A meta-analysis. *Journal of music therapy*, 41(3): 192-214.

Phillip, Kreager and Elisabeth Schroder Butterhill. (2005).Ageing Without Children: *European and Asian Perspectives*, New York, Beghahn Books.

Piore, M.J, (1979). *Birds of Passage: Migrant Labor in Industrial Societies*, Cambridge University Press, New York.

Punia, D. and Punia, S. (2003). Personal problem of retired elderly in Haryana.*Indian Psychological Review*., 60(2): 91-96.

Ramamurthi, P.V. (1968). *A study of some related factors related to adjustment of urban aged man.*Doctoral Dissertation. Tirupathi: S.V. University.

Ramamurthi, P.V. and Jamuna, D. (1993). Are religiosity and external locus of control associated with good adjustment in old age? *Personality Study and Group Behaviour*, 13, 59 – 63.

Rao, A. Venkoba (1990). Family Jointness, family and social Integration among the Elderly, Indian *Journal of Social Psychiatry*, 3(8): 81 – 104.

Ravenstein, E. G. (1885).The Laws of Migration, *Journal of Royal Statistical Society*, 48(2): 167-235.

Rob Vos, Jose Antonio Ocampo and Ana Luiza Cortez.(2008). *Ageing and Development*, London and New York, Zed Books.

Sahai, Paramjit and Kathryn Dominique Lam. (2013). Migration from Punjab to Itlay in the Diary Sector: The Quiet Indian Revolution, CARIM- INDIA Research Report2013/ 10.

Sasikumar, S.K. and Zakir Hussain (2008).*Manageing International Labour Migration from India: Policies and Perspectives*, ILO Asia-Pacific Working Paper Series. Available at http://www.ilo.org/wcmsp5/groups/public/ asia/ ro-bangkok/ sro-New_Delhi/documents/publication/wcms 123412.pdf.

Savikko, N. (2008). Loneliness of older people and elements of an intervention for its alleviation.Annales Universitatis Turkuensis. Nro 808.Turun yliopisto.Hoitotieteen laitos.Doctoral thesis.

Kieran Walsh., Thomas Scharf, and Norah Keating. (2007). Social exclusion of older persons: A scoping view and conceptual framework, *Ageing, 14*(1): 81-98.

Schlossberg, 2004, Life events and adjustment in elderly. *Indian J. Psychiatry*, 44(1): 42-48.

Shea, G.F. (1991). *Managing Older Employees*. San Francisco: Jossey-Bass.

Singh, Gurharpal and Tatla D.S. (2008).Sikh in Britain: *The Making of a Community*, London, Zed Books Ltd.

Sjaastad, Larry A. (1962). The Cost and Return of Human Migration, *Journal of Political Economy*, 70(5):80-93.

Soodan, K.S. (1972). Changing roles of the aged. *Indian Journal of Gerontology*, 4, 50 – 52.

Streib, G.F. and Schreider, J.S. (1971).*Retirement in American Society: Impact and Process*. New York: Cornell University Press.

Stuck, A.E. et al. ( 1999). Risk factors for functional conditions decline in community-living elderly people: a systematic literature review. *Social Science and Medicine*, 48(4):445–469. Available at: http://www.sciencedirect.com/science/article/pii/ S0277953698003700 [Accessed: November 21, 2015].

Subaiya, L., Bansod, D.(2011). *Demographies of Population ageing in India: Trends and Differentials*. BKPAI Working Paper No.1, United Nations Population Fund(UNFPA), New Delhi.

Susanne, N and Tim, S.(2014). Well-being and Mobility: A Theoretical Framework and Literature Review Focusing on Older People,*Mobilities*,9(1), 104-129.

Szirmai, A. (2005). *The Dynamics of Socio-Economic Development: An Introduction*, Cambridge: Cambridge University Press.

Thakur, Vasundra.(2012). The Demograhic Dividend in India: Gift or Curse? A State level analysis on differing age structure and its implications for India's economic grwoth and prospects,*Internatinal Development*,LSE, Working Paper Series No:12-28.

Thandi, S.S. (2013). The Punjab Paradox: understanding the failures of diaspora engagement, *Diaspora Studies*, 7(1):42-55.

Thorson, G.R. (1983). Spiritual Well-being in the Secular Society. *Generations*, 7(3):10 – 11.

Tilly, C. and Brown C, H, (1967). "On Uprooting, Kinship and Urban Unemployment in Less developed Countries", *The American Economic Review*, LIX (1), pp.138-148.

Waltron, Roberts. (2004). Returning, Remitting, Reshaping: *Non-Resident Indian and the Transformation of Society and Space in Panjab, India*, Working Paper series 01-15, RIIM, Vancouver, pp.78-103.

Wenmeng Feng. (2010). Social Exclusion of the Elderly in contemporary China: One Empirical Study based on the surveys in six provinces, available at https://www.oecd.org/dev/pgd/46837621.pdf.

William, A; Ota, H; Giles, H; Pierson, H.D. Gallois, C; Ng, S.H; Lim, T.S; Ryan, E.B; Somera, L; Maher, J; Cai, D; and Harwood, J.(1997).Young People's beliefs about intergenerational communication: an initial Cross-cultural analysis. *Communication Research*, 24, 370-393.

Wisman Jon D. (2010). The moral imperative and social rationality of government guaranteed employment and reskilling, *Review of social Economy*, 68(1): 35-67.

World Migration Report. (2013). *Migrant and Wellbeing Development*, United Nations Publications.

Yatish Kumar and Anita Bhargava, (2014) Elder abuse in Indian families: Problems and Preventive Actions, *International Journal of Scientific and Research Publications*, 4(10):1-8.

Yuchan Wu and Chang Zhang. (2011). The Impact of Isolation and Loneliness on Elderly well- Being, Bachelor's Thesis: Novia, University of Applied Sciences.

Zelizer, V.A. (2005).*The Purchase of Intimacy*, Princeton, New York, Princeton Press University, pp.1-14.

## Notes

1. Growing older in the UK, British Medical Council, available at http://www.bgs.org.uk/pdfs/2016bma growing older in uk. pdf, retrieved on 02 Nov, 2017.

# IV

# Policies, Legislation and Institutions for Older Persons in India and Uk

## Introduction

This chapter began with depiction of older age and ageing. It defined that there are three interrelated processes of ageing: physical, psychological and social. The aspect of ageing also includes internal differentiation of class, gender, region, religion, educational background etc. hence it would be interesting to analyze three factors in the field. Whether these factors also prevail in the universe of our study. Further, this chapter has revealed how United Nations defines ageing. We have found that the United Nation defines a country as ageing where the proportion of the people over 60 years. United Nation has also estimated that there 10.38 Crores of population which is 60 years and above in the world. Therefore United Nation has revealed number of policies so that older people can live dignified life.

Apart from UN, this chapter has also recorded the national policies and programs for elderly in India. Apart from the general articles of the constitution which upholds the rights of individuals, we have mapped the legislation for the elderly in India. For instance, Hindu adoption and Maintenance Act 1956 envisages that a Hindu child (male/female) will take care of his aged and infirm parents. In the same vain along with sons and daughters, there are obligations on the State to take care of elderly in India. The state has entitled old age pension schemes which provide Rs200 per month per person. However, it can be argued that in today's time it is not a sufficient amount to survive. More over there is a National Pension System as well which depends on how much a person has contributed while he was young. There are also health related policies by the state and private sector both. Above all the Government of India has brought 'Senior citizen Act

2007' which provides number of privileges to the senior citizens. For instance, it has made maintenance of parents and senior citizens by children and relatives obligatory, establishment of Old age home for senior citizens. Ministry of Social Justice and Empowerment has been a nodal ministry to look after the specific problems of the elderly. Different other ministries like Health and Family Welfare, Railways, Ministry of Civil Aviation, Telecommunications etc have been asked to provide these facilities and privileges to the senior citizens.

Further, this chapter has also analyzed the programs and policies available for the senior citizens in Punjab. For instance, there exists, 'Old age allowance' scheme from person who attain age of 65 years. In Punjab along with this, there are many other policies and programs for the elderly women also, like for instance elderly woman above 60 years enjoy free travel in Punjab.

Along with these programs and policies at the national and state level we have mapped the programs and policies that prevail in the UK as well. At the outset, we have recorded what are the ways in which senior citizens can migrate to UK? What is the specific policy in this regard? It is interested to note that UK allows senior citizen visas who can demonstrate that they need long term personal care because of their illness. Apart from these, there are number of legislation and constitutional provisions to safeguard the rights of the elderly in UK. Free passes for buses, discounts in trains and trams, free passport, free gas safety checks, state pensions, funeral payments, winter fuel payment etc are few facilities available to the elderly in UK. There is also a facility of old age, homes, free home checkups and medical facilities in UK. Last but not the least this chapter has also recorded the roles of NGOs for the welfare of the elderly in UK and India. In the light of this review of programs and policies for the elderly in UK and India, it would be interesting find out in the field whether these programs and policies are being implemented or they are only on paper. It would also be interesting to check that whether the respondents are aware of these programs and policies for their welfare and lastly what do they feel about these programs and policies. Are the satisfied or not?

This chapter further informs us that the population of elderly/senior citizens is increasing day by day. This trend is seen in every part of the world. According to the UN, approximately 20.7 per cent of the world's population would be elderly by 2050. On the other hand, World Health Organization (WHO) has argued that the Southeast Asian regions would have increased life expectancy and hence by 2050 SEAR will have 21.4 per cent of its population above 60 years. Hence, this analysis also suggests that as the ageing population would increase in future, it would become necessary to have effective programs and policies for the senior citizens in place or they will be left out to suffer. In this light, this chapter has made the researcher to analyze the need for future preparation for our ageing population.

## Understanding Old Age

"Old age is the inexorable stage of human life, which is determined both by biological and economic conditions determine. There are three interrelated processes of ageing that is physical, psychological and social. It is a series of transition from one set of role to another which is structured by the social system rather than mere biological one" (Mishra, 2004). Chaudhary opines, "A life course perspective on ageing recognizes that older people are not one homogenous group and individual diversity increases with age as the old people do not belong to the same gender, economic class, marital status, family background, religious status, health status, mode of living, professional background, and educational attainment, and they respond to the old age differently, face different needs, hopes, fears and problems according to a given specific situation" (Chaudhary, 2004).

## Understanding Ageing Elderly Population in Global Context

"The U.N. estimates and projections show that in 1995. There were children 31.3 percent in the world`s population. The elderly were 9.5 percent of the world`s population. By 2050, children would be 20.5 percent of the total while the elderly would be 20.7 percent of the total. In 2100, there would be 18.3 percent children and 27.7 percent elderly in the total population. By 2150, there would be 17.5 percent children and 30.5 percent elderly in the total population" (Bose, 2000). "In USA, the total number of those aged more than 65 years was 35 million, and it is expected to double by 2030 A.D. Of those, people aged more than 85 years was 4 million in number. This is expected to double by 2030 A.D" (Srivastava, 2000).

It is reported that range from 10 percent in Japan and 90 percent in Sweden, persons aged more than 65 years of age live alone in developing and developed countries. Married and widowed older persons usually live with their children and grandchildren because of traditional multigenerational households hence the range is smaller in developing countries. "The life expectancy at birth in most developed countries is 70-75 years for men and 76-81 for women. It is 11 years less in developing countries" (Joshi and Sengupta, 2000). "France took 155 years to double its older person`s population from 7 percent to 14 percent. China, Thailand and Colombia took 25 years" (Nampudakani, 1999).

The WHO has classified the SEAR countries as (South East Asian Region: Bangladesh, Bhutan, India, Indonesia, Maldives, Myanmar, Nepal, Sri Lanka and Thailand). Life expectancy in these countries exhibited upsurge. In 1983, three of the member states showed a life expectancy at birth of 60 years and more. By 1997, this had been reported by seven of the member's states. In 1980, there were 5.3 percent elderly reported. By 2050, this was expected to become 12.4 percent in the SEAR countries. In 1995, the proportion of the elderly population in the SEAR countries was 18.1 percent of the world total. This was expected to become 21.4 percent by 2050 A.D. This was double in population from 1995. By this time, the proportion of males in these countries was expected to be 11.6 percent for females 13.2 percent (Wibwo, 1999)."In Britain, the compulsory retirement age for men was 65 years and for women was 60 years. Of those above 65 years, 95 percent stayed in dwellings rather than in hospital or homes for the elderly" (Srivastava, 2000).

## What does United Nations mean to have an Ageing Population?

"Globally, the number of older persons is growing faster than the number of people in any other age group. As a result the share of the older persons in the total population is increasing everywhere"(World Population Ageing, 2015:2). As per 2011 Census, total population of Senior Citizens (people aged 60 years and above) is 10.38 crore, Seven percentage of which population of males and females was 5.11 crore and 5.27 crore respectively"(Ministry of Social Justice, Government of India)."Principles on older persons adopted by General Assembly resolution 46/91 of 16 Dec 1991 encourages Governments to incorporate the following principles into their national programs whenever possible" (United Nations,1991).

## United Nations Principles on Independence

"Through the provision of income, family and community support and self-help, elderly people should have access to sufficient food, water, shelter, clothing and health care. The elderly must get an opportunity to earn. They should have access to suitable educational and training programs. They should be able to live in environments that are safe and adaptable to personal preferences and changing capacities. Older persons should be able to reside at home for as long as possible". (United Nations, 1991).

## United Nations Principles on Participation

"Participation by elderly people to lead an active life is must. By participation, they can voice their demands for formulations and effective implementation of policies that directly affect their well-being. They should share their knowledge and skills with younger generations. Elderly people should take part in serving the community as a volunteer according to their interests and capabilities. By joining volunteer association, the elderly people express their views to bring about positive changes in the society" (United Nations, 1991).

## United Nations Principles on Care

"Elderly people must receive support from family and community. Their protection should be in accordance with each society's system of cultural values. The elderly must have access to healthcare system to maintain the maximum level of physical, mental and emotional well-being and to prevent or delay any kind of illness. The older persons should have proper legal services to retain their rights and protect themselves. Institutional care needs to be in a humane and secure environment. Rehabilitation of the elderly should be done carefully. While living in any shelter, or treatment facility, they must be treated respectfully. Their beliefs and customs should not be hurt. In any such sort of place, they must be allowed to maintain quality of life" (United Nations, 1991).

## United Nations Principles on Self-fulfillment

"Elderly persons should be able to advance prospects for the full development of their potential. Society must provide educational, cultural, spiritual and recreational resources to the older persons" (United Nations, 1991).

## United Nations Principles on Dignity

Elderly persons must enjoy dignity and security and be free of exploitation and physical or mental abuse. They should not be discriminated due to age, gender, racial or ethnic background, disability or other such status. Their contribution to the nation, community should be acknowledged independently' (United Nations, 1991).

## National Policies for Elderly in India

The central and the state government have launched various healthcare schemes and policies for the welfare of the elderly in the last decades. A separate fund allocation to fund various schemes and policies are allocated with the help of which well-being of the elderly people is maintained.

## Constitutional Provisions

In the constitution of India, every state in India has the duty to apply in the purview of Directive Principles of State Policy the following principles while making laws. The following provisions have been protected in the constitution of India.

Under the Directive Principles of State Policy the state to secure a social order for the promotion of the welfare of the people (Constitution of India, Article 38).

The Indian Constitution talks about the right to an adequate means of living for citizens for both men and women (Constitution of India, Article 39).

The Indian Constitution provides that the State shall, within the limits of its economic capacity and development, make effective provision for securing the right to work, to education and to public assistance in cases of unemployment, old age, sickness and disablement, and in other cases of underserved want (Constitution of India, Article 41).

The Indian Constitution provides that the State shall promote with special care the educational and economic interests of the weaker sections of the people, and shall protect them from social injustice and all forms of exploitation. Thus, the welfare of senior citizens is mandated by the Constitution of India (Constitution of India, Article 46).

The state shall regard the raising of the level of nutrition and the standard of living of its people and the improvement of public health as among its primary duties (Constitution of India, Article 47).

## Legislation and the Elderly in India

### Senior Citizens Act, 2007

Under the provision of Act 2007, the maintenance and welfare of parents and senior citizens guaranteed and recognized under the Constitution. It also covers up incidental matters. Section 2(h) explains 'Senior Citizens' being a citizen of India, who has attained the age of sixty years or above. Maintenance and welfare are the two components of this Act. Provisions of food, health care, recreation centers and other amenities necessary for the senior citizens.

According to this Act, children are under obligation to provide maintenance to older parents so that they may lead a normal life. Tribunal constituted under the Act laid down certain procedures to get allowances. Senior citizens are free to revoke transfer of property in case of negligence by children or relatives. In case of abandonment of Senior Citizens, legal provision is available to fight their case. Old Age Homes for Senior Citizens need to be established in case they need such services. This Act also ensure medical facilities and security for older persons. Every state needs to enforce this Act and required to take effective measures for its implementation. Frame Rules under the Act; Assign maintenance officers; Establish maintenance and appellate tribunals; create public and official sensitization and awareness for welfare of Senior Citizens; recommend a comprehensive action plan for the protection of life and property (The Gazette of India, Ministry of Law and Justice).

## National Council for Senior Citizens

"In keeping with the provisions of the National Policy, Government of India constituted a National Council for Older Persons (NCOP) in May 1999 with the following objectives. Advice the government on policies and programs Provide feedback on the implementation of the NPOP and programs. Provide a nodal point at the national level for redressing the grievances of individual. Lobby for concessions, rebates and discounts for older persons both with the government and corporate sector. Represent the collective opinion of the older persons to the government. Suggest the steps to make old age productive and interesting. Suggest measures to enhance the quality of intergenerational relationships" (National Council of Senior Citizens, 2007).

## Nodal Union Ministries/departments responsible for the senior citizens in India

The following Ministries and Departments of government of India ensures need-based entitlements.

## Ministry of Social Justice and Empowerment

"The National Policy on Older Persons (NPOP) was announced in January 1999 to reaffirm the commitment to ensure the well-being of the older persons. The policy envisions state support to safeguard financial and food security, health care, shelter and other needs of older persons, equitable share in development, protection against abuse and exploitation, and availability of services to improve the quality of their lives. The primary objectives are to encourage individuals to make provision for their own as well as their spouse's old age; to encourage families to take care of their older family members; to enable and support voluntary and non-governmental organizations to supplement the care provided by the family; to provide care and protection to the vulnerable elderly people; to provide adequate healthcare facility to the elderly; to promote research and training facilities to train geriatric care givers and organizers of services for the elderly; and to create awareness regarding elderly persons to help them lead productive and independent live" (Ministry of Social Justice and Empowerment, Government of India).

### Ministry of Health and Family Welfare

"The Ministry of Health and Family Welfare (MOHFW) provides the following facilities to the Senior Citizens a separate queue for older persons in government hospitals.

National Institutes on Ageing at New Delhi and Chennai are set up. Geriatric Department in twenty five medical colleges are set up; twice in a year the PHC(Primary Health Care) nurse or the ASHA(Accredited Social Health Activists) workers will conduct a special screening of the 80plus population of villages" (Ministry of Health and Family Welfare, Government of India).

### Ministry of Railways

"The Ministry of Railways offers the following facilities to the Senior Citizens. These are separate ticket centers for Seniors Citizens at various Passengers Reservation Systems (PRS).Provision of lower berth to male passengers of 60 years and above female passenger of 45 year and above. 40 percent and 5o percent concession in rail fare for male passengers aged 60 years and above and female passengers aged 50 year and above respectively. Provision of wheel chair for older persons" (Ministry of Railways, Government of India).

### Ministry of Finance

"The Ministry of Finance offers the following facilities to the Senior Citizens. These are Income Tax exemption for Senior Citizens of 60 years and above up to Rs 2.50 Lakh per annum. Income Tax exemption for Senior Citizens of 80 years and above up to Rs 5.0 Lakh per annum. Deduction of Rs 20,000 allowed to an individual who pays medical insurance premium for his or her parents, who is a senior citizen and deduction of the amount spent or Rs 60,000, whichever is less for medical treatment of a dependent senior citizen" (Ministry of Finance, Government of India).

### Ministry of Civil Aviation

"Air India, a national carrier under the Ministry of Civil Aviation provides airfare concession upto50 percent for male passengers aged 65 years and above female passengers aged 63 years"(Ministry of Civil Aviation, Government of India).

### Ministry of Consumer Affairs, Food and Public Distribution

"Under Antyodaya scheme, the families under Below Poverty Line (BPL) which also include older persons are provided food grains at the rate of 35 Kgs, grains at Rs.3 per Kg. and rice at Rs.2 per Kg. Older persons above 60 years from the BPL category are given a unique identification. Senior citizens who remain uncovered under the old age pension scheme by the state and union territory are the beneficiary of food grains free of cost. The older persons having ration cards are given priority in "Fair Price Shops" (Ministry of Consumer Affairs and Distribution, Government of India).

### Department of Pensions and Pensioners Grievances

For facilitating Senior Citizens, the government of India launched a pension portal to enable them to get information regarding the status of their application. The portal also provides the information in regard to pensions documents required if any. The senior citizens can also lodge of grievances (Ministry of Finance, Government of India).

### Department of Telecommunications

Priority category with VIP flag for senior citizens to register Faults or complaints; Under N-OYT Special Category, Senior citizens are allowed to register telephone connection (Ministry of Communications, Government of India).

### Legal rights for senior citizens in India

Certain legal rights are in place to ensure the safety and security of the older persons. Some of them are discussed below:

### Hindu Adoption and Maintenance Act, 1956

"Section 125 (1) (d) of the Code of Criminal Procedure 1973, envisages the right of parents without any means to be supported by their children. Section 20(3) of the Hindu Adoption and Maintenance Act, 1956, envisions a statutory recognition to the well-established normal obligation of a Hindu child (male or female) to maintain his aged or ailing parents. The children need to maintain their older parents as long as they are not in position to maintain themselves independently" (Department of Legal Affairs, Ministry of Law and Justice, Government of India).

### Code of Criminal Procedure, 1973

"Section 125(1) (2) makes it compulsory for a person having adequate means to maintain his father or mother who is unable to maintain himself or herself and on getting proof of neglect or refusal, may be ordered by a First Class Magistrate to make a monthly allowance not exceeding Rs.500 Such legal provisions are available irrespective of their religious faith and religious persuasions. It also includes adoptive parents. The Supreme Court in its ruling gave directions to the lower courts to make daughters and sons, married or unmarried, equally responsible to maintain their parents" (Department of Legal Affairs, Ministry of Law and Justice, Government of India).

## Provisions of Medical Care for Senior Citizens in India

"Every state encounter huge challenges to provide medical care to the senior citizens. The state shall ensure that hospitals shall provide beds for all senior citizens as far as possible, facilities for treatment of diseases. Mental health of older person depends upon various factors such as socio-economic and psychological" (Ministry of Health and Family Welfare, Government of India).

## Protection of Property Rights

"As per Sec.22 of the Act, the state government shall recommend a comprehensive action plan for providing of life and property of senior citizens" (Ministry of Social Justice and Empowerment, Government of India).

## Privileges and benefits for older persons in India

## Economic Security

"The government of India lunched Indira Gandhi National Old Age Pension Scheme (IGNOAPS) for the economic security of the older persons. All BPL families are covered under this scheme. All persons above 60 years belonging to a household below the poverty line (BPL) are eligible to avail this scheme. Under IGNOAP, the central assistance shall be at the rate of Rs. 200 per month per beneficiary. States are urged to give equivalent amounts. It is noted that some states have been giving additional amounts to assist the older persons below poverty line. The amount for this scheme is directly credited into the account of the beneficiary who are supposed to open up account either in a post office or any public sector bank. After disbursement of the amount, the states and union territories are required to furnish a certificate that all eligible persons have been covered under IGNOAPS"(Government of India).

## National Pension System (NPS)

"This scheme is a voluntary scheme. Under this scheme, the individual's funds are pooled into a pension fund which are invested by Pension Fund Regulatory and Development Authority (PFRDA). Government bonds, bills, corporate debentures and shares are diversified by professional fund managers. These contributions would grow and accumulate over the years, depending on the returns earned on the investment made. It is a flexible and simple and regulated scheme. The National Pension System (NPS) administered by the Pension Fund Regulatory and Development Authority (PFRDA). Under the Atal Pension Yojana(APY), the subscribers would receive the fixed minimum pension of Rs. 1000 per month, Rs. 2000 per month, Rs. 3000 per month, Rs. 4000 per month, Rs. 5000 per month, at the age of 60 years, depending on their contributions, which itself would be based on the age of joining the APY. The minimum age of joining APY is 18 years and maximum age is 40 years. Therefore, minimum period of contribution by any subscriber under APY would be 20 years or more. The benefit of fixed minimum pension would be guaranteed by the Government. Fixed pension for the subscribers falling between Rupees 1000 to Rupees 5000, if she or he joins and contributes between the age of 18 years and 40 years. The contribution levels would vary and would be low if subscriber joins early and increase if he or she joins late" (Ministry of Finance, Government of India).

## Varishtha Mediclaim for Senior Citizens

"This scheme is intended to cater to the needs of Senior Citizens. It covers Hospitalization and Domiciliary Hospitalization Expenses as well as expenses for treatment of Critical Illnesses. Coronary Artery Surgery, Cancer, Renal Failure, Stroke, Multiple Sclerosis, Major Organ Transplants, Paralysis and blindness at extra premium are covered under this scheme. Hospitalization and Domiciliary Hospitalization sum Insured covered is Rupees 1, 00,000 and under Critical Illness cover Sum Insured is Rupees 2, 00,000. Any older persons between 60 to 80 years of age can avail the benefits of this scheme. In case renewal of policy, age limit will be extended up to 90 years in which case the premium of 76 years to 80 years age band will be loaded by 10 percent up to 85 years and 20 percent up to 90 years of age" (Department of Financial Services, Government of India).

## Hope - Health of Privileged Elder

"Health of Privileged Elder (HOPE) was launched by the Oriental Insurance Company for Med claim Policy for the senior citizens. The policy covers citizens above 60 years. Hospitalization, older patients with chronic diseases are covered. The sum insured of Rupees. 1 lakh to Rupees 5 lakh can be opted. The premium bands and sum insured are based on 47 years of age and it ranges from Rupees 4500 to Rupees 29000. 10 per cent extra to be borne by fresh takers of the policy. 20 per cent has to be borne by the insured compulsory. The Co-pay optional will reduce 10 to50 percent of the total insured amount. Up to one lakh, cashless payment through Third Party Administrators (TPA) facility is available under this scheme" (Oriental Insurance Company).

## Old Age allowances for Senior Citizens in Punjab

Eligibility for 'old age allowance' by five years has been reduced by the Punjab government. Those who are at the age of 65 shall get 5 percent old age allowance which was earlier available at 70 years of age. Further, 10 percent old allowance is given at the age of 80 years which was earlier available at the age of 75 years. The old allowances are applicable to all pensioners including the civil servants. Senior citizens are also eligible for 50 percent travel concession for travelling in state run transportation (Government of Punjab). The following schemes have been made operational in Punjab in the financial year 2012-13. It also includes schemes for various target groups including the elderly (Table 4.1).

**Table 4.1: Major Social Schemes for the Elderly in Punjab**

| *Type of Scheme* | *Name of the Scheme* | *Year of Implementation* | *Eligibility Criteria* | *State/Central Scheme* |
|---|---|---|---|---|
| Exclusively for Older Persons | | | | |
| Income Security | Old age Pension Scheme | 1964 | Females aged 58 years and above and males aged 65 years and above at the time of application | State Scheme |
| | Indira Gandhi National Old age Pension Scheme | 1995 | BPL house hold applicant aged above 60 years or above | Central Scheme |
| Healthcare | National Program for Health care of Elderly people | 2010 | Males and Females above 60 years or above | Central Scheme |
| Residential Care | Home for the aged and Infirm, Hoshiarpur | 1961 | Males (aged above 65 years) and females (aged above 60 years) who are destitute or infirm | State Scheme |
| Old Age Identity | Scheme for the issue of identity cards to Senior Citizen | NA | The applicant must be aged 60 or more years at the time of application | State Scheme |
| Subsidized Travel | Concessional Bus Travel Facility for Women | 1997 | Only women who are residents of Punjab and are 60 years or above are eligible | State Scheme |
| Older Schemes | | | | |
| Income Security | National Family Benefit Scheme | 1995 | BPL households where primary breadwinner has died between 18-64 years of age | Central Scheme |
| | Indira Gandhi National Widow Pension | 2009 | BPL widows in the age group 18-79 years | Central Scheme |

| | | | | | |
|---|---|---|---|---|---|
| | Scheme | | | | Central Scheme |
| | Indira Gandhi National Disabled Pension Scheme | | 2009 | Persons with severe or multiple disabilities aged 18-79 years belonging to a BPL household | |
| Physical Activity | State Protective Homes, Jalandhar | | 1951 | Neglected or destitute or infirm older persons of both sexes (women above the age of 60 years and men above the age of 65 years) | State Scheme |
| Nutritional Security | Atta Scheme (ADS) | Dal | 2007 | Households with annual income less than Rs 60,000 from all sources, or cultivable landholding less than 2.5 acres | State Scheme |
| | | | | Households owning AC or four-wheeler or the head being income tax or service tax or VAT assesses or professionals or registered industrialist or permanent employees in central/state government/public sector undertaking/ municipal corporations/boards are excluded from the Scheme | |

*Source:* Department of Social Security and Development of Women and Children; Department of Health and Family Welfare; Department of Food Civil Supplies and Consumer Affairs, Government of Punjab, Chandigarh.

## Immigration to UK

Older migrants can follow a number of ways to gain entry to UK. All older non- EU national's generally require a visa to enter UK. In the case of the older persons, family visa is most availed.

In family reunification category, older migrants obtain family visa. In most cases, British citizens can sponsor older parents. There are certain legal conditions that needs to be fulfilled by son or daughter while sponsoring older parents. For example, a person sponsoring older parents must be a British citizen. His income should be sufficient so as to support the older parents. Before arrival, the older parents need to procure medical insurance for treatment of any kind in case of emergency. This is required in case of older parents who stay for a temporary period. Those who are British citizens automatically eligible for free medical healthcare services.

## National Policies for Senior Citizens in England (UK)

The UK Immigration and Citizenship department has laid down certain rules and policies for eligibility to immigrate for older persons. However, older person groups are very specific individuals who generally immigrate to join their sons or daughters who are British citizens. Older parents need to apply for immigration visa and wait for some time since it takes a number of years. The limit is not given by the Immigration and Citizenship Department, UK. The government of United Kingdom has laid down certain benefits for older persons such as free prescriptions and free eye tests. The old age benefits falls under different categories.

### Equality Act 2010

"The Equality Act 2010 offers without discrimination general protection that older migrants may need to avail public services. Age and race are protected characteristics under this Act. Under the ambit of this Act, age discrimination is prohibited except for any stated reason for differential treatment. Older persons are the beneficiary to avail concessions such as cheap haircuts, cut price or free travel and winter flu injections."(Equality and Human Rights Commission UK, 2017).

### Human Rights Act (HRA) 1998

"As like an ordinary citizens, older migrants are also protected under Human Rights Act. European Convention on Human Rights ensure older migrants to claim the human right it covers. The right to life, freedom from torture and inhuman or degrading treatment are included. It also ensures the older persons to family support. It safeguards the older persons or any other individual from discrimination of any sort such as race, age, and ethnic. It is not a freestanding right. This Act also directs the local authorities to provide public services such as planning, commissioning and monitoring home care services" (Human Rights Act UK,1998).

### Care Act 2014

"Care Act is intended to simplify obligations on local authorities and to introduce new social care duties based on individual wellbeing. Older migrants receiving social care are from a local authority are encompassed in the general responsibility of these duties. Various duties and responsibilities are involved while giving care and protection to the older migrants such as provision of social care including assessment of care needs, arranging care funding and provision of prevention services. A duty to promote well-being and promote integration between health and social care services. Duties with respect to safeguarding of adults receiving social care" (Care Act UK, 2004).

## Mental Capacity Act 2005

"Mentally ill people are unable to make some or all decisions for themselves. The ability to understand and make decision by an older person is known as mental capacity. Older migrants experience language difficulties in accessing public services. Some of the challenges such as income and poverty; isolation; language barriers; health and social care; cultural expectations and culture diversity are experienced by the older migrants" (Mental Capacity Act, 2005). Healthcare system is run and manned by the National Health Service (NHS). Under the NHS, all legal citizens and immigrants are eligible for critical and non-critical medical care without any out-of-pocket payment" (Mental Capacity Act UK, 2005).

## Travel

"For older persons above 60 years in UK, travel concessions are available. These travel concessions offers discount to the older persons who are likely to travel by bus or train. Senior citizens also get bus and train discount cards. Some other concessional provisions are by the UK government such as Freedom Pass and Free Passport for those who were born before 1929. The cost of the Rail or bus card falls between 30 pounds for a year and 70 pounds for the whole year"(Government of UK).

## Council House for the Elderly

"The council provide a house for the elderly people. The house is provided to those who either do not have or are kicked out of the house due to family dispute. The eligibility criteria for council house varies from council to council in UK. The council provide all facilities to the older persons at discounted rates" (Government of UK).

## Pension Benefits

"Pension benefits varies from person to person. Low income people are entitled to Pension Credit. It has been divided into two parts and no tax is payable on both. Under. Guarantees Credit, a single person above 60 years get £155.60 per week. And for a partner £237.55 per week. Under Savings Credit, a single person above 65 years who have saved towards their retirement. For a single, it pays up to £13.07 per week and for partner £14.75 per week. Those who retired after 2006 are eligible for the Guarantee Credit Council tax and housing benefits. Older persons are eligible for discounted funeral payments and winter fuel payment" (Government of UK).

## National Level Voluntary Organizations working for older persons in India and UK

Non-Government Organizations help the older persons by facilitating them in income generation and rehabilitation projects for the older persons. The following voluntary organizations having national and international presence. There have been working to ameliorate the wretched condition of old age people in India and UK.

### Caritas India

It is a member of CARITAS international. Cartis in India is a national organization which provide services to the sick, aged, handicapped and destitute.

### Age-Care

Older persons experience difficulties after retirement. Age-Care is recognized by the United Nations. It helps the older persons to lead a healthy and dignified life after retirement. It works under the patronage of the United Nations.

### The Agewell Foundation

The Agewell foundation provides legal assistances to the older persons. This organization helps them to find out suitable employment for those elderly who want to work after retirement.

### Help Age India

It was set up by the Help the Aged of UK in 1980 in India. Help Age (India) offers financial support to the non-government organizations which are working for the welfare of the older persons.

## Conclusion

This chapter began with depiction of older age and ageing. It defined that there are three interrelated processes of ageing: physical, psychological and social. The aspect of ageing also includes internal differentiation of class, gender, region, religion, educational background has been analyzes these factors in the field. We have found that these factors are prevailing in the universe of our study. Further, this chapter has revealed how United Nations defines ageing. We have found that the United Nation defines a country as ageing where the proportion of the people over 60 years. United Nation has also estimated that there 10.3 Crores of population which is 60 years and above in the world. Therefore United Nation has revealed number of policies so that older people can live dignified life.

**Table 4.2 : Understanding Elderly Population in Global Context Percent Elderly by Age: 2000 to 2030**

| *Region* | | *Year* | *65* | *years* | *75 years and* | *80* | *years* |
|---|---|---|---|---|---|---|---|
| | | | *and over* | | *over* | *and over* | |
| Europe | | 2000 | 15.5 | | 6.6 | 3.3 | |
| | | 2030 | 24.3 | | 11.8 | 7.1 | |
| North America | | 2000 | 12.6 | | 6.0 | 3.3 | |
| | | 2030 | 20.3 | | 9.4 | 5.4 | |
| Oceania | | 2000 | 10.2 | | 4.4 | 2.3 | |
| | | 2030 | 16.3 | | 7.5 | 4.4 | |
| Asia | | 2000 | 6.0 | | 1.9 | 0.8 | |
| | | 2030 | 12.0 | | 4.6 | 2.2 | |
| Latin | America | 2000 | 5.5 | | 1.9 | 0.9 | |
| Caribbean | | 2030 | 11.6 | | 4.6 | 2.4 | |
| Region | | Year | 65 | years | 75 years and | 80 | years |
| | | | and over | | over | and over | |
| North East/North Africa | | 2000 | 4.3 | | 1.4 | 0.6 | |
| | | 2030 | 8.1 | | 2.8 | 1.3 | |
| Sub-Saharan Africa | | 2000 | 2.9 | | 0.8 | 0.3 | |
| | | 2030 | 3.7 | | 1.3 | 0.6 | |

*Source:* An Ageing World:2001, op. cit., p. 9.

**Table 4.3: Global Situation of older person (1995-2150)**

| *Year* | *Population* | *% aged* | *% aged* | *% aged* |
|---|---|---|---|---|
| | *(Billion)* | *60+* | *65+* | *80+* |
| 1995 | 5.687 | 9.5 | 6.5 | 1.1 |
| 2000 | 6.091 | 9.9 | 6.8 | 1.1 |
| 2025 | 8.039 | 14.6 | 10.8 | 1.7 |
| 2050 | 9.367 | 20.7 | 15.1 | 3.4 |
| 2075 | 10.066 | 24.8 | 19.1 | 5.3 |
| 2100 | 10.414 | 27.7 | 22.0 | 7.1 |
| 2125 | 10.614 | 29.2 | 23.6 | 8.6 |
| 2150 | 10.806 | 30.5 | 4.9 | 9.8 |

*Source*: World Population Projections to 2150. Department of Economic and Social Affairs, Population Division (United Nations, 1998).In the context of this global information, it is important to have the outlines of National policies and programs to understand a perspective from the elderly viewpoints.

Apart from UN, this chapter has also recorded the national policies and programs for elderly in India. Apart from the general articles of the constitution which upholds the rights of individuals, we have mapped the legislations for the elderly in India. For instance, Hindu adoption and

Maintenance Act 1956 envisages that a Hindu child (male/female) will take care of his aged and infirm parents. In the same vein, along with sons and daughters, there are obligations on the State to take care of elderly in India. The state has entitled old age pension schemes which provide Rs200 per month per person. However, it can be argued that in today's time it is not a sufficient amount to survive. Moreover, there is a National Pension System as well which depends on how much a person has contributed while he was young. There are also health related policies by the state and private sector both. Above all, the Government of India has brought 'Senior citizen Act 2007' which provides number of privileges to the senior citizens. For instance, it has made maintenance of parents and senior citizens by children and relatives obligatory, establishment of Old age home for senior citizens. Ministry of Social Justice and Empowerment is a nodal ministry which looks after the specific problems of the elderly. Different other ministries like Health and Family Welfare, Railways, Ministry of Civil Aviation, Telecommunications etc. have been asked to provide their facilities and privileges to the senior citizens.

Further, this chapter has also analyzed the programs and policies available for the senior citizens in Punjab. For instance, there exists, 'Old age allowance' scheme for older persons who attain the age of 65 years. In Punjab along with this, there are many other policies and programs for the elderly women also, like for instance elderly woman above 60 years enjoy free travel in Punjab.

Along with these programs and policies at the national and state level we have mapped the programs and policies that prevail in the UK as well. At the outset, we have recorded what are the ways in which senior citizens can migrate to UK? What is the specific policy in this regard? It is interested to note that UK allows senior citizen visas who can demonstrate that they need long term personal care because of their illness. Apart from these, there are number of legislations and constitutional provisions to safeguard the rights of the elderly in UK. Free passes for buses, discounts in trains and trams, free passport, free gas safety checks, state pensions, funeral payments, winter fuel payment etc. are few facilities available to the elderly in UK. There is also a facility of old age homes, free home checkups and medical facilities in UK. Last but not the least, this chapter has also recorded the roles of NGOs for the welfare of the elderly in UK and India. In the light of this review of programs and policies for the elderly in UK and India, it would be interesting to find out in the field whether these programs and policies are being implemented or they are only on paper. It would also be interesting to check whether the respondents are aware of these programs and policies for their welfare. And lastly, what do they feel about these programs and policies. Are they satisfied or not?

This chapter further informed us that the population of elderly/senior citizens is increasing day by day. This trend is seen in every part of the world. According to the UN, approximately 20.7 per cent of the world's population would be elderly by 2050. On the other hand, World Health Organization (WHO,2017) has argued that the Southeast Asian regions would have increased life expectancy and hence by 2050 SEAR will have 21.4 per cent of its population above 60 years. Hence, this analysis also suggests that as the ageing population would increase in future, it would become necessary to have effective programs and policies for the senior citizens in place or they will be left out to suffer. In this light, this chapter has made the researcher to analyze the need for future preparation for our ageing population.

## References

Age Care, New Delhi. http://www.age-care-india.org/

Agewell Foundation, New Delhi. http://www.agewellfoundation.org/

Constitution of India, Government of India.

Cartis India. http://caritasindia.org/

Help Age, India. https://www.helpageindia.org/

Ministry of Civil Aviation, Government of India. http://www.civilaviation.gov.in/

Ministry of Consumer Affairs, Food and Public Distribution, Government of India.

Ministry of Finance, Government of India. https://www.finmin.nic.in/

Ministry of Health and Family Welfare, Government of India. https://mohfw.gov.in/

Department of Pensions and Pensioners Grievances. http://persmin.nic.in/

Ministry of Railways, Government of India. http://www.indianrailways.gov.in/railwayboard/

Ministry of Social Justice and Empowerment, Government of India. http://socialjustice.nic.in/

Department of Telecommunications. http://www.dot.gov.in/

Mishra, A.K. (2004) the Process of Ageing in India. http:/socialwelfare.delhigovt.nic.in/nationalpolicy.htm.

United Nations.

World Population Ageing Report.(2015)."Department of Economic and Social Affairs Population Division, New York, United Nations.

# V

# Family Structure and Socio-economic Status of Elderly Punjabis in Punjab

## Introduction

This chapter emphases on the different dimensions of elderly Punjabis living in Doaba regions of Punjab. The family structure is the key issue which will be investigated in this chapter. We will try to gauge why do people prefer to live in a certain type of family? Several studies indicate that joint family was quite prevalent in the Punjab society but later joint families are found to be disintegrating. Hence, we would like to investigate what are the reasons because of which joint families are disintegrating. Secondly, we would also analyze whether this disintegration of the joint family is leading to formation of nuclear or extended family. This chapter will further try to record how the nuclear and extended family emerge and sustain in Punjab in which elderly Punjabis live. This chapter will also examine the types of occupations in which the elderly Punjabis are involved in Doaba region of Punjab and the universe of the study. Are they looking after their grandchildren or they actively participate in business or petty shops of their adult children? The researcher would like to note how do the elderly Punjabis spend time when they are at home? What are the role of the friends and relatives in the life of the left behind elderly will also be examined?

Further, this chapter will also include the views of the respondents about the healthcare services available to them in Doaba region of Punjab. This chapter will also try to understand their opinions about the health centers in Doaba region of Punjab. For ascertaining economic status of elderly Punjabis which is another aspect, this chapter will also study the role of remittances in the life of the left behind elderly Punjabis. How much are the remittances important for their survival in their old age, will be probed? This chapter is constructed on primary as well secondary data collection. The primary data collected from the respondents is by visiting and talking to them personally. The field work is conducted in Jalandhar, Hoshiarpur and Kapurthala. We had administered interview schedules to the respondents selected through snowball technique and extracted relevant data for the study. We have used observations and informal interactions to substantiate our argument about the family structure and health facilities given to the elderly in Punjab. It is interesting to note that most of the respondents lacked fluency in English language and therefore the questions are translated into English. Secondly, the relevant data collected is then translated from Punjabi to English. Last but not the least, we have used data from books, reports and census to analyze further our point of study.

## Overview of Family Structure

Family is a social institution. In the modern days, the family is found to be disintegrating. The disintegration process has made impact on the structure and functions of the family. "Of all the groups that affect the lives of individuals in a society, none touches them so intimately or as continuously as does the family" (Baldassa et al., 2007: 102). "Though socialization is a continuous process that influences human beings throughout the life cycle, it is the family that firstly inculcates in a person, social, cultural or any other behavioral norms and values. Every one of us, with statistically small exceptions, will be a member of a family for the larger part of his life. The family gives us our principle identity and even our very name, which is the label of this identity, in the larger society of which we are a part" (Baldassa et al., 2007:128). Over the last five decades, a drastic change in the family structure has been observed. Several variations have been created. The major three types of families such as Joint family, nuclear family and extended family are prevalent. In this context, the following types of families are discussed to understand and analyze the migration and wellbeing of the Punjabi elderly.

## Understanding Family

Family is an important social institution. It is the base of society (Molla, 2016:64). According to Malinowski (1954:9), "The typical family, a group consisting of mother, father, and their progeny is found in all communities, savage barbarians and civilized: everywhere it plays an important role and influenced the whole extent of social organization and culture. It is undeniable fact that the family is universal and sociologically more important than the clan which is the evolution of humanity is preceded and outlasted". Desai argues, "the family is the first line of defense especially for children and a major factor in their survival, health, education, development, and protection. It is also a major source of nurturance, emotional bonding and socialization, and a link between continuity and change. It has the major potential to provide stability and support when there are problems. Human development can, thus, be enhanced by enriching family life. It is the head of the family who takes household economic responsibilities" (Desai, 1995a:228).

A woman plays a vital role in continuing the family. Traditionally, children are supposed to provide food and medical care to the elder people. "The Indian family is by and large patriarchal in structure" (Kapadia, 1982:230). According to Mullatti (1995), "The patriarchal set up is changing slowly towards equalitarian interaction among the educated, urban middle-classes and also among some rural set ups. Even in matrilineal and matrilocal cultures patriarchy seems to be prevalent in the form of power held by the bother and not by the women herself". Mujahid opines that "family is the central institution with responsibility for elderly care in most countries in South – East Asia. Although not the only form of family support, co-residence is the main component of family support because a substantial portion of the informal care of the elderly takes place among household members" (Mujahid, 2006:28).

## Evolution of Various Types of Families in Punjab

## Understanding Joint Family

The joint family in Punjab is still prevalent. In the rural villages of Punjab, it has been observed that members of the family prefer to live joint families but considerably lower percentage (Singh, 2004:145). "The majority of older Indians prefer to live with adult children in multi-generational homes arrangement long widely considered to be the most "normal" and proper" form of ageing and family in India"(Sarah Lamb,2009:3). However, in the urban areas members of the family are found scattered due to employment or some business activities. Living in a joint family has several advantages. Working children can depend upon parents to look after their grand-children.

Ramurti and Jamuna (2004:65) argue, "The paradigm shift in the value system of the ancient agrarian society has resulted in disintegration, disorientation and collapse of the joint family care and support system". "Yesterday`s practices of elder care as a dutiful task of a primary care given has been dwindling due to lack of time, commitment and dearth of resources for care giving. Similarly, the older parents get emotional and psychological support while living with children. The vantages of a joint family are enumerated such as cradles of social virtues, insurance against olds, division in labor, and socialism in wealth, an agency of social control, avoids fragmentation of land. "Regardless of the structure of the family, the role women in the family has been subordinate to men consistent with a patriarchal Indian system in which women`s sexuality is strictly controlled" (Dommaraju, 2015:1245).

Historically, a joint family was quite prevalent in Indian society particularly before the onset of industrialization and increased urbanization. In the light of the above discussion, the researcher has discussed about the joint family and analyze the viewpoints of the respondents. For instance, 68-year -old male from a Chitti village from district Jalandhar opined that "Since decades we all living in a joint family. Brothers, sisters and their children live under one roof. Our ancestors taught us the merits of living in a joint family. I am a 68 -year -old farmer. My wife left for England to take care of my children and adult young grand –children. After her departure, I never felt alone since there are brothers, sisters, and grand-children to look after me in case of emergency. I am a diabetic patient hence need a constant help".

Similarly, 75- year -old male from Basti Sheikh, an urban area of district Jalandhar argued that "We are four brothers. Our parents died a few years back. All of us live together. Our grandchildren are married but they also live with us. I am happy to see the faces of grandchildren. We all sit together and discuss our problems and resolve. Our parents always taught us to live together so we are living together". Yet another 66- year -old male of village Kang in district Hoshiarpur narrated his family story in the following ways, "Our family is a big family. My deceased father had four brothers; all lived together. Today, my sons and daughters and their children live together under one roof. It is always a consolation to live together. My opinion is that joint family is the best family". In a similar vein, 72- year -old widow of village Rampur in district Kapurthala told that "We have 12 members in the family; all live together. It is a tradition in our family. Some men work outside the state but their families live with us. I and my husband are old now. I believe the joint family is the proper site of elder care".

Apart from this, the researcher has conducted interviews with the children of the same family to extract their views about the various types of families and its impact on their life to analyze and substantiate this study. Following the discussion, 32 –year- old daughter eloquently expressed her love for her migrated parents that, "I am a married woman having one daughter. My husband is a bank employee. He has been transferred to Rajasthan. We all live in a joint family. My in-laws are very helpful to me particularly in the absence of my husband". Yet another 42 –year- old son responded in the same way that, "I am a working man. I am an officer in the department of Income Tax posted at Amritsar. My wife and little son are living with my parents. My unmarried brother and sister also live in the same house. We all live together and are happy".

## Understanding Nuclear Family

There are several reasons for emergence of nuclear families as cited by Singh (2004:135) these are because of industrial development, rural to urban migration, divorce etc. Sociologist Sonawat (2001:180)argues, "Families in India are undergoing vast changes like increasing divorce and separation rates, domestic violence, inter-generational conflicts, social problems of drug abuse, juvenile delinquency etc. consequently growing stress and strain in the families".

Muraleedharan (2005:1035) stated that changing social set up from the co-family living to nuclear families results in losing the familiar support to the old aged people. Increased labor force participation by women in formal and informal sectors resulted in the loss of support from women, the ultimate care-given to the family especially the aged. Migration to the urban and semi-urban areas for employment and better opportunities also accentuates this phenomenon as it forces youngsters to leave their homes and their parents at their native places. Even in the case of urban-based nuclear families, both the husband and wife have to go out in search of livelihood leaving the parents and aged people living with them in distress. All these result in old-aged people left uncared and unwanted at homes either in the concrete jungles of urban areas or deserted homes at the rural areas.

"In addition, the emergence of financially independent, career-oriented men and women, who are confident of taking their own decisions and crave to have a sense of individual achievement, has greatly contributed to the disintegration of joint family. For many, nuclear family is a safer matrimonial home to a woman. In villages, the size of joint family has been substantially reduced or is found in its fragmented form. Some have split into several nuclear families, while others have taken the form of extended or stem families. Extended family is, in fact, a transitory phase between joint and nuclear family system" (Singh, 2004).

Talcott Parsons (1954) argues, "modern industrial society had led to the growth of what he calls it isolated nuclear family. This family is structured isolated as it does not form an integral part of the wider kinship group. Parsons theory of emergence of the isolated nuclear family can be seen in terms of his general theory of social evolution. The evolution of societies involves a process of structural differentiation". Mason discussed, "the probable effects of urbanizations and industrialization on migration and family structure and care of the elderly. Evidence about changing family support for the elderly in Asia is thus reviewed. Mason concludes that future changes in Asian countries and areas seem to erode traditional family based systems of care for the elderly, even if the overall welfare of the elderly improves due to higher incomes. Problem faced by elderly woman are likely to be acute and may require special policies to deal with them" (Mason, 1996:15). Young and Willmot hold that nuclear family has proved to be functional in one respect. Due to strengthening of conjugal bonds and the employment and education of women, the power equation within the family has become more symmetrical. Women enjoy equal status as their husbands and equally participate in all decision-making processes (as quoted in Arya Priya, 2017:28).

The researcher conducted in-depth interviews with the respondents and analyzed the same. In this context, 68- year-old male from Mithapur, district Jalandhar shared his experience unexcitingly. According to him, "Earlier, we all used to live together under one roof but now everyone is out either for work or due to education of children. My elder son went to Mumbai for his job. Wife of my younger` son does not want to live with us. She forced my son to live separately due to adjustment problem in the family. I do not know what is happening to the families. This negative thought is spreading fast in the society which is dangerous especially for the older persons like us". In the same vein, another 67 -years old female of village Kanpur in district Hoshiarpur related this situation that, "I and my husband live alone. My elder son immigrated to England. My elder daughter married and went to Bengaluru with her husband. Our whole family is disintegrated. What to do the society is like that only". Yet another 65 -year -old female of district Kapurthala revealed, "My husband immigrated to England leaving behind my son and me. Later on, my son also migrated to England on a study visa. Currently both of them are living in England. I am alone in Kapurthala.

## Understanding Extended Family

Extended family consist of uncles, aunts, cousins and grandparents. Gordon (1972:1625) states that, "the extended family is, typically, a residential unit composed of husband, wife, dependent offspring, and married sons and their spouses and offspring." In this definition, marital status and sex (married sons and their nuclear families (are also viewed as essential criteria of the extended). "A recent study on the living arrangements of Mexican immigrants in the United States has also found that the migration process accentuates the pattern of the extended family household formation, with recent immigrants more likely to live in the extended family households than non-immigrants in the United States of America and Mexico" (Van Hook and Glick, 2007:235).

In this context, the researchers conducted in-depth interviews for data collection with the respondents and tried to understand strengths and challenges of the extended family and the data was analyzed. Some observations are also made to substantiate this study. For instance, 78- year -old male from Jalandhar told that "My elder son went to England and married a NRI Punjabi girl. Before he left for England he was married and had two children. There is lot of stress and strain in the family. In a similar vein, 66 -year -old female from Hoshiarpur responded that "My elder daughter married with a Punjabi man.

She has one son aged 13years. Her husband migrated to England. He married a second wife in UK and now her husband has three children in UK. However, he sends money to my daughter but never visited her in the last ten years. The whole family is disturbed". Yet another 69 -year -old male from Kapurthala narrated as story of her only daughter that, "My

**Table5.1:Socio-Economic Profile of left Behind Elderly Punjabis in Punjab.**

| *Particulars* | | *Percentage* | *Families* |
|---|---|---|---|
| Age | 60-80 years | - | - |
| **Income** | | | |
| Remittances(a) | | 60 | 30 |
| Government Pension and Petty Business(b) | | 20 | 10 |
| Both (a+b) | | 20 | 10 |
| **Visit/Staying** | | 20 | 10 |
| Visit(Social occasions) | | | |
| 1)do not want to stay because of harsh weather and | | 80 | 8 |
| English language hindrance in the host society | | | |
| 2) want to stay because they want to avail dual citizenship | | 10 | 1 |
| benefits | | | |
| **Awareness** | | 90 | 48 |
| Not aware of old age pension benefits | | | |
| Not aware of public transport concession | | 90 | 45 |
| **Health** | | 100 | 50 |
| Health Problems | | | |
| Private hospital services | | 75 | 38 |
| Mentally depressed in the absence of loved ones | | 100 | 50 |
| Dependent on immediate relatives during health problems | | 90 | 45 |
| Depressed and isolated | | 100 | 50 |
| **Expenditure(50 families )** | | | |
| Food and Medical | | 80 | - |
| Other Expenses | | 20 | - |
| a) Extend financial help to relatives and friends | | 75 | - |
| b) Donations to Sikh religious organization. | | 25 | - |

Souce: Data Collated from field work

daughter completed higher studies (M.Tech) and got married to an NRI in UK. She was sponsored by her husband. After arrival in UK, she came to know that her husband is already married. She came to know about this after giving a birth to a daughter in UK. Her whole life is shattered.

Table 5.1 shows a survey of 50 families in three districts: Kapurthala, Jalandhar and Hoshiarpur in Doaba region of Punjab in the Indian subcontinent. 30 families living together are depended upon remittances sent by their children to meet day to day expenses. 10 families draw government pension and have income source from the petty business. 10 families getting i.e. remittances as well as government pension and income from the petty business. Some children sponsored their parents and they immigrate to the United Kingdom and are currently living with their children such 10 families keep on visiting Punjab to meet their close relatives and friends on social occasions. 08 families keep on visiting the United Kingdom and do not prefer to stay permanently in the United Kingdom due to harsh weather and language barriers. 01 family out of 50 families already immigrated and settled permanently in the United Kingdom.

Punjabi people maintain a close relationship with the homeland. The emigrated elderly people particularly stay in touch with the relatives and friends in Punjab through various modes of communication such as phone, video conferencing etc. This study has observed that 48 families do not know about welfare schemes of the government of Punjab for the older persons. 45 families are not aware of concessional fares available in Punjab for the senior citizens. The health issue is a challenge, especially for the elderly people. This study has found that 50 families have a health issue. The elderly people between 60-80 years have a chronic disease such as arthritis, heart problem, knee pain, and bronchitis. The shortage of qualified doctors and medical care staff and inadequate facilities in the government hospitals in the state of Punjab are the key challenges for the elderly people. 38 families prefer to go to a private practitioner or private hospitals in the event of illness. This study found that in the absence of children 45 families depend upon close relatives for extra help in case of sudden hospitalization, death in the family, or social function. Without their sons or daughters, the left behind elderly seek the assistance of friends and relatives if there is a need. Loneliness and isolation are prevalent among left behind elderly in 50 families. This study has found that in order to pass their time happily, the elderly in 50 families take active participation, if health permits, in religious activities. The elderly people feel satisfied spiritually when they go to a religious institution. This study has found that older people share their joy and pain in the company of like-minded people when they visit a religious institution.

## Understanding Economic Status of Left behind Elderly in Punjab

The researcher has tried to examine the economic status of the left behind elderly Punjabis in Punjab. In this context, it is significant to understand the concept of remittance. The researcher has consulted various previous studies conducted by the social scientists. The researcher has conducted in-depth interviews to gauge the views of the left behind elderly about the remittances and its importance in their life for meeting day to day expenses.

Dandekar and Kumundini (1996:1192) analyzed ageing and related problems. The study concluded with the trials and tribulations of the elderly due to poor health, nonworking status, adverse socio-economic conditions and lack of independence. Lucas and Stark (1985:912) opines that migration as a group decision in which the family invests in the migration of one of its members according to new Economics of Migration. Family members expect to receive remittances in times of need to protect themselves against calamities such as drought and other national disasters or illness. Economic status of the elderly relates to the family care. "It may be noted that the elderly with high economic status tend to be more self-dependent than those with lower socioeconomic status". (Cowgill and Holmes, 1972:32). "Poorer elderly tend to have more difficult lives and have to depend more on care from their families" (Reed et al., 1995:63). "However, one study shows that elderly with sufficient income were more likely to receive care in terms of moral and mental support than those without sufficient income" (Esterman and Andrews, 1992:279).

"Poverty is one of the obstacles for families to be able to take care of the elderly, despite social norms' and social expectations" (United Nations, 1994a). Caffrey found, "Households in which an elderly person was responsible for him/herself, had less land and less yearly income, while those households that maintained the traditional pattern of the youngest daughter remaining in the home as the caregiver had more land under cultivation and a higher yearly income. The problem for caregiving is not that children don't want to care for their parents, but that their resources for doing so are limited because of the economic pressures of raising their own families" (Caffrey, 1992:125). "However, a study conducted by Pyke and Bengtson (1996:382), found no differences in care received by the elderly between families with different economic status".

Bengston and Harootyan (1994) found that in the United States, a large majority of adult children reported some contact with their ageing parents at least weekly, either by telephone or in person. Geographical proximity was an important variable in maintaining such intergenerational communication. Practically adult children were little prepared to take on a caregiving role, still assuming that parents are there to help them, although most agreed they had a responsibility towards their ageing parents and closeness between adult children and their parents grew as people aged. Lee et al. found, "In Taiwan richer sons are more likely to have parents living alone and provide financial support to parents instead of co-residing with them" (Lee et al., 1994:1022).Harper writes, "there is a concern that emotional strain will increase within families as large number of older people become reliant on decreasing number of children to care for them in old age. Increased longevity equaled the increased number of older people requiring care while declining fertility will lead to the shrinking of the reservoir of family care for the old and place increasing pressure on the middle-aged coping both with dependent children and ageing parents" (Harper,2006:125).

The following narratives of the responded are included to understand the views about the remittances. In this context, 85 year-old- male from Bootan Mandi from district Jalandhar explained that, "I have no source of income. I and my wife depend heavily on the money sent to us by my son from UK. My wife was admitted to the hospital due to a kidney problem. All the hospital expenses were met by my son. Without his financial help, we cannot survive". Similarly, 79 year old male from Nurpur village of Kapurthala responded that "We wanted to marry our daughter. As you know, parents have to spend a lot of money on marriage. It is farce when people say they do not want dowry. In Punjab, it has become a fashion to demand more dowry from the parents especially when people come to know that they have a family member living in a foreign country. My son could not come due to his job engagement but he sent the whole money to arrange dowry and marriage function". In a similar vein, 68 year-old male from Hoshiarpur told that "We wanted to construct a new room in the house. The amount which I had was not sufficient so I requested my son in UK to help us. He sent money to us, therefore, we could complete the room". From the above narratives, it is evident that remittances are used for various purposes by the elderly parents. The remittances for the left behind parents are absolutely significant for meeting different kinds of expenses.

The questions such as what are the economic resources available with the elderly Punjabis how remittances sent by their children play a key role in their daily life? These questions were deeply investigated by the researcher. In this context, the narratives of the respondents are analyzed to substantiate our arguments regarding economic status of the elderly Punjabis in Doaba. On the basis of facts given by the respondents, we can safely argue that the elderly feel secure and safe with financial resources and assets which currently exist at their disposal. It gives them liberty to make choices.

Dandekar(1996) and others argue that help as, "by the age of 60 years people are assumed to have fulfilled their various responsibilities, many of them involving money, for instance, education of the children, their marriage, and may be their jobs. All this could possibly lead to a drain on the savings. Retirement usually brings a decline in their income and thus financial status. Retirement could also result into poverty, which could further lead to dependence in old age on children, grand- children or even relatives". "In a similar context established, "the financial problems are more common among widows and among elderly in nuclear families and also indicated economic insecurity to be having some bearing with the social strata of class and caste" (Singh et al., 1987).

The following narratives of the respondents are discussed and analyzed. In this context, 68 year-old male from Bootan Mandi in district Jalandhar told that, "I retired as an Engineer from Punjab State Electric Board. I draw a monthly pension of Rs 8000. My wife is a housewife. We have only this source of funds to run our life. My elder son migrated to UK and settled there. He is a bank employee and also works part- time in a shopping mall on Saturday and Sundays. He regularly sends money to us which is quite sufficient for both of us. If there is any extra need such as repair of the house or extension or untimely hospitalization, we request him for more money. He is quite helpful to us. His money to us works like an oxygen". Yet another, 75 year-old male from Nurpur village in district Kapurthala responded that "I am a farmer. My only income was from the farming. Now I am too old to work in the fields hence I leased the entire agriculture land to a third party. For the last few years, the income from the harvest have reduced drastically. My wife is a diabetic patient. We have only a daughter who is married to a NRI Punjabi in UK. My son-in-law is a good person. My daughter is working in a cloth factory in UK. Both are earning good money. My daughter sends money to us and support. Sometimes, I do not feel good to have money from my daughter since in Punjabi culture a daughter is a '*Parayadhan*' but we are helpless. A lot of money goes to meet medical expenses for my wife". Similarly, 80 year-old- female from Badowal in district Hoshiarpur narrated that, "I am a widow. My husband died a few years back. I have no source of income since my husband was a peon in a private firm. I used to work in the fields to earn my livelihood but now I am too old to go to the fields. My only son reached UK via Italy. He sends money to me but not regularly. However, I can manage my life even with irregular flow of money".

However, elderly left behind receive money from their sons and daughters who have migrated to UK but sometimes the amount of remittances is not sufficient as t maintain day to day expenses. A distressed and worried 85 year-old- male from a village Lambra in district Jalandhar responded that "I retired as a clerk from the Punjab Irrigation Department. My monthly pension is Rs 2500/-. The department has taken my bank account but no amount of pension has been credited to my bank account for the last six months. I am an old person. I cannot go to the department since I am bed-ridden. I asked my brother`s son to check my bank account and withdraw if it is credited. He told me, a clerk in the pension department demands a bribe for releasing the pension. This is the current situation in the state of Punjab. Top politicians and government officials talk about the welfare of the older persons but nothing in reality on the ground. My son in England also stopped sending the money because he told me that he lost his job". I am surviving on the rent income".

From the above discussion with the respondents, we can infer that the left behind elderly Punjabis depend heavily on the remittances from their children. The researcher also found from the respondents that the retirement pension is not adequate to defray the necessary expenses. The absence of social security for the unemployed has added further vows to the day to day problems of social the older people. In addition to that, the sky rocketing prices of essential commodities and the rising cost of medication and hospitalization are the key challenges, particularly for the older persons. The researcher found that the retirement pension system is sluggish and also infected with corruption at the local level.

Baldassar et al (2007) established that transnational migrants participate in care giving across national borders in four main ways: through (a) transnational communication, (b) return visits to give emotional, practical and personal care to their ageing parents in times of need, (c) bringing their parents to Australia to care for them on a long term basis and (d) repatriating their homeland to care for their parents there.

Srivastava (1968:77) argued that migrants continually send money to their relatives left behind who had spent more money than before on agricultural implements and fertilizers. Nambiar (1995) examined the socio-economic background of migrants and their characteristics. The author concludes that although migrants brought in comfort and luxury to the people at home, it involved suffering and degradation.

The researcher has tried to find out what are the modern electric appliances available in the households of the left behind elderly Punjabis and why are they? The majority of the left behind elderly parents possess modern electric appliances and fully furnished house not particularly for their use but for the usage of their NRI children and grandchildren who keep on visiting the older parents. We have found that 50 families have *pucca* houses and have modern electric appliances such as refrigerator, fans, and air-conditioner.

The researcher through in-depth interviews tried to find out from the respondents about who gives money for the modern electric appliances and furnishings. The following respondents during the interview proudly described the possession of electric appliances.

For instance, 69- year -old male of district Jalandhar described that "Our children are in the UK. They bought Refrigerator, Washing Machine, Colored Television, Music Systems and Air Conditioner for us. They come once a year to India. Their children need all this. Now- a- days these are the essential utilities, not the luxuries".

In district Hoshiarpur a male responded aged 72 that, "In contemporary times, grand-children are addicted to all sorts of electronic gadgets. My elder son brought many electronic gadgets from England. Some items such as TV, Fridge, and washing machine were purchased by the money sent by my son. Today society has changed. Luxury items in the house, of course, have become a social status in the society". Describing the necessity of the electronic gadgets, another 79 -year -old male from district Kapurthala reflected that, "Refrigerator, washing machine, gas stove items are the necessity. One should have if one can afford. In our case, children send money from England whenever we need to buy". It is evident from the various interviews that the left behind elderly Punjabis possess all kinds of modern electronic appliances and furnishings. This is because of the money sent to them by their children to buy modern items. Children and grandchildren use all these items when they visit their older parents. Punjabi are known for the ostentation of wealth since they believe strongly that ostentation and magnificence elevate their social status in the family.

## Understanding Isolation and Loneliness among Elderly in Punjab

"Social isolation is defined as an objective state of having minimal social contact. Loneliness is a subjective, unpleasant feeling in which the person yearns for intimate companionship or social connectivity" (Krist, 2017). Gurudas (1989:236) observed that "men who lived with their spouse had more satisfaction with life than those who had lost their spouse". Jindal (1987:186) found that "isolation was more prevalent among the widowers than among the married ones. Loneliness was also significantly lower in the aged couples who were not living with the family as compared to the widow or widowers who were living with the family".

Nayyar (1982:18) observed that, "aged living with the family were happier than those living alone. Therefore, it can be seen that the aged who were living alone or those who were widows/widowers were experiencing more loneliness than the aged who were living with their life partner". To understand the dynamics of isolation and loneliness in the life of the elderly left behind parents, the researcher has conducted in-depth interviews to substantiate the universe of the study. In this context, 83 year-old – male from Chitti village in district Jalandhar responded that "I feel lonely because my children have migrated to UK. My friends have also left because they have shifted to the city. I live with my wife in this village because we have house as well as a piece of agriculture land which I have given on lease to a third party. I and my wife spend whole day either watching TV or sleeping. We both are unhappy since we miss our children and grandchildren". In a similar vein, 69 year-old- male from district Kapurthala told that "My wife died a few years back. My elder son migrated to Australia and settled there permanently with his family. He never came back even on the death of his mother because he was not a citizen of Australia. I feel very depressed. It is very difficult to spend time without a companion. I do not have anyone to talk to me. My elder brother lives in the city. Now-a-days, he is sick hence he cannot come to stay with me. I do not want to be burden on anybody". A female from district Hoshiarpur boringly narrated that, "My husband went to the Gulf country and did not return back. I do not know even if he is alive or dead. My only daughter migrated to UK and married Punjabi NRI. She does not come to India since her husband whole family live in UK. She calls me sometimes but not regularly. I cannot go to her because I am sick. I am depressed".

From the previous literature and current discussion, the researcher has found that the elderly left behind parents are isolated and lonely. They miss their children. They want them to call them regularly. From the respondents, it is also observed that money does not matter much but love and care do.

## Understanding Social Exclusion in Punjab

Caste is a reality in the Indian society. The prevalence of caste in the state of Punjab is no exception. Social scientists such as Kumar (2014), Ram (2007), Puri (2003) and Jodhka (2002), Judge (2004) have done an elaborate research on caste and social exclusion.

Discussing caste and untouchability in rural Punjab (Jodkha, 2002:1817) writes that, "Segregation of individual castes or groups of castes in the village was the most obvious mark of civic privileges and disabilities. There were also restrictions on the kind of work an individual could do. Each caste was expected to consider a particular occupation as its legitimate calling. The prevailing ideology of caste discouraged individual choice of occupation, even employing coercion, if required, as a means to keep the system of occupational hierarchy going." Understanding the contours of social exclusion, Kumar(2014:38) writes that, "the social exclusion of an ex-untouchable is so overpowering that even though he attains economic and political mobility or even beyond the national boundaries through his hard labor, he is not accepted by the castes located higher up in the caste hierarchy as an equal. His social identity remains stigmatized and his achievements are basically associated with that social identity". Similarly, Puri (2003:1148) argues that casteism has continued to exist in the Sikh community. Sikh panthic organizations are very powerful in Punjab and works exclusively for the upper caste Jat Sikhs. (Ram, 2007) states that, "all the important Sikh Panthic organizations are under the control of the Jats and they are adamant not to share their management with dalits". From the above literature, we can conclude that social exclusion is prevailing in Punjabi society and the victims belong to the marginalized sections of the society.

In the backdrop of discussion on caste, the researcher has tried to understand this social exclusion prevailing in the Punjabi society. It is, therefore, empirical data was collected through in-depth interviews from the elderly respondents. In this context, 74 year-old male from village Talan from district Jalandhar told that "I belong to a Scheduled Caste community. There are three Sikh temples in the village. The Sikh temple is occupied by the Sikhs and they do not allow any other caste man or woman to occupy a position in the management of the temple. The caste system is prevailing till date. Sometimes, Sikh people also indulge in caste atrocities. The poor scheduled castes who happen to work in the Sikh agriculture fields are subjected to various kinds of humiliations and abuses because of the caste system".

In a similar vein, 81 year-old-male from Nurpur from district Kapurthala responded in anguish that, "In what kind of society we live today. We have been suffering due to the caste system since centuries. The Sikh people claim that Guru Nanak teaching opposed the practices of discrimination on the basis of caste system. It is nothing but hollow rhetoric. I do not know when it will end. Discussing existence of discrimination in the educational institutions of Punjab, 68 year old retired teacher explained that, "I was a teacher in a Government Senior Secondary School in Hoshiarpur. The upper caste teachers in the school discriminated with me because I belong to Scheduled Caste community. For Instance, they always tell the parents of the students that this teacher belongs to the lower caste. It discouraged me a lot. I found that the majority of the upper caste people in Punjab do not want to see a Scheduled Caste man or woman to rise up in life socially and economically. We cannot change their mentality since it is embedded in them. I also noticed during my service that the upper caste teachers discriminate with the students belonging to the marginalized sections of the society". I found that I was discriminated when I was in service due my caste. This continued even after my retirement among my colleagues".

Similarly, 73 year-old male running a shop in the main bazaar of Jalandhar district explained that "I run a cloth shop in the main bazaar. My clients are from different religions and castes. In the market, the upper caste people always speaks ill of the lower caste people. Reservation is always a topic over which they shout and abuse openly. We have a Shopkeeper Association. The association is managed by the upper caste people. My name was proposed by a like-minded shopkeeper but it was rejected because of my caste. I strongly believe the caste system will never die in India. Now people are carrying this cancer to the western countries and to some extent the upper caste people have succeeded in spreading this cancer".

## Understanding Engagements of the Elderly Punjabis in Punjab

The researcher has tried to examine day to day engagements of elderly Punjabis in Punjab. This is important and significant to discuss in relation to their wellbeing. The following narratives reveal how the elderly Punjabis engage themselves in their daily life. In this context, 68-year-old male of village Khurla Kingra from district Jalandhar explained that "After retirement, I invested in setting up a cloth shop in the city. I believe that it is better to be engaged in some activities to maintain a good health and sustain financially. I do not like to depend on my children in any manner". In yet another respondent, 65 -year -old male of district Hoshiarpur revealed that "I took voluntary retirement and invested the whole money in starting a construction company with the help of my younger son. The elder one has migrated to UK. I am doing well in business. My son also sends money whenever he is comfortable to send". In a similar vein, 60-year-old male of district Kapurthala working in a temple as a Granthi told that, "I am a Granthi in a Sikh temple. I go to people`s house for conducting religious ceremonies. I am very satisfied. My son and daughter are in England. We go to them once a year and stay with them for a few days and come back before the winter starts."

Another 67 year-old female from district Jalandhar shared her feelings told, "I am an illiterate. My whole life is spent in taking care of children and grand-children. It is very satisfying that my role in the house keeps happy one and all". In another case, 73-year-old female of a village district

Hoshiarpur, explained that her engagements in educating the children from the marginalized sections of the society. According to her, "My two children migrated to UK. I am a retired teacher from a government school. I and my retired husband have been running a coaching classes in the village to educate children belonging to the marginalized sections of the society". Yet another, 68 -year-old woman from district Kapurthala told that "I spend my time in the Sikh temple. I daily go to the nearby Sikh temple and clean the floor. I also wash utensils sometimes. It gives me spiritual satisfaction. You know, working in a Guru house (Sikh Temple) is a blessing for a woman like me". From the above discussion, we can deduce that the elderly Punjabis remain engaged throughout the day if their health permits them. It helps them to satisfy their social necessities by interacting with others. The researcher has also found that the engagement of the elderly Punjabis in various social activities help them in fighting loneliness and isolation.

## Understanding Elderly Abuse in Punjab

"Elder abuse is defined as a single or repeated act or lack of appropriate action occurring within any relationship where there is an expectation of trust which causes harm or distress to an older person"(Bhatia et al., 2008). Elderly abuse is common in all societies across the globe and Punjabi society is no exception. Elderly parents are commonly abused in the families. BKPAI (2011) having done study on the status of the elderly in Punjab reported, "Elderly abuse is growing concern for the ageing population".

"Almost 11 percent of the elderly in Punjab have reported facing abuse after turning 60. With the proportion of abuse being slightly higher in rural areas as compared to urban areas'. There are various types of abuses that elderly parents face during their old age" (BKPAI, 2011:23). "Physical abuse includes hitting, striking, beating, pushing, shaking, pinching, kicking, slapping. Emotional and psychological abuse includes verbal assaults, intimidation, humiliation, threats, insults, harassment" (Yatish and Bhargava, 2014).

In a similar vein, Kapur (1997) mentions, "incidences of elderly abuse by family members ranging from neglect to physically throwing the old age parents out of the house". This study study found that the elderly who have savings and property in their name get more love, respect, and care than those who do not have. Those who do not have financial and property resources are occasionally abandoned by the children. In the absence of their children, the role of immediate family members are significant in the life of older person 's.According to a study conducted by Kemi (2014) social network, colleagues and acquaintances are important to ward off loneliness and isolation. Some of them reported exploitation at the hands of close relatives and friends. The common complaint is that the elderly people are deceived by their own close relatives and friends when it comes to the property matter.

The following narratives illustrates the nature and dynamic of elderly abuse existing in Punjabi families in Punjab. In this context, 78 year-old-male from district Jalandhar argued that "the time has changed so the children. My elder son came from UK. He has been telling me to sell ancestral property and give his share so that he can repay the loan in UK. After consistent refusal, he started quarrelling with me and his mother. One day, under the influence of liquor he pushed me to the wall consequently my writs bone broke. I told him, come what may, I shall never sell my ancestral property". In a similar vein, 83 year-old-female narrated that, my daughter-in-law along with son and children came from UK to visit us. My daughter-in-law is quite quarrelsome. She gets upset over trifle matters. One day, she was insisting to sell a piece of land. I refused. She did not like it. She went back to UK with my son. Because of her ferocious behavior, I do not like to go to UK and stay there permanently".

## Understanding Healthcare System in Punjab

A general understanding endorses that elderly are intense users of health services and many need assistance in undertaking day today activities. The factors that determine the utilization of healthcare system by the elderly needs to be understood. It is important and significant to discuss the healthcare services available in the state of Punjab for the elderly to review their health status. The researcher has tried to find out the status of current healthcare system in the state of Punjab by collecting empirical data from the respondents. The researcher conducted in-depth interviews with the respondents tried to understand views of the elderly people with regard to the healthcare services available in the state of Punjab. The interviews conducted in the rural areas of Punjab revealed pathetic conditions of healthcare services available to the elderly. The healthcare services are inadequate in these areas despite several welfare schemes exist for the older persons. Before we analyze the narratives of the respondents in the state of Punjab specifically on this issue, we need to know about the existing welfare schemes for the older persons from secondary data in general.

World Health Organization (WHO), "considers health to be a fundamental right of every human being" (WHO, 2018). The Twelfth Five Year Plan (2002-2017) aims at achieving Universal Health Coverage in the country where each individual will have access to basic services at reasonable prices. The World health statistics reveal that the public health spending in India is amongst the lowest in the world whereas the private health expenditure is very high in India as compared to other nations. Nearly 70 percent of the total health spending is private, making Indian health the most privatized in the world (Ahluwalia, 2000).

The delivery of healthcare services in Punjab by public and private sector play a vital role. According to Registrar General of India (RGI, 2016), "the number of elderly (aged 60 and above) in the state of Punjab grew from 1.01 million to 2.87 million, which constitutes 10.3 percent of total state`s population". "Longevity of males and females in Punjab has increased by 14 percent and 26 percent as against 28 percent and 38 percent at the all-India level between 1970-75 and 2006-10. The life expectancy at birth of an average person in Punjab was estimated to be 69.3 years during 2006-10 as compared to 68.9 years in Tamil Nadu and 67.2 years in Karnataka. Elderly women experience greater longevity in the older age as compared to men. A relatively high percentage of elderly (65%) were not formally educated and migration after marriage among the elderly women was found to be significantly high. The health status of elderly in rural Punjab (18%) and 22% in urban areas rated poor by the report" (BKPAI, 2013). A study by Srinivasan, (2010) to explore current health status, showed that more than four-fifth of total elderly (85 per cent) reported that they suffered from at least one medical problems. Another study by (Ghosh and Arokiasamy, 2009) show a high prevalence rate of chronic illness among the aged population in India.

"The Health and Family Welfare department in the state of Punjab provide preventive, promotional and curative Health Services to the people of the State. This is done through a network of medical institutions such as sub-centers, subsidiary health centers (dispensaries/Clinics), primary health centers, community health centers, sub-Divisional and Districts Hospital, Government Medical and dental Colleges. (Government of Punjab) Punjab signed a MOU with the Government of India on June 15, 2006, for implementation of the National Rural health Mission" (NRHM) (Government of Punjab).

In a bid to provide better health facilities and cashless health care services to farmers "Bhagat Puran Singh Sehat Bima Yojana" scheme launched (Government of Punjab). Several studies indicate that the poor are forced to go for expensive medical private doctors and hospitals due to inadequate infrastructure and poor medical facilities. In article published in Indian Express quotes a statement of Director General Labor Welfare, Government of India: "Punjab has not fared well in implementing the "Rashtriya Swasthya Bima Yojana" for below poverty line (BPL) families" Mahendra Dev(2006) rightly pointed out in regard to the inequalities in health sector. He argued that "In the health sector, there are significant inequalities in expenditures across classes, regions, and gender. A review of policies and programmes shows the well-known fact of deterioration in the quality of services in public healthcare system. The poor cannot afford the private health systems because of high costs".

Although, multiple welfare schemes are available in the state of Punjab for the healthcare of general and older population yet the people in general face lots of challenges in the delivery of the healthcare services. The narratives of the respondents from the rural and urban areas of the Punjab demonstrate that a large number of elderly was unhappy with the healthcare services. In addition to that unprofessional attitude of the staff of the government, hospital is another cause of unhappiness. In this context, 75 -year- old male argued the worst condition of the government hospitals in Jalandhar, "My children migrated to the UK 12 years back. I live with my wife in this house. I am a heart patient. I cannot drive because of poor eyesight. The condition of the government hospital in this village is the worst. Doctors do not have sympathetic feelings for the older people. The attitude of the nursing staff towards the older people especially whose children are abroad is greedy and insensitive. The ambulance in case of emergency are not available at all".

In Jalandhar district, 67-year-old female narrated that, ".Whenever I go the government hospital the doctor refer to me to a private hospital. There is a nexus between doctors of private and government hospitals in Jalandhar. I had to go to a private hospital for a knee operation". Stating with a heavy heart, 69-year-old male from rural area of district Kapurthala told that, "We have only one government hospital in the whole area. Most of the time, it is overcrowded with patients. Therefore doctors are very busy. This hospital is under-staffed. I am a diabetic patient. The nurses treat older people as if we are beggars. The rooms are dirty. The sweepers are greedy. They always demand this or that. Dogs and cats frequently roam in the medical wards.

While explaining the worst conditions of the government hospital, 72-year -old female from Hoshiarpur shared her bad experience with the hospital staff and reflected that "I had a heart stroke last year. I went to a government hospital but I was treated very badly there. I will never go to a government hospital because the doctors are insensitive. My elder son is in the UK. He always sends money to meet hospital expenditure. Now, *I* prefer to go to a private hospital. I do not know what kind of free healthcare facilities are available for the older people in the government hospital". While remembering his encounter with the government hospital, 66 -year-old male from a village Chhiti in district Jalandhar told with a heavy heart the condition that exists in the government hospital. Accordingly, he argued that "We have a government hospital in our village. The present condition of the hospital is the worst. Doctors and nurses never reach on time. The villagers with the help of the foreign Punjabi donors donated money to buy wheelchairs and beds for the hospital. I came to know from my friend that the gifted items are either broken or dispappeared. Doctors working in the Government hospital are busy to earn an extra money. They have opened up their personal clinics and devote much of time in their private clinic or hospital. They enjoy good rapport with the doctors of good private hospitals in the city and refer most of the patient to them. It is quite popular among the people that these types of greedy doctors get commission by referring a patient to a private hospital".

Yet another, 69 year-old male from Bootan Mandi in district Jalandhar revealed that "I was admitted to a government hospital in Jalandhar for my kidney operation. I was in the general ward where dogs and cats run freely. On the very first day, I did not get any attention from the doctors or nurses. I was lying on the bed as an abandoned body. Luckily, I knew a nurse through my relative working in the same hospital but in another department. She helped me a lot. She introduced myself to the doctors and nurses as her uncle. The operation was successful. I was discharged from the hospital after a week. I had to go to the government hospital because my UK son stopped sending money to me. My current source of income is meagre and therefore I could not afford private hospital".

From the above discussion, the researcher has found that the majority of the respondents are not satisfied with the prevailing healthcare services in the state of Punjab. The condition of the government hospitals especially in the rural government hospitals are quite challenging. The elderly respondents were very unhappy and have very bad image of the government hospitals. They feel facilities like ambulance, wheelchair, beds etc. are not available. The worst part is lack of cleanliness in the government hospitals.

## Conclusion

This chapter has tried to understand and analyze the socio-economic status of the elderly Punjabis in three districts of Doaba region of Punjab namely Jalandhar, Hoshiarpur and Kapurthala. This chapter is constructed on primary and secondary data. The primary data was extracted from the respondents with the help of preformulated interview schedule. The researcher conducted in depth interviews in the local language as the respondents lacked fluency in English language. Later on, the narratives were translated into English by the researcher himself. The secondary data was collected to substantiate our arguments and findings from the field. A number of health reports and government documents were consulted for the same.

First and foremost, we have discussed theoretical dimensions of the family. After this, the chapter has dealt empirically the issues of family structure in three districts of the universe of the study. Through observation and general conversation, we have found that joint families are still prevalent in big way in Punjab. The data reveals that because emotional support and social security, Punjabis choose living in a joint family system. Due to industrialization, urbanization, and migration, However, the joint family system has been breaking. The researcher has found the members of joint family have migrated because number of reasons. Such as in search of occupation, education or lack of adjustment. Migration abroad is also major cause of disintegration of joint family. However, we have found in our studies that elderly prefer joint families with their immediate sons and grandchildren.

The next aspect of analysis was the financial status of the elderly in the universe of the study. We have found that most of the elderly in Punjab who are receiving help from their children or who are settled abroad are very satisfied with their economic condition. In these cases, the respondents were having double income one from their retired job and second from their sons, daughters or other relatives.

Secondly, most of the houses who have their sons or daughters living abroad they have well-furnished houses with all electronic goods. However the respondents revealed that these electronic items are not bought specifically for the elderly rather it is bought for their sons, daughters or other relatives living abroad. It is so because they will need when they come back to India. Thirdly, we have found that the economic condition of those people are very bad who survive only on their pension. It is difficult for them to live happily.

We have also tried to understand the experience and perception of elderly about the health services in three districts of Punjab where this study is conducted. The researcher has found that in spite of number of health schemes for elderly and general people in Punjab, the citizens do not get any satisfaction from public health department, doctors, and nurses. The respondents, the elderly men, and women have revealed the pathetic condition of the health services available in Punjab. The behavior of doctors and nurses are worse. There is lack of security about the suffering of the elderly patients. There is rampant corruption in the government hospitals. The medicines are not available. Even most essential facilities for elderly such as ambulances and wheel chairs are missing. Asked if they would like to visit the government hospital if private hospitals are available and affordable. The elderly replied that "they would never like to visit a government hospital again".

In this context, most of the elderly those who can afford go to a private hospital and are happy. However, those who survive on their meager pensions have to visit government hospitals are very unhappy and feel lots of stress and strain. Some elderly were found to be in strain because their sons and daughters stopped sending remittances to their old parents. The elderly have also revealed existing caste based exclusion in the Punjabi society. The elderly feel unhappy when they are alone in the absence of their loved ones hence they feel isolated and lonely.

## References

Arya, Priya. (2017). From Joint to Nuclear Family: Some Observations on the Changing Pattern of Family as a Social Institution, IOSR, *Journal of Humanities and Social Sciences,*22(6):28-31.

Baldassar, Baldock, and Wilding. (2007). *'Families caring across borders; Migration, Ageing, and transnational care giving*, Palgrave Macmillan, New York.

Bengston.V.L. and Harootyan.R.A.(1994). *'Intergenerational Linkages*', Springer Public Company and AARP, New York.

Caffrey, R.A. (1992). 'Family care of the elderly in Northeast Thailand: changing patterns'; *Journal of Cross -Cultural Gerontology*, 7(2), 117-134.

Cowgill, D.O., and Holmes, L.D. (1972). '*Ageing and Modernization'* New York: Appleton-Century-Crofts.

Dandekar and Kumunduni. (1996). 'The Aged, their problems, and social intervention in Maharashtra, *Economic and Political Weekly*, Vol. XXXI, 1188-1994.

Desai, M. (1995a). Towards Family Policy Research, *Indian Journal of Social Work*, (56), 225-231.

Dommaraju,Premchand.(2015). One person househodls in India, *Demograhic Research*,32(45),1239-1266.

Esterman, A and Andrews, G.R. (1992) Southeast Asia and the Pacific: a comparison of older people in four countries. In *Family support for the Elderly: The International Experience*, H.L. Kending, A. Hashimoto and L.C. Coppard eds. Oxford, United Kingdom: Oxford University Press.

Ghosh, S and P. Arokiasamy, (2009).Morbidity in India Trends, Patterns and Differentials.*Journal of Health Studies*, 2, 136-148.

Gordon, Michael. (1972). The Nuclear Family in Crisis: *The search for an alternative*, Harper, and Row, p.48.*Economic and Political Weekly*, 38(26), 1620-1632.

Gurudas S, Lakshminaraynan, T.R. (1989). A study of life satisfaction in relation to marital status among the aged.*Indian Journal of Social Welfare*, 50,236-8.

Harper Sarah (2006) Addressing the implications of global ageing, *Journal of Population Research,* 23(2), University of Oxford, 112-132.

Jindal B.L. (1987). Alienation among the ageing males, *Ageing and society*, 5(2), 183-95. Jodhka, Surinder S. (2002). Caste and Untouchability in Rural Punjab, *Economic and Political Weekly,* 37(19), 1813-1823.

Kapadia, K. M. (1982*). Mar* Desai, M. (1995a).Towards Family Policy Research, *Indian Journal of Social Work*, (56), 225-231.

Krist, Pamela. (2017). Social Isolation and Loneliness among seniors, available at https://www.colebrookvillage.com/wp-content/uploads/2017/10/Social-Isolation-Loneliness-New.pdf.

Kumar, Vivek. (2014). Inequality in India: Caste and Hindu Social Order, *Trans science*, 5(1):36-52.

Puri K Harish. (2003). The Scheduled Caste in the Sikh Community- A Historical Perspective, *Economic and Political Weekly*, 42(2): 1145-1156.

Lee.Y.J Parish W.L and Willis.R.J (1994) 'Sons, Daughters and Intergenerational Support in Taiwan', *The American Journal of Sociology*, 99(4):1010-1041.

Lucas Robet and Oded Stark (1985) 'Motivation to Remittance: Evidence from Botswana, *The Journal of political Economy*, 93(5): 901-918.

Malinowski, B. (1954). *Sex and Repression in Savage Society*, New York: Brace Company.

Mason Oppenheim Karen (1996) '*Family change and support of the elderly in Asia*': what do we know? Article presented in East-West Centers program and populations U.S.A., pp. 13-32.

Molla, Nasiruddin. (2016).Concept of Family: Causes of disintegration of Joint Family in Indian Perspective, *Remarking an Analisation Journal, 1(ix) 64-67.*

Mujahid .G. (2006) 'Population ageing in East and South East Asia'. 1950 – 2050, Implications for elderly care, Asia – Pacific population Journal, 21(2):25-44.

Muraleedharan.K (2005) 'Dynamics and consequences of population ageing- A comparative inter-regional perspective of Asian economics', *Asian Economic Review*, April 47(1):1032-41.

Nambyar.A.C.K (1995) '*The Socio Economic Condition of Gulf Migrants*', Common Wealth Publication, New Delhi.

Nayar PK. (1982).*The State and the old in the developing countries in world congress of the International Sociological Association*: Mexico City.

Pyke, K.D., and Bengtson, V.L. (1996). Caring more or less: Individualistic and collectivist system of family eldercare, *Journal of Marriage and the Family*, 58(2):379-392.

Ramamurti, P.V; and Jamuna.D. (2004).*Handbook of Indian Gerontology*, New Delhi: Serial Publications.

Ram Ronki (2007). Social Catastrophe in the *Making*: Religion, Deras, and Dalits in Punjab, available at http://www.ambedkartimes.com/ronkiram % 20 page % 201. htm # social.

Reed, D. Santarino, W.A., Gildengarin, G., Mc Mahon, K., Fleshman, R. and Schneider, E. (1995) 'Health and functioning among the elderly of Martin Country', California: A Glimpse of the Future, *Journal of the Future*. 15 (2): 61-69.

Sarah E. Lamb. (2009). *Ageing and the Indian Diaspora:* Cosmopolitan Families in India and Abroad, Bloomington, Indiana Univeristy Press.

Singh, J.P (2004). *'The contemporary Indian family'*, in Bert N. Adams and Jan Trost (Eds.), Handbook of World Families, California: Sage Publications Inc., pp. 129-166.

Singh AK; Singh M and Singh, DS.(1996). Health problems in rural elderly at Varanasi, Uttar Pradesh.Journal of *Association Physicians India*, 44(3):540.

Sonawata, Reeta. (2001).Understanding Families in India: A Reflection of Societal Changes, *Psychologies: Theoria e Pesquisa Mai-Ago*, 17(2):177-186.

Srivastava.S.L. (1968) 'Impact of emigration on structure and relations in a village in Eastern Uttar Pradesh', *Journal of Social Research*, 3(2): 73-86. Talcott, Parsons (1954). *Essays in Sociological Theory*, New York: Free Press.

Van Hook J and Glick JE. (2009). Immigration and living arrangements: moving beyond economic need versus acculturation, *Demography*, 44(2):225-49.

# VI

# Family Structure and Socio-Economic Status of Elderly Punjabis in England (UK)

## Introduction

This chapter focusses on the different dimensions of Elderly Punjabis living in different regions of England (UK). The issue of family structure is one of the first issue which will be probed here. We will try to find out why do people prefer to live in a particular type of family? Why do people live in joint families in England also? It is in this context, we would also try to understand why joint families are breaking in England among Punjabi Diaspora. The researcher will also analyze what type of family are evolving with the disintegration of joint families in England.

This chapter will also record how and why do existed families come into existence in England. Apart from nature of emergence and disintegration of various types of families, this chapter will also record types of occupations in which elderly are involved in England. This means the researcher will like to note how do this spent time when they are at home? Are they involved in helping their adult children in domestic work or they actively participate in their business as well? Further, this chapter will also include the views of the respondents about the health facilities available for the elderly in England. How do they feel about the experience when they visit health centers or in the hospital?

Last but not the least, this chapter would analyze the nature of integration of elderly Punjabis in British society. If at all the elderly Punjabis want to return to homeland in their old age it is important to note that an important characteristic of diaspora is 'wish of return to homeland' as given by Safran argues, "A diaspora exists once people have been dispersed from a specific original center to two or more peripheral or foreign regions and they regard their ancestral homeland as their true, ideal home and as the place to which they or their descendants would or should eventually return" (Safran, 1991:83). Here it becomes pertinent to look into this fact with reference to elderly Punjabis live in England. This chapter is constructed on primary and secondary data. Primary data was collected form the respondents by visiting and talking to them personally. The field work was conducted in Southall, Birmingham and Wolverhampton. We have administrated interviews schedule to the respondents selected through snowball technique and relevant data was extracted. We have also used observation and informal interactions to substantiate our argument about the family structure and health facilities given to elderly in England (UK). Last but not the least, we have also used secondary data from books, reports and census to further analyze the issues in our study.

The family is a social institution. In every society, there are different family structures and different roles and relationships within the family structure. Joint, nuclear, and extended are the types of families form in various types of societies. Survey indicates that Joint family is still prevalent in rural and urban areas of India. Due to industrialization, and migration people are turning towards a nuclear family in India and England (UK).

## Understanding Family

A classic sociological definition was propounded by George Murdock (2015:225). According to him, "a family is a social group characterized by common residence, economic cooperation, and reproduction. It includes adults of both sexes, at least two of whom maintain a socially –approved sexual relationship, and one or more children, own or adopted of the sexually cohabiting adults".

Britain is traditionally observed as a country of emigration got encouragement because of UK liberal immigration policies. Migration to the United Kingdom followed different patterns. Those who migrated during colonial times and later came to the United Kingdom formed a family. At the beginning of migration, the size and structures of the family were small. The man was considered to be a head of the family. In the later phase of migration, people of the same family started migrating to the United Kingdom. The majority of the families in earlier days preferred to marry a girl from Punjab. According to Jone (2009:49), "most marriages among Asians living in Britain are still arranged marriages involving a partner from the Indian sub-continent, usually from the locality and caste of origin. It is because of nature of migration and marriages, the Punjabis have produced particular types of family structure in England which we will analyze in the present chapter subsequently".

Desai argues that "the type of family is not to be determined by the fact of co-residence, commensality, or the size of the group. It is the relationship between the members of a household among themselves and with those of another household that determines the type of family of that household" (Raina, 1988:8). In a similar vein, Das Gupta, "a marriage does not therefore necessarily create a new household, rather imports another woman into the households, "to bear children and carry out the other tasks assigned to females". Cain has also argued that a typical household in North India is patriarchal and usually multigenerational. In this type of arrangement, "it is the responsibility of fathers and their brothers to use household resources to arrange marriages of daughters" (Burholt and Wenger, 2003:16).

According to Beteille (1964:240), "in spite of socio-economic and political changes, family life and family structure have remained as an integral part of Indian society with the ` spirit of family solidarity` as the sustaining power". It is because of this fact that even when Indians migrate they take along with them this basic social institution wherever they go and UK is no exception. On the basis of mere observation the researcher during this field work in UK, at the outset, found that Punjabis are living in different types of families. Therefore, before analyzing the empirical data, it is essential to define and distinguish the patterns of the families in view of change in the structure of the family. The various family patterns such as Joint family, nuclear family and extended family are discussed below.

Joint family is still prevalent in many societies of the world. Irawati Karve (1953:125) defines: "A joint family is a group of people who generally live under one roof, who eat food cooked at one hearth, who hold property in common and who participate in common family worship and are related to each other as some particular type of kindred". Ross (1961:31) describes, "the Indian joint family as, family-centered, characterized by intimacy, mutuality of interest, strong primary group controls and mutual assistance in time of need. In it family tradition and pride are strong and individual members are dominated by the opinions of the larger group. "Older Japanese perceive co-resident family members as especially important for social support. However, as with the modified extended families in western countries societies, older people also reported support from non-resident children and other non-resident kin. An expectation for support from non-kin was limited, particularly by other people having low functional health. Older women were found to have fewer close kin available than older men but the women were more likely to expect social support from neighbors are friends" (Kending et al.,1999:192). Gore states, "The fraternal or collateral joint family was never the most common form. In a similar vein, Goode also asserts that the large joint family was not common at any time in India perhaps because of the great forces of fission, initially between daughters-in-law and later between brothers"((as quoted in Naranjan et al.:287).

## Evolution of Various Types of Families in UK

## Understanding Joint Family

It is in this context the researcher has found different reasons for the disintegration of joint family structures in UK. Both men and women have narrated their experience with regard to separation from an existing family structure. Each individual gave his/her own reason which ranges from privacy adjustment with in-laws, generational conflict, and freedom to job location, to death of spouses, to quote just a few are various reasons because of which family structures are disintegrating. We are aware that historically Punjabis back home have been living in joint families. They try to maintain the same but under different circumstances; they are not able to maintain the joint family structure.

To begin with, an in-depth interview with the respondents took place. In this context, a 45-year-old married woman narrated, why did she break from her joint family? In her own words, "for few years after marriage, we lived with our elderly parents however we could not get any privacy living with them. We did not have a separate room because of which I could not talk to my husband in private which was very disturbing. Also, we were always crowded with family members. Hence, we can observe that small size of accommodation and low level of privacy were the reasons because of which the family disintegrated". Similarly, a 35- year-old man from Birmingham also told that because of the small size of accommodation our children could not feel free because they were always guarded by their grandparents. The grandparents would want children to follow the traditional family norms, which used to create lots of conflict in the house. Hence we have moved into a separate accommodation".

Apart from privacy, freedom and small structure of the house adjustment with the elderly in-laws is also another reason because of which either families disintegrating or there is unrest within the families among the Punjabis living in the UK takes place. For example, a married male aged 47 narrated his story with regard to the disintegration of his family. In an interview with the researcher, accordingly, he argued that "I married a girl from Punjab and sponsored her to the UK as my spouse. I was living in a joint family in Wolverhampton in the UK. However, my wife could not adjust herself within this joint family. The whole atmosphere of the family got affected, I felt very disturbed. On the one hand there was my wife and on the other hand, therefore, my elderly parents. Ultimately I had to leave my parents and move to a rented house. This was both emotional and an economic loss. But I had to bear it"

Apart from this, the researcher has also found that, few cases of intergenerational conflict which has forced individuals living in the UK in three different places after break from their joint family. A 49-year-old man living in Southall, London narrated his painful story. In his own words "I invited my aged parents to the UK from India to look after my young children. They used to live with us on the same floor in the house. However, my children who were being raised in the western culture, like eating with spoon, fork, and knife, did not like my parent's habit of eating with a hand and used to regularly complain. Above all my children could not cope up with the snoring sound of my parents and were greatly disturbed. Hence with a heavy heart, I had to shift my parents to the basement". Similarly, a 35 year old woman from Birmingham also told the researcher that, "While living with the elderly grandparents my children experienced social and cultural restrictions in terms of their dress and food patterns." Hence he had to change the house and hire an independent accommodation.

Another unique and surprising reason responsible for a break of the joint families in the UK, which was unearthed by the researcher during fieldwork was the language of the parents. A young person revealed that his parents did not speak English. He sponsored his old parents from a village Chak Kehlen in district Hoshiarpur, Punjab to live with them in Southall, England. The Punjabi boy married an English speaking white woman. The English speaking wife faced an extraordinary problem in the presence of her mother-in-law. The mother-in-law speaks only the Punjabi language. During conversation between a son and mother, the English speaking wife feel uncomfortable and also a stranger. In addition to that, the English speaking wife could not converse with her mother-in-law in the absence of her husband.

In the light of theoretical and conceptual explanation of different types of families propounded by various social scientists, we will examine the existing nature and structure of family existing among the Punjabis in UK. On the basis of observation and discussion in the field that is three cities of UK i.e. Southall, Birmingham and Wolverhampton the researcher has found that the Punjabis family structure has been disintegrating in the western world in spite of the fact that they know the advantages of the joint family such as sociability, flexibility, and security. However, as the time moved most of the couples started creating their own independent families. However, it is not only the nuclear family in which they lived in but they also lived in extended families as well. It is in this context we will analyze the reasons why did respondents chose to live in a particular type of family.

It is instructive to note that social scientists like (Mala Kapur et al., 1996), Sarah Lamb (2009) and (Irudaya Rajan et al., 2015:236) argue that the joint family has its own advantages. In the joint family responsibility and duties are shared to relieve the social and economic burden. However, some studies endorse that inter-generational differences can emerge due to different attitudes and beliefs. These differences can cause strain, tension, and antagonism between younger and older generations. Western culture is modern and cosmopolitan in terms of freedom of choice. Children born and brought up in Britain‘s multicultural society are often found rapidly changing their outlook and becomes rebellious whereas older parents are old-fashioned. Talcott Parsons stated that youth culture exits embodying values in conflict with those of the adult world as early as 1942. He characterized it as being "more or less specifically irresponsible", with a heavy emphasis on having a good time, much cross-sex socializing and a certain recalcitrance to the pressure of adult expectations and discipline (Parsons, 1963). Migrants still prefer to live in a joint family but due to an official occupation of the children at different places, they need to live in a nuclear family (Distler, 1968).

## Understanding Nuclear Family

Nuclear family constitutes two-parents with children. The concept of nuclear family is quite prevalent in the industrialized nations. Parsons (1964) argues, "The isolated nuclear family is the only type which is functional for urban industrial society". Davis (1949:127) in his study observed, "The effects of industrialization on the family. He notes that "a modern society characterized by an elaborate industrial technology, a high degree of urbanization and a greater amount of geographical and social mobility, has steered away from the extended kinship bonds".

Ross viewed, "industrialization, urbanization, education and occupational differentiation as new sources of change and anticipated gradual breakdown of the joint family and the emergence of the nuclear family"(as quoted in Rayada, 2000:20). According to Cohen, "households have reputedly been shrinking in size for ten thousand years or more, right up to the present, and this is the result of an evolving technology that requires fewer co-operating people to secure food, rear children, and look after the sick( as quoted in Netting et al.,1984).

Punjabi families in the United Kingdom have been moving toward the nuclear family formation. There are several reasons behind disintegration of the joint family. A few prominent reasons were observed by the researchers after an in-depth interviews with the respondents. In a joint family, all members of the family cannot be alike. There are different attitudes and behaviors exist among all the members of the family. It is well known among the Punjabi families that one member might not agree with all the family members consequently there would be a quarrel or argument in the family. While answering to this question, one 37 year -old male from Southall opined that I came England ten years back. We used to live together. All members of the family were happy and enjoyed cordial relations among themselves but my wife could not develop cordial relationship with my mother. From day one, there were arguments over arguments consequently peace of the family got vitiated. It also affected my children adversely. Because of noisy and quarrelsome arguments between my mother and wife, the study of children affected badly. Because of verbal violence, they were psychologically disturbed and that attitude started reflecting in their behavior. It also brought bad name for the family in the neighborhood. At last, I bought a new house and shifted with my wife and children. My elder parents live separately. My wife and children are happy now. Independent life brought us more responsibility, autonomy as well freedom".

Apart from this, the researcher has found that some cases where we observed that older Punjabi parents try to impose Punjabi culture and language on the grandchildren. The grandchildren born and brought in a cosmopolitan city like London often defy the dictates of the older parents. It is also observed that Punjabi parents want their children and grandchildren to wear a turban, a Sikh identity, however, in the western world children want to cut their hairs according to the prevailing customary fashion in the British society. The argument over religious beliefs sometimes give impetus to a fight between the youngsters and the elders. Responding to a question, a 35 year -old female from Birmingham revealed that, "I have one son who was born in the UK. He is a grown up boy aged 16 years. He goes to an English medium school. He has friends from different nationalities. Most of them do not wear a turban. My husband invited his old parents from Punjab. My father-in-law a staunch Sikh started teaching my son Sikh religious beliefs and rituals. My son did not like it. The argument between my father-in-law and son always disturbed a peace of the family. Because of this, my husband requested my father-in-law to stay with his younger son. So, they both shifted to his younger son. And in the event, our joint family was reduced to nuclear family.

In some case, we have observed that due to job locations at a distant place working children need to live separately. For instance, a 79 year –old female from Wolverhampton revealed that earlier time was good when my children and grandchildren used to live with us. The factory in which my son used to work got shut down in Wolverhampton. He got the job in other city of London which is far-off from the town in which we have a house. For few weeks my son travelled between the new place of job and the house but at last, he decided to move with his immediate family since it was not feasible physically and economically to go to London everyday where he is employed. Now, we live alone in our family home. Separation is unbearable. We feel insecure and unsafe".

## Understanding Extended Family

"The extended family systems existed in various cultures and regions of the world. "The rise in the number and proportion of immigrants from less developed countries where extended family structures are more common" (De Vos, 1995). Spencer explained that during First World War, Punjabis went to different British colonies and served as soldiers. Migrants also included families and relatives of already settled seaman and semi-skilled workers recruited from the merchant shipping industry" (Sheetal, 2013:17).

Dow and Werner (1983) state, "The members of the extended family are generally held together by what has been described as an extensive kinship network of reciprocal social and economic obligations". In the same vein, Ruggles states, "horizontally extended households contain family members from the same generation or other related lines such as uncles, brothers, sisters, and aunts. Vertically extended households contain more than one generation of adults" (Ruggles, 1987:216). Similarly, we can discuss the economic characteristic of an immigrant group, Kibria (1994:85) in his study found that the economic characteristic of an immigrant group also affect extended family living because pooling resources among family members in the households constitute a viable strategy for survival among those facing economic hardship in their new country. Sharma (2013) holds, "previous generations of immigrants have strived hard to maintain ties with their families back home. Families remains in touch, even after establishing separate nuclear families".

In the light of the above discussion regarding extending family, we would like to analyze that how and why they were born in the Punjabi diaspora in the universe of our research.

Family structure is sometimes disturbed by the extended family. The life of the family members experiences as separate, disjointed, fragmented or independent from each other. Women in the family experience loss of power and freedom. (Sonuga and Mistry, 000:135) state, "children in extended families fared better, but their mothers fared worse than their nuclear family counterparts. In extended families where social support was likely to be most available mothers were at greatest risk, while their children profited and this advantage seemed to be linked to the grand-maternal presence".

"Punjabis migrated to different British colonies; some came back after the completion of the job, and some stayed back. Those who stayed back in African countries entered into transnational marriages and raised their family in Africa" (Chanda and Ghosh, 2012:25) the researcher met a few respondents who narrated their stories. For instance 75 year -old male from Southall told his story with nostalgia that, "I went to Uganda to work. I married with an African woman. I had two children from my first wife. However, my first wife died due to cancer. After that, the Ugandan government threw us out in 1972 so I came to England with my two children. Due to family pressure and advice by my close friends, I married a Punjabi woman from Punjab. I sponsored my second wife. She came to England and currently, we have one daughter. My second wife has one son back in Punjab. I am a retired person. I draw an old age pension. Similarly, a 68 year -old wife from Birmingham narrated her story that when I came to England I was already married in Punjab having one son from my deceased husband. I married second NRI widower and have two children. Later on, I got sponsored my son and currently, he has been living with us. All of us live together. Children do not have any problem and they have adjusted comfortably. We can see that however although they are one family but they do not share one roof and maintain separate ways. Yet another, 73 year -old female from Wolverhampton responded that my son died in England due to a heart attack leaving behind his three children. It is difficult to live a life without a companion especially when children are grown up. I married to a Punjabi businessman whose wife died a few years back. He had one grown-up son. We all live together".

Apart from the views of the elderly Punjabis, the researcher has interviewed children of the same family to substantiate the present study and discussed and analyzed also their views also.in the purview of the extended family. During the interview schedule, the researcher discussed with the children belonging to the extended family. For instance, 38 year - old son from Southall argued that my father was already married and had two children in Punjab. My first father died in a car incident in Southall. My mother married to another person from Birmingham. My second father had already two children. However, we all live separately but we meet during social or family functions. In a similar vein, a 42-year-old daughter from Birmingham responded that after the death of my mother, my father went to Punjab and secretly married to a Punjabi divorcee. The divorce has already two children living in the village of Bassi in district Jalandhar (Punjab). When I go to Punjab I meet my father, mother and their two children.

In this way on the basis of observation and empirical data collection from the field through in-depth interviews, we can infer that extended families have also emerged within the Punjabis living in the UK. We have found mostly extended family have emerged because of the death of the spouses. Secondly, in most cases, the members live under separate roofs and do not share same hearth. Further, there are members who are born out of either diseased husband or diseased wife. However, they all maintain a familial connection.

## Understanding Economic Status of Elderly Punjabis in UK

Migration of South Asian populations to the developed countries is generally assumed to offer socioeconomic advantages in the form of improved and employment opportunities, better housing and access to healthcare (Nazroo, 2011). Older citizens are entitled for old age pension and social security in UK. However, there are different regulatory frameworks on old age, disability and survivors. Retired men or women are eligible for basic state retirement contributory and non- contributory pension. "Noncontributory pension is paid those who resided in the UK for 10 years in any 20 –year consecutive period after age 80" (Government of UK, 2011). The researcher has discussed the economic status of the elderly Punjabis and tried to understand how much pension they are getting from the UK government and analyzed the issue to substantiate this study. Most of the respondents happily disclosed their pension income during the field study. We have included here a few cases of pensioners to ascertain their source of income. For instance, 86 year-old male from Southall respondent that, "I gets 850 pounds per month as pension after tax deduction. This includes my work pension (650 pounds) and old age pension (200 pounds). I was a factory worker. I retired at the age of 65 years. Now, I am now 86 years and eligible for old age pension also. Yet another, 75 year-old male from Birmingham told that "I get 600 pounds per month after tax deduction. It includes my work pension (400 pounds) and disability pension (200 Pounds). I was working in the government hospital as a security guard. I did not complete my service period. I applied for a voluntary retirement due to health reasons. So, I get two pensions, one is work pension and other is disability pension. Similarly, 82 –year-old female explained that "I get only old age pension. I am a house-wife. My old age pension is 250 pounds per month. It is sufficient for me. I am thankful to the government of the UK. I save money to buy an air ticket for India. Almost every year, I visit my relatives and friends in Punjab and stay with them for two to three months. An economically upset 84 -year -old male respondent that, "Day by day there is a deep cut by the government of UK in the sum of pension. Earlier, I was getting 350 pounds per month after tax deduction but now I get only 275 pounds. This cut in the pension by the government of UK has economically disturbed the older persons like me. Let me tell you frankly, with the cut in the pension, the attitude of my own children changed towards me because I get less money."

## Household Engagements of the Elderly Punjabis in UK

"Occupation is described as actions or series of actions in which one is engaged" *(*Ingeborg, 2006:5*)*. "The occupation has often been used as a synonym for activity and task" (Henderson, 1996:141). Fisher states that, "Activity is used as a description of doing but with no emphasis on meaning or purpose, while the task is used to refer to what is or was done. Furthermore, this reasoning leads to the idea that the doing of a task (task performance) that has meaning and/or purpose is synonymous with occupation". Kielhofner implicitly described, "Engagement as involvement in the sense of being involved in the performance of a task. He also stated that engagement is important for well-being" (as quoted in Ingeborg, 2006:6). Gore (1992:269) argues that "a fully supportive family would also provide its elders with meaningful family's roles. If elders can take part in caring for and bringing up their grandchildren, in housework, in contributing in other ways, and be recognized and valued for such roles, they would feel as if they were an integral part of the family instead of being bored and emotionally estranged".

In the light of explanation of occupation, job, task, activity or involvement we would like to analyze the nature and type of activities or jobs in which the elderly Punjabis in the UK are involved. Most respondents, in this case, are over 65 years old. This study found that the majority migrated elderly Punjabi men and women are retired from an active job. The elderly Punjabi men and women assist the children in taking care of the grandchildren. Older women are found largely occupied in house responsibilities. The following narratives illustrate the engagement of the elderly Punjabis in the household chores in UK.

The researcher also asked the respondents about their daily engagement. We asked such question only to those elderly men and women who were physically fit to assist their children in their household jobs or in their business. Responding to a question a retired 64 year- old male from Wolverhampton explained that how he is engages in the cloth factory run by his son. In his own words, he said that "I am a retired class one officer from the government of India. My children sponsored me to live with them and assist them in their business. My son and daughter-in-law run a cloth factory". I am a qualified administrator hence I help them in administration work of the factory. In a similar vein, 68 year -old male from Southall explained that, "After my retirement, I migrated to UK to live with my children and grandchildren. I pass my time in the companion of my grandchildren. I drop and pick them up from the school and sometimes take them to a nearby shopping mall if the weather permits. This is how I spend my time happily". Yet another, a 72 year-old female from Birmingham explained that "I love my grand-children. I prepare a variety of food for them. I drop them at the school. I take them to a nearby park".

From the above narratives of the respondents, it is observed that the majority of the elderly Punjabis in the UK remain engaged in some or other activity associated with their families to lead a happy life. Anne McMunn et al., (2009:183) in their study on socially productive participation of the older persons demonstrates that "participation in social activities is associated with higher levels of wellbeing among post-retirement age people in England". "Older volunteers (aged 60+years) experienced greater increase in life satisfaction, and improvement in perceived health as a result of the time the spent volunteering than younger volunteers"(Willigen,2000:309).

## Understanding Isolation and Loneliness among Elderly Punjabis in UK

"Late in life immigrants are often at risk of psychological stress, and social isolation because of number reasons. For instance, it may be because of language barriers, small social networks, and cultural differences from their host society" (Emami, et al., 2000:172). "Older immigrants are more isolated than elders with other migrants background, followers of children being among the most isolated in spite of the strong kinship ties"(Weeks and Cuellar, 1983:127). "Duffy argues, "because of their recent arrival, unfamiliar social environment, poverty, poor health and communication problems, it is difficult for them to participate effectively in the economic, social, political, and cultural life. As a result, they become alienated and isolated from the mainstream society" (as quoted in Hossen, 2012:1). Similarly, Maiter found, "difficulties in understanding media news reports, reading newspapers and magazines or making use of public transportation to visit friends or shop reinforce their sense of loneliness and social isolation"(as quoted in Hossen, 2012:1). Kiefer et al state, "because of the cultural norms, financial condition and expectation of physical and emotional care, the elderly tend to live in multigenerational households. This living arrangement is complicated and does not shield the elderly from feeling lonely; sometimes it exacerbates the situation. Some studies have found that multigenerational households can reduce loneliness and stress levels and facilitate adjustment to a new society" (as quoted in Hossen, 2012:1).

"Gold found that multigenerational living is likely to increase stress and conflict and cause dissatisfaction"(as quoted in Hossen, 2012:1). Kim et al describe, "Their dependence on kin leads to conflict, particularly with respect to filial expectations from their married sons" (as quoted in Hossen, 2012:2). Yu and Wu found, "this dependency, however, can threaten intergenerational solidarity and negatively impact older immigrants if families are not able or willing to provide assistance. Adult offspring may not be able to assist their parents because of their own struggles in adjusting to a new country" (as quoted in Hossen, 2012:2). Isshi- Kuntz found, "other offspring may prefer to live in non-ethnic neighborhoods and chose not to live with their parents" (as quoted in Hossen, 2012:3).

The researcher has conducted in-depth interviews to understand the nature and dynamic of isolation and loneliness in elderly Punjabi in UK. In this context, 81 year-old-male from Southall opined that "My children are working. My son and his wife are working in shift duties. Whenever anyone is at home; he or she either busy in household work or buying grocery. I am always alone at him even in their presence. Nobody has time to sit and talk with me. It is not like that they do not want but they do not have time for me. Their job and household responsibilities are huge. I do not know what will happen to them when they will have a baby. I spend whole day watching Punjabi programmes on Television. I cannot go alone because of cold weather. I feel as I am in a gold cage. In England, nobody has time for the older people. I am lonely and depressed. My wife came and went back because she did not like. I might stay for a few days and go back". In a similar vein, 79 year-old-male from Birmingham narrated that, "I came to England to see some historical places. My son insisted me and so I came. After landing, I found my son and his wife behaved differently and did not take me to go for sightseeing. I feel as if sometimes has kidnapped me and put me in a prison. I spend my time in the room watching TV. It is mostly Punjabi songs. I do not know English so I cannot go alone to the market since I can neither read sign boards in English nor catch a bus by myself. I feel lonely and depressed".

Yet another 72- year-old female from Wolverhampton revealed that "Life in England is lonely otherwise it is a wonderful country. The government is liberal. For older people, there are number of facilities such as a separate pedestrian walk, wheel chair in the shopping mall, a designated seat for the older people in the bus or train. I really appreciate the kinds of healthcare services are available for the older people like us. The problem is that in the home nobody has time for the older person. Everyone is occupied in his or her job. There is a huge intergenerational gap between the children and grandparents. Language barrier is the biggest problem for communicating even with the grandchildren. Most of the time grand - children speak English. Neither I can speak nor understand English. I feel depressed and lonely even in their company. I sit in the corner and watch them talking, playing. Cold weather also embolden isolation and depression". From the above discussion, we can safely assume that the elderly Punjabi feel isolated and lonely even in the company of their children and grandchildren mostly because of intergenerational gap between grandchildren and grandparents. The movement of the elderly Punjabis in UK is also restricted because of language barrier. Their dependence on children and grandchildren also reinforce isolation and loneliness since the children and grandchildren are occupied in their professional and household tasks.

## Understanding Elderly Abuse in UK

"The abuse of older people by family members dates back to ancient times. Mistreatment of older people – referred to as elder abuse was first described in British scientific journals in 1975 under the term Granny Battering" (Baker, 1975:125). "The definition developed by Action on Elder Abuse in the United Kingdom and adopted by the International Network for the Prevention of Elder Abuse states that: "Elder abuse is a single or repeated act or lack of appropriate action, occurring within any relationship where there is an expectation of trust which causes harm or distress to an older persons" (Sebastian and Sekhar,2010:54). "Older adults who are abused physically, sexually, or psychologically exhibit serious negative physical and mental health consequences, including depression, fear, stress, early nursing home placement, and increased mortality" (Dong et al., 2009:521).

The researcher has tried to understand elderly abuse among Punjabi families living in UK and collected empirical data with the help of in-depth interviews. In this context, 78 year-old male from Southall narrated, "In England, it is difficult to handle grandchildren since they are born and brought in English culture. The influence of the peer groups is quite enormous. The children of white and black in England are socialized in different manners". In this context, the peer group included the white and black British kids born and brought up in their own culture. They do not tolerate if father or mother scold them either in home or at public place. In the company of such obstinate children, our school going grandchildren also learn many bad things. We teach our grandchildren Indian cultural values and customs yet they sometime become ill-mannered and disrespectful. In a similar vein, 82 year-old- male from Birmingham told, "My grandchildren are very nice but when they go out and mix with white and black boys and turn rowdy. For instance, one day my grandson came home from the school and started breaking the plates because the food prepared by his mother was not according to his choice and taste. He threw a plate on me which hit my shoulder painfully. Such things are common in UK". Yet another 84 year-old-female from Wolverhampton opined, "I get a pension of 645 pounds every month. I asked my son to withdraw half the money so that I can spend whenever I go to the market with them. My elder grandson steals my money when I am sleeping or taking bath. I noticed several times but he always refused by saying that he did not do it. When I complained to his father. He scolded him mildly but he did not stop even after that. At last, I stopped keeping the money at home".

### Understanding Healthcare System in UK

Apart from family structure, nature of job the researcher has also discussed the health related issues of the elderly Punjabis living in three locales of the universe. The respondents talked about healthcare services and formed a positive opinions about the healthcare providers. According to McDowell and Newell, "During history, health has been viewed in terms of survival, freedom from disease, and ability to perform daily activities, or described using themes like happiness, well-being". In the same vein, Wilcock has defined health as, "the absence of illness (but not necessarily disability), balance in occupation, enhancement of capacities, community opportunities, and social integration and support. She also stated that underlying factors can be influenced by occupational engagement and subsequently influence health in a positive way" (as quoted in Ingebor, 2006:7).

The UK healthcare services are run by National Health Services (NHS) which was established in 1946. "As per a study of eight industrialized countries, the UK`s healthcare system is one of the most efficient in the world" (Dixon, 2002:175). In regard to access to care, "The UK has relatively short waiting times for basic medical care and non-emergency access to services after hours but has longer times for specialist care and elective, non-emergency surgery" (WHO, 2017). "Health services in England are largely free at the point of use. Established in 1948, the NHS provides preventive medicine, primary care and hospital services to all those ordinarily resident in England. Over 12% of the population is covered by Private Medical Insurer (PMI), which mainly provides access to acute elective care in the private sector. Citizens were entitled to a local General Practitioner (GP) and might expect to be cared for in an emergency at any hospital in UK" (Boyle et al., 2011).

The respondents acknowledged the quality of healthcare services particularly for the older persons in the UK. For instance, 69 year -old female from Southall explained her own experience in this way that. "I appreciate the quality of healthcare services for the older people in this country. Sometimes, my children are on the job. They fix up an appointment with the hospital if I need medicine or regular check-up. The hospital will send a vehicle and a nurse on duty to pick and drop me from my residence. It can never happen in India. Last time, I went to India to attend a marriage of my sister`s daughter I observed that the elderly people are badly treated in the government hospitals". She compared health services in India and UK which cannot be appropriate. Similarly, explaining the services of the health department, a 73 year-old male from Birmingham explained that, "I do not have any financial problem since the day I migrated to this country. In this country, the older people can enjoy all medical facilities. For Instance, hearing aids are costly in the market but I got my hearing aids free of cost from the hospital".

In a similar vein, 82-year-old male from Birmingham applauded the healthcare services in this manner, "I suffered from a heart attack last year. I was taken to the hospital. I stayed for fifteen days in the hospital. The medical staffs in the hospital were so caring and loving that one cannot imagine. My children and grandchildren used to visit me once a weak, even then I never felt alone. Moreover, I did not pay even a single pound to the hospital. This respondent was so much impressed and mesmerized by the healthcare services in this country that he claimed, "I want to live and die only in this country". Yet another 86 year-old female from Wolverhampton explained the helping nature of the medical staff in the government hospitals in UK. According to him, "I had my knee replaced in the government hospital. Nurses were so nice to me that I did not encounter any problem. Meals were served to me in time. Once in a month, doctors with a nurse visit me at my residence and had thorough medical check-up of mine before prescribing medicine if required".

Housing Benefit (HB) provides help with rent and some service charges and is administered by local authorities (Age UK, 2018). The applicant has to apply to the local government. The inspector of the area would come to the applicant and ascertain and verify the reasons given in the application.

The applicant has to fulfill some prescribed criteria before getting a council house. For instance, 80- year -old female living alone in Wolverhampton explained, "I live in a council house. I had a quarrel with my daughter-in-law because of which I left my son`s house. I approached the government and it gave me a one-bedroom set fitted with all essential electronic items that I can use easily. I am physically fit and can do a number of activities. Whenever there is any medical emergency I can call 911".

From the above discussion and analyses of the narratives of the respondents, we come to know that the elderly Punjabis are happy about the quality of health services offered by health department of the UK government. Those who happen to live alone due to family dispute feel safe in case of emergency.

## Understanding Integration Experience of Elderly Punjabis in UK

It is significant to understand the integration of elderly Punjabis in a British society. The researcher has conducted in-depth interviews with the respondents living in UK and tried to deduce their experience to substantiate the universe of the study. According to McNeill and Adams (1978:99). Integration and assimilation of the immigrants in Western Europe are thus made difficult by at least two groups of factors, even in cases where permanent immigration results in spite of official policy. The barriers to integration and assimilation are consequences, on the one hand, of the "alien policy", and on the other, of the immigrants "own past". A third barrier indirectly affecting the immigrants results from structural factors affecting the native population. "Migration is a process of social change where individuals leave one geographical area for permanent residency in another. Typically, they transfer knowledge and expressions of distress with them and when settled, their identity is likely to change" (Bhugra, 2004:132).

"The first immigrants to Britain struggled for social integration because of two reasons first, the problems of communicating in English; and second, the memories of British colonial domination were still fresh in the minds of the communities. Also, the first generation of migrants did not command much respect as they worked mainly as manual laborers. Survey indicates that Indians are better integrated into mainstream British culture as compared to other religious and ethnic communities"(Sharma,2012). "Families play an important role in social integration because they shape the social relations between men and women and between generations" (Isfahani, 2013:4). "Those who follow this strategy experiences less distress and achieve "better adaptions". Lastly, "there are some individuals who have little interest in retaining their cultural heritage, which may not always be a choice and little interest in their host culture, this referred to as 'marginalization"

(Berry,2005:702). "The immigrants do not abruptly lose their earlier religious beliefs, but rather assimilated the new ones and amalgamated some of the old ones in to them. This is what happens to immigrants in the society to which they have come. The immigrants gradually lose the memory of place and of landscape, and this in its turn furthers the loss of culture, that is, of language, beliefs, and images. The loss of culture alone would not be traumatic; it becomes so on reflection. The reflection sometimes magnifies the loss. The immigrants are bound to have some influence on the culture of their host society; especially if the society into which they come is liberal and democratic. All the great cultures of the world have been amalgamated cultures. It is naïve romanticism to believe that the culture with which immigrants come to a foreign country has an integral purity, a mixing of which with any other culture would be a tragic loss" (McNeill and Adams, 1978:417-418). "In Great Britain and France, for instance, it was thought that assimilation of ethnically alien groups would be injurious to the central culture. This is not the case today" (McNeill and Adams, 1978:407).

Sharma (2013) states that "the first generation in the diaspora invariably remains nostalgic about their country of origin. They maintain contact with family, watch Indian movies, listen to Hindi music and folk songs, and are keen to retain cultural and spiritual links with India. Retried elderly people also devote time and energy to protect and propagate the cultural and religious heritage of their communities" (McNeill and Adams, 1978:421) conclude, "the assimilation of immigrants into the society in which they settle is necessary for the well-being of the society".

Integration into the British society is a great experience for the elderly Punjabis. The researcher conducted in depth interviews and tried to understand the views of the elderly Punjabis in relation to integration into the British society. In this context, "75-year-old male from Birmingham told that I immigrated to England in 1943 on a work permit. I used to work in a metal factory. At that time, most of the work was done manually. It was very difficult. My whole life is spent in the UK. My whole family lives with me. I never even dream of going back to India. Now the UK is my homeland. Some people want to go to their homeland but they have neither property nor any family members left behind". In a similar vein, 81-year-old- female from Southall opined that "I am the only daughter in the family. My old parents died a long time back. Our ancestral property was usurped by our relatives. I was sponsored by my NRI husband. His whole family is in the UK. I hear stories about India from my friends but never went back. I did not even felt the necessity to go back".

Yet another a disabled 72-year-old male from Wolverhampton explained while discussing his helplessness that, "I met with a car incident on the highway. My health is deteriorating day by day. I wanted to visit my village but unable to fly. I curse my helplessness. I really wish to see my village, relatives, and friends. Till day, I did not go. I do not know when that time will come in my life before death".

From the above discussion, we have reached a conclusion that the elderly Punjabis are fully integrated in the British society. This argument is also supported by the findings of Bhachu (1985) wrote, "Punjab Sikhs have found it easier to integrate in the UK due to their lack of ties to India". In this same context, the BSR(2013) reported, "95 percent of Punjabi Sikhs were proud of their 'Britishness' and preferred the term 'British Sikh' in reference to their identity". The ICM also revealed that during interview of 500 British South Asian, they prefer to be called as British Sikh" (2007).

## Conclusion

This chapter has tried to anlayse the family structure of the Punjabi families, However, due to industrialization, capitalism, and migration, the young people are drifting towards nuclear families. The inter-generational gap is prevalent in a cosmopolitan society of Britain. The family conflict arises when the older people stick to traditional norms and values and the young one defies traditional norms and values. Elderly who are currently living with their children depend on children for financial matters. Hence, most of the daily needs of the elderly parents are taken care of by the children.

Socially, they feel alienated and depressed because of English language barrier. The elderly parents living with the children have to depend on them for going to the market or to the place of relatives and friends. Cold weather is also one of the factors due to which these elderly Punjabi parents remain, most of the time, within the four walls of the house. Sometimes, these elderly parents get worried about their left-behind children in Punjab. The loss of close relatives and friends back in the homeland also disturbs them emotionally. Sometimes, it can also cause mental depression.

So far household engagements of the elderly Punjabi parents are concerned, the field survey found that the majority of the elderly Punjabi parents finds themselves engaged in the care of the grandchildren. Women remain busy in performing household chores. Despite social and economic disadvantages in an alien society, the elderly Punjabis feel satisfied with the quality and timely services provided by the healthcare centers run by the UK government. For older Britain citizens free medical services are an added advantages. From regular medical check-up to hospitalization, all the medical services in the UK for the older citizens are free. "The United Kingdom provides public healthcare to all permanent residents, about 58 million people Healthcare coverage is free at the point of need, and is paid for by general taxation" (Josh Chang et al., 2009). The respondents during the field survey informed that they are quite satisfied with the medical services in UK. "More than two thirds of people over the age of 65 say they are satisfied with the NHS, compared to just over half of 25-34 year olds. 91percent of people over the age of 65 are satisfied with their Gross Product (GP), compared to 74percent of 25-34 year olds. The same pattern is repeated for inpatient and outpatient care. For social care services, Social Services Inspectorate inspections of services for older people regularly show user satisfaction rates of around 80percent" (UK Government Report, 2011). Despite all excellent healthcare facilities available for the older people in UK, they still feel lonely and isolated. Sometimes, they encounter humiliations and abuses at the hand of the grand-children.

## References


Anne McMunn, James Nazroo, Elizabeth Breeze (2009). Inequalities in health at older ages: a longitudinal investigation of the onset of illness and survival effects in England, *Age and Ageing*, 38(2):181-187.

Baker, A.A. (1975) Granny-battering. *Modern Geriatrics*, 5(20).

Berry, J. W. (2005). Acculturation: Living successfully in two cultures. *International Journal of Intercultural Relations*, 29, 697-712.

Beteille, Andre (1964). Family and Social Change in India and Other South Asian Countries, *Economic and Political Weekly*, .6(5):.237-244.

Bhachu, P. (1985). *Twice Migrants: East African Sikh Settlers in Britain.* London: Tavistock.

Bhugra, D. (2004). Migration, distress, and cultural identity. *British Medical Bulletin*, 69:129-141.

Boyle, Seam. (2011). United Kingdom (England): Health System Review, Health Systems in Transition 13(1), European Observation on Health Systems and Policies, available at http://www.euro.who.int/ data/assets/pdf file/0004/135148/e94836 .pdf.

British Sikh Report. (2013). BSR 2013.Retrieved from:http://www.britishsikhreport.org/british-sikh-report download-2013.

Burholt, V and Wenger, Clare.W. (2003). Families and Migration: Older People from South Asia, South Asia Regional Report No.2, DFID, United Kingdom, Available at http://citeseerx.ist.psu.edu/viewdoc/download?doi=10.1.1.1024.894&rep=rep1&type=pdf.

Chanda, Rupa and Ghosh, Sriparna. (2012). *The Punjabi Diaspora in the UK: An Overview of Characteristic and Contributions to India*, CARIM, and IIMB.

Davis, Kingley. (1949). *Human Society*, Macmillan Co.

Distler, L.S. (1968). "*The Adolescent "Hippie" and the Emergence of Maristic Culture*".American Psychological Association Convention, San Francisco, California.

Dixon, A.L.(2002). *The Relationship Among Ethnic Identity, Acculturtaion, Mattering and Wellness in minority and nonminority Adoloscents*, University of North Carolina.

Dong XQ, Simon M, De Leon CM, Fulmer T, Beck T, Hebert L, et al. (2009). Elder self-neglect and abuse and mortality risk in a community-dwelling population. *Journal of American Medical Association*. 302,517–526.

Duffy, K. (1995). *Social Exclusion and Human Dignity in Europe*. Council of Europe: Strasbourg.

Emami, A., Torres, S., Lipson, G., and Ekman, S. (2000). An Ethnographic study of a day care center for Iranian Immigrant seniors. *Western Journal of Nursing Research*, 22(2): 169-188.

Gold, S. (1989).Differential Adjustment among new Immigrant Family Members. *Journal of Contemporary Ethnography*, 17(4): 408-434.

Gore, M.S.(1992). Family Support to Elderly People: The Indian Situation. In H.L. Coppard(Eds), Family Support for the elderly: The International Experience(pp-260-270), Oxford University Press.

Hendricks, J. (1996). The Search for New Solutions, *Gerontologist*, 36,141-144.

ICM Research. (2007). Report retrieved fromhttp://www.icmhsr.org.

Ingeborg, Nilsson. (2006). Occupational Engagement among older people: Evaluation, Repertoire, and Relation to Life Satisfaction, Sweden, and Umea University.

Irawati Karve. (1953). *Kinship Organization in India*, Deccan College Ishii-Kuntz, M. (1997).Intergenerational relationships among Chinese, Japanese and Korean Americans. *Family Relations*, 46(1): 23-32.

Isfahani-Salehi, D. (2013). "*The Role of the Family in Social Integration in the Middle East and North Africa*" DIFI Family Research and Proceedings, Virginia Tech and Brookings Institution.Health Care System in Eight Countries: Trends and Challenges', European Observatory of Health Care Systems, available at http://www. revmed. unal. edu.co/red/documentos/varios /8paises.pdf, retrieved 23 May 2017.

Irudaya.Rajan, Varghese, Aswini Kumar Nanda. (Eds). (2015). *Migration, mobility and multiple affiliations: Punjab in a transnational world*, London, Cambridge University Press.

Jones, Gavin .W. (2009).Indian Overseas Migration, Marriage Markets and Citizenship Issues, Working Papers No.9, available at http://lib.jnu.ac.in/sites/default/files/ pdf/ imds p/IMDS May 2009 WP 9.pdf.

Kending, Hal. Koyano, W., Asakawa, T and Ando, T.(1999). Social Support of Older People in Australia and Japan, *Ageing and Society*, pp.185-207.

Kibria, N. (1994). Household structure and family ideologies: The dynamics of immigrant economic adaptation among Vietnamese refugees. *Social Problems*, 41, 81-96.

Kiefer, C. W., Kim, K., Choi, L., Kim, B. Shon, S., and Kim, T. (1985) Adjustment problems of Korean American elderly, *The Gerontologist*, 25, 477-482.

Kim, K., Kim, S., and Hurh, W. (1991).Filial Piety and Intergenerational relationship in Korean immigrant families. *International Journal of Ageing and Human Development*, 33(3): 233-245.

Kiyotaka Sato (2010). Division among Sikh Communities in Britain and the Role of Caste System: A Case Study of Four Gurdwara in Multi-Ethnic-Leicester, *Journal of Punjabi Studies*, pp.1-26.

Mala Kapur Shankardass and Kumar. (1996). A Sociological analysis of support networks in old age in India. In Kumar (Eds) *Ageing: Indian Perspective and Global Scenario*, All India Institute of Medical Sciences, New Delhi, pp.195-97.

Maiter, S. (2003). The Context of Culture: Social Work practice with Canadians of South Asian background. In A. Al-Krenawi and J.R. Graham (Ed.), *Multicultural Social Work in Canada* (pp. 365-387). Oxford University Press. Canada.

McNeill, William H. and Adams, Ruth S. (1978).*Human Migration Patterns and Policies*, Bloomington and London, Indian University Press.

Murdock, G. P. (2015). *Social Structure*, Chizine Publications.

Netting, Robert McC. Wilk, Richard, R. and Arnold. (1984). *Households: Comparative and Historical Studies of the Domestic Group*, Berkeley, and University of California Press.

Niranjan, S., Sureender, S. and Rao, G. Rama. (1998). Family Structure in India-Evidence from NFHS. *Demography India*. 27(2): 287-300.

Raina, Jawaharlal Lal. (1988). Structural and Functional Changes in the Joint Family System: *A Study of D.C.M. Workers*, New Delhi. Concept Publishing Company.

Rayada. (2000). The Indian Family: Change and Persistence, New Delhi, Gyan Publishing House.

Ruggles. (1997). Prolonged Connections: *The rise of the extended family in 19th –century England and America*. Madison: University of Wisconsin Press.

Sarah, E. Lamb. (2009).Ageing and the Indian Diaspora: Cosmopolitan Families in India and Abroad, Bloomington, Indiana Univeristy Press.

Safran, William. (1991). Diaspora in Modern Societies: Myth of Homeland and Return, *Journal of Transnational Studies*, University of Toronto Press, 1 (1): 83-89.

Sebastian and Sekhar, T.V. (2010). Abuse and Neglect of Elderly in Indian Families: Finding of Elder Abuse Screening Test in Kerala, *Journal of the Indian Academy of Geriatrics*. 6, 54-60.

Sharma, Sheetal. (2013). Immigrants in Britain: A Study of the Indian Diaspora, *Diaspora Studies*, Routledge, pp.14-43.

Sonuga-Berke E.J. and Mistry, M. (2000). The Effect of Extended Family living on the Mental Health of three Generations within two Asian Communities, NCBI, available at https://www.ncbi.nlm.nih.gov/pubmed/10895357.

Weeks, J., and Cuellar, J. (1983). Isolation of Older people: The influence of Immigration and length of residence. *Research on Ageing*, 5, 369-388.

World Health Organization. (2013). "Measuring overall health system performance for 191 countries, available at http://pages.stern.nyu.edu/wgreene/Statistics/WHO-COMP-Study-30.pdf,retrieved 20 June 2017.

Yu, L. C., and Wu, S. C. (1985).Unemployment and family dynamics in meeting the needs of Chinese elderly in the United States. *Gerontologist*, 25, 472-476.

# VII

# Elderly Punjabis in Punjab and England (UK): A Comparison

## Introduction

This chapter tries to analyze the nature and dynamics of ageing in a comparative perspective. Here we will compare the structure and processes in which elderly Punjabis live in Punjab and England. For doing the same we will highlight the differences and similarities in socio-economic status of the elderly Punjabis living in three different districts of Doaba region of Punjab and three districts of England. We would like to understand in a comparative perspective how do the elderly survive in Punjab and how do they do it in England. That means what is the source of their income after they retire for their wage. It is in this context this chapter will also record the role of remittances. How it is utilized by the parents in their old age? Apart from economic status, this chapter will also analyze the nature of conflict parents suffer in the old age. We would like to record, what are the main causes of conflicts, which elderly suffer in both the societies. Whether conflict is cultural, financial, and generational or it is problem of differences in two different cultures, that is Punjabi native culture and western culture.

This chapter would also record nature and crises of isolation, loneliness and abuse suffered by aged Punjabis in both the societies. What are reasons because of which old age parents suffer isolation and loneliness in Punjab and England? Or it is because the children are working specifically in England? Whether language and traditional value system are responsible for this isolation and loneliness of old age members of Punjab society in Punjab and England? Why do aged people suffer physical, verbal and psychological abuse among the Punjabi families? This will also be probed in this chapter. A comparison has been made on the basis of healthcare facilities available for the elderly in the two societies that are in Punjab and England.

We would like to record the impact of the healthcare system in two societies on the elderly people. Whether there is an alternative residence for the old age persons if they want.to leave the house of their children because of domestic conflict and violence of different types. Apart from these conditions influencing the lives of the old age persons. This chapter has specifically recorded the role of weather in forcing the old age people in England to fell in isolation and depression. Hence on these various facts, this chapter would record the differences and similarities between the lives of old age persons in Punjab and England. Although two societies have different socio-structural and cultural elements yet a comparison can be made between the elderly livings in two societies.

## Economic Status of left behind Elderly Punjabis in Punjab

The researcher has tried to examine the economic status of the left behind elderly Punjabis in Punjab. It is a common knowledge that those who do not work or have no source of income heavily depend upon remittances from the children. The researcher has consulted various previous studies conducted by the social scientists. The researcher has consulted previous studies on old age pension and social security available for the older persons in Punjab. The researcher has also conducted in depth interviews to gauge the views of the left behind elderly about their economic conditions and how they manage their life in meeting day to day expense with or without remittances. (Dyson and Moore, 1983:12) wrote, "Punjab remained demographically a better performing states with many of its vital parameters showing improvements dating back to early 1980s or even earlier. The economy of Punjab remained a symbol of economic prosperity and role model of economic development among the Indian state for more than three decades since the ushering in of the green revolution". "A high proportion of the elderly in Punjab -85 percent males and 98 percent females –reported not receiving any work-related benefits such as prescribed ages for retirement and pension" Singh, 2005). "The rural Sikhs in Punjab are still predominantly engaged in agriculture and allied agriculture activities" (BKPAI, 2011). "The left behind elderly parents mostly depend upon remittances for meeting day to day expenses". (Ghuman, 2012:90).

## Economic Status of Elderly Punjabis in England (UK)

This present study found that the elderly Punjabis in England (UK) are financially sound as compared to the elderly Punjabis in Punjab. Those who migrated to UK in the first phase during 1959s and 1965s worked in foundries, factories, and construction sector. During those times employment opportunities were plenty in UK. This was because the country was undergoing a complete change from agricultural settings to industrialization. There was neither age and nor gender discrimination in employment. The Equality Act 2010 allows employers to voluntarily appoint under-represented groups under specific circumstances.

This study also found that the older citizens over the age of 65 years are eligible to get old age pension in UK. Those who worked are also eligible for retirement pension. Elderly men or women get two types of pension-one is work pension and other is old age pension. The elderly who comes and goes back to India are not eligible for any type of old age pension. The state pension is only for those who fulfill eligibility criteria as laid down by UK government. There is also a state disability pension. Those elderly who are disabled due to some unanticipated incident are eligible for disability pension. The respondents during the interviews revealed that the state pension and work pension is sufficient as to lead a very comfortable life. The majority of the elderly who draws such pensions do not depend financially upon the children. Rather, they sometimes help their relatives, friends back in Punjab if they need financial help.

The researcher has conducted in-depth interviews with elderly Punjabis in UK to understand the economic status of the elderly. In this context, 89 year-old- male from Southall revealed, "I am a retired factory worker. I get two pensions; one is work pension and other is old age pension. A total 845 pounds per month I get after tax deduction. I live with my children and grandchildren. We live in a joint family. Fifty percent I deposit in my bank account and fifty percent I give to my son who is manageing the house. My married daughter is living in the village Chitti in district Jalandhar. I send money and gifts to my daughter. If she needs money due to emergency I send money to her either through bank or through Western Union. It is easy and prompt. Sometimes, I donate money to the Sikh temple. I get a request from the board of trustees of the Sikh temple to support them to buy some electric appliances such as fan, water pump etc. Believe me, till this age I never spread my hands for money before my children or grandchildren rather I give money to them. It gives me satisfaction and I feel proud and dignified father".

In a similar vein, 74 year-old-female from Birmingham told, "I never worked in life. Now I get old age pension 350 pound per month after tax deduction. This money is sufficient for me. My children are earning well hence they do not demand anything from me. I save my money. I buy lot of gifts for my sister`s children who lives in Punjab. Once in a year, I go to Punjab and stay there for almost three weeks. I spend all my savings during my visit to Punjab. UK is known as a paid old age homes for older persons. When I listen that older people in Punjab get a small amount of old pension or sometimes they need to pay bribe to the officials to get their old age pension I get disturbed. It is a shame on the bureaucratic system".

Yet another 83 year-old female from Wolverhampton explained, "I get 735 pound per month. I worked as a sweeper at the London airport. I retired with pension so I get two pensions that is work and old age pension respectively. I am as free to buy my own things as I desire. Sometimes, I buy gifts for my grandchildren. I do not have any relative left in Punjab. I had one sister who died a few years back. Her children and husband do not keep communication with us because I could not sponsor them to England. I love this country because it takes care of the older people with respect and dignity".

In a similar vein, 76 year-old male from Wolverhampton opined, "Without money, nothing is possible in this country. I get 650 pound per month. It includes work and old age pension. I live separately because of my daughter-in-law. My wife died long time back due to kidney failure. My son is a gentleman. I do not want to disturb the peaceful atmosphere of the family because of my daughter-in–law so I applied for the council house. The Municipal department gave me one room set flat. I live alone and spend my pension to meet daily expenses. My son visits me with grandchildren but my daughter– in-law does not. My son brings food items and sometimes cloths for me".

## Remittances, Pension and Social Security in Punjab

"Remittances refer to the money and goods that are transmitted to households by migrants working outside of their original communities, either in urban areas or abroad" (Adam et al., 2014). In a similar vein Certin and Munzele argue, "remittances from a family welfare system that facilitate consumption, alleviates liquidity constraints and provides a form of mutual insurance. The vast majority of remittances go to family members who are either spouses or parents who are at the old age and who really need support in both kind and cash. Invariably women head many recipient households" (as quoted in Nangia, 2015:197).

According to World Bank report (2017), "Punjab is a largest recipient of the remittances of non-resident Indians and persons of Indian origin". "An estimated US$413 billion in remittances are sent to India by immigrants in 2016"(UN Report, 2017). Remittances for elderly parents work like an oxygen particularly for those who do not earn or draw any type of private or government pension. The utilization of remittances as studied by Seema found, "remittances are mainly utilized for living expenses, debt repayment, marriage expense, and improvement in housing, purchase of land for a house or buying a new house and furthering emigration of other family members. In a few cases, however, part of remittances was invested in agricultural land and equipment's as well as small business ventures to augment the family income" (Seema, 2005).

Migrated children from England usually send money to the older parents for their day to day expenses. Older parents who get remittances regularly are happy. In the case of children who are currently under the process of settlement in UK are not in a position to send money regularly to the older parents. This causes fear and sadness to their hearts and minds. Older parents usually spend money on consumption such as buying food, medicine, and paying utility bills. In this context, Levitt argues, "monetary remittances have the potential to improve health outcomes. Ultimately, both aged men and women of the 70-79 age brackets (suffering from old age, illness; diabetes and hypertension) used remittances in cash to go for checkups (consultation, lab test) and buy related medications" (Levitt, 1997:935).

In case of some major family function, they make a request to the children for extra money. A widowed mother tended to receive more than older men. Elderly people, particularly in rural areas are found to be socially active in religious functions. Some are found to be an active member of Sikh temples in the village of their residence. Donation to the Sikh temple is a regular feature. Those who are financially sound donate generously for building a room or paying for electric fans, wooden or iron furniture. Some rich families contribute to the village gate. Such financial contribution brings them a sense of pride in the village community.

Death of an older person in the family attracts social function in which close relatives and members of the family are served food. Remittances are used for the funeral ceremony. Remittances are used to pay for loans to fund the migration costs of the children. Foreign remittance plays an essential role in meeting day to day expenses and reducing poverty rates of elderly parent's households. Foreign remittances impact the economic well-being of older parents. It also improves the health of old-age parents.

"Pension system should ensure income security during old age for all and, as a minimum, need to provide benefits that place recipients above the poverty line or any other socially acceptable minimum standard. Pension system may be privately or publicly administered but the ultimately the responsibility to guarantee, regulate and supervise the delivery of a basic pension lies solely with the government. Estimates of poverty among older persons in other developed countries with extensive pension coverage are often based on a concept of relative poverty" (Rob Vos et al., 2008:126

and128). "In developing countries, few have access to pension benefits and most have to rely on other, often insecure source of income. Those who were poor during their prime working years have a high probability of remaining poor during old age. During old age, people tend to rely on for main income sources(a) private transfers from the family and social networks;(b)public transfers from pension and other cash transfer programmes;(c) labour earnings; and (d) financial and other assets, including private pensions"((Rob Vos et al., 2008).

According to United Nations, "Social security was established as a right in the Declaration concerning the aims and purpose of the International Labour Organization (ILO) adopted in Philadelphia, Pennsylvania, on 10May 1944, and is integral to the implementation of the Universal Declaration of Human Rights (10 December 1948) which states, "Everyone has the right to social security and is entitled to realization of the economic, social, and cultural rights indispensable for his dignity (Article 22). "Everyone has the right to a standard of living adequate for the health and well-being of himself and of his family, including necessary social services, and the right to security in the event of unemployment, sickness, disability, widowhood, old age or other lack of livelihood in circumstances beyond his control" (Article 25).

While analyzing the narratives of the respondents the researcher found that the majority of the elderly parents (men and women) are not eligible for a private or government pension. The amount of state pension for the older people is meager. Even to avail pension, the process is cumbersome. Many of the older people are not aware of the pension or welfare schemes of the state of Punjab. In the absence of social security and adequate old age pension, there is hardly any economic security for the older people hence the majority of the older people are economically weak and dependable.

"Families and community invest in the next generation convinced that this is how society progresses. The next generation, in turn, will reciprocate and be better prepared to care for younger and older generations while advancing the well-being of societies" (Butts, 2010:4). There was a mixed response in regard to the support of the children to the elderly parents. Children who have regular income come forward to support their elderly parents. Children who are in the process of settlement and do not have a regular job are unable to support their elderly parents financially. The following narratives of the respondents are included to understand the financial status of the elderly Punjabis in Punjab and the importance of remittances in their life in meeting household and other essential expenses.

In a similar vein, 82 year-old female from a village Dholowal from district Hoshiarpur told, "I am a widow. My husband died a few years back due to heart failure. He was a diabetic patient. I have only son who left for England when my husband was alive. My husband sponsored his immigration cost to the UK. My husband was an inspector in the department of Punjab Police. He could not complete his full services due to a sudden demise. He was eligible for a job pension so I get Rs 1500 per month. This is a very small amount to meet sky rocketing prices of essential commodities. Addition to that, I am also not keeping good health. I have high blood pressure and my eyesight is also weak. In this situation, I always give a call to my son to send money to me. I am a lucky mother who is supported by children in this old age. For me remittance is indispensable".

## Pension and Social Security in UK

During field work, the researcher found that the majority of the elderly aged 65 years get state pension in the United Kingdom. Those who are retired also get work pension. It is further found that the elderly men or women get two types of pension- one is work pension and other is old age state pension from the state. The elderly who comes and goes back to India are not eligible for any type of pension. The state pension is only for those who fulfill eligibility criteria as laid down by the United Kingdom government. There is also a state disability pension. Those elderly who are disabled due to some unforeseen incident are eligible for disability pension. The respondents during the interview revealed that the state pension and work pension is sufficient as to lead a very comfortable life. The majority of the elderly who draws such pensions do not depend financially upon the children. Rather, they sometimes help their relatives, friends back in Punjab if the relatives or friends need financial help.

Social support between older parents and children is reciprocal. Peter and Kaiser argue, "the elders do reciprocate the aid they receive". Similarly, Wentkowski argue, "the elders reciprocate in relation to all the types of relationships they maintain" (as quoted in Litwin, 1998:239).) "Sons generally carry the major responsibility for taking care of their older parents and daughters fulfill the son`s roles when sons are not available". (Spitz and Logan (1990:427). It is observed that a daughter remains quite sensitive as compared to son and provide care and financial help to the older persons. The permanent migrated elderly parents do not expect financial support from the children because they receive old age pension and social security. Some of the elderly respondents revealed that they support financially their relatives, friends back in the homeland. They also help their left behind brothers and sisters in Punjab in case they demand. Their only expectation from the children is love and care. The majority of the elderly parents reluctantly answered few questions related to the children support. Their mixed response indicated that the elderly parents are not fully satisfied. Similar is the case with the grandchildren.

## Healthcare Services in Punjab

There is a wide gap between government and private health services and infrastructure in the state of Punjab. The welfare of the older people is at risk due to inadequate medical facilities and the shortage of qualified medical staff. As per CRRID Annual Report (2013-14), "Most of the health institutions lack basic facilities while there is also a shortage of staff in almost all the health institutions". According to the field survey, the researcher found that the majority of the elderly people prefer to use the services of private hospital because of better and upgraded infrastructure and qualified and efficient medical staff. The older people still prefer to go to a private medical practitioner despite government hospitals or dispensaries in Jalandhar, Hoshiarpur, and Kapurthala districts of Punjab.

The analyze of narratives from the respondents from urban as well rural areas of the Punjab demonstrate that a large number of elderly people are unhappy with the healthcare services prevail in the state of Punjab. Unprofessional behavior of the medical staff of the government hospitals remains a cause of unhappiness among the elderly. In this context, 75-year-old male explained the worst condition of the government hospitals in Jalandhar in his own words, "My children migrated to UK 12 years back. I live with my wife in this house. I am a heart patient and needs a regular help especially at night. I cannot drive because of poor eyesight. The condition of the government hospital in this village is the worst. Doctors do not have sympathetic feelings for the older people. The attitude of the nursing staff towards the older people especially whose children are abroad is greedy and insensitive. The ambulances in case of emergency are not available at all".

In Jalandhar district, 67 year-old female opined, "Whenever I go to the government hospital I found doctor is either in a meeting or on vacations. There is a nexus between doctors of private and government hospitals in Jalandhar. I had to go to a private hospital for my knee operation". Stating with a heavy heart, 69-year-old male from rural area of district Kapurthala told that, "We have only one government hospital in the whole area. Most of the time, it is overcrowded with patients. Therefore doctors are very busy. This hospital is under-staffed. I am a diabetic patient. Dogs and cats frequently roam in the medical wards.

While explaining the worst conditions of the government hospital, 72-year-old female from Hoshiarpur shared her bad experience with the government hospital staff and revealed, "I had a heart stroke last year. I went to a government hospital but I was treated very badly there. I will never go to a government hospital because the doctors are insensitive. My elder son is in UK. He always sends money to meet hospital expenditure. Now, I prefer to go to a private hospital. I do not know what kind of free healthcare facilities are available for the older people in the government hospital".

While remembering his encounter with the government hospital, 66-year-old male from a village Chhiti in district Jalandhar narrated, "The prevailing condition in the government hospital is the worst. He further argued, "We have a government hospital in our village. The present condition of the hospital is the worst. Doctors and nurses never reach on time. The villagers with the help of Non-resident Punjabis and donated money to buy wheelchairs and beds for the hospital. After few years, all the donated items have disappeared or broken. Doctors working in the Government hospital are busy to earn extra money. They have opened up their personal clinics and devote much of their time in private clinic or hospital. They enjoy good rapport with the doctors of reputed private hospitals in the city hence refer most of the patient to them. It is a common knowledge among the people of Punjab that greedy doctors get commission by referring a patient to a private hospital".

Yet another, 69 year-old male from Bootan Mandi in district Jalandhar revealed "I was admitted to a government hospital in Jalandhar for my kidney operation. I was in the general ward where dogs and cats run freely. On the very first day, I did not get any attention from the doctors or nurses. I was lying on the bed as an abandoned body. Luckily, I knew a nurse through my relative working in the same hospital but in a different department of the hospital. She helped me a lot. She introduced myself to the doctors and nurses as her uncle. I was discharged from the hospital after a week. I had to go to the government hospital because my son living in UK stopped sending money to me. My current source of income is meagre and therefore I can not afford hospitalization in a private hospital".

From the above discussion, the researcher has found that the majority of the elderly respondents are not satisfied with the prevailing healthcare services in the state of Punjab. The condition of the government hospitals especially in the rural areas of Punjab are quite challenging. The elderly respondents are very unhappy and carry a bad image of the government hospitals. Shortage of doctors and nursing staff, wheelchairs, beds especially in the rural areas of the government hospitals in Punjab is a cause of annoyance among the elderly. Lack of cleanliness in the government hospitals is another cause of distrust in the healthcare services of Punjab.

## Healthcare Services in UK

The National Health Services (NHS) was founded in 1946 and is responsible for the public healthcare sector of the UK. "As per study conducted in eight industrialized countries, the healthcare system of the United Kingdom is one of the most efficient in the world" (Evans et al., 2002:45). "The UK has relatively short waiting times for basic medical care and non-emergency access to services after hours but has longer times for specialist care and elective, non-emergency surgery" (Chang et al., 2010).

This study found that the elderly people are overwhelmingly satisfied with the health care services and medical infrastructure. The majority of the elderly people asserted that the welfare care services for the older people in UK are par excellence. Doctors and nurses are so kind as to take of every older patient. Ambulance service for an emergency call is available for 24x7 without any charges. During the interview, the researcher found the elderly Punjabis compliant about old age diseases including knee pain, bronchitis, diabetes, blood pressure. It has been also observed that elderly people are sensitive to cold weather, especially during the winter season.

The respondents also revealed that in case they do not go for a medical routine check, they get a letter from the hospital for visiting the hospital. The hospital staff come to the elderly home and pick and drop in case the children are unable to take the elderly parents to the hospital. Some critics allege that there is sharp deterioration taking place in the delivery of National Health Services (NHS) over the last decade. The NHS faced criticism of the public due to overcrowded healthcare services, inadequate number of medical staff, decreased efficiency, cost cutting and consultation with patients. With the increase of the demand of the older people in UK, much longer wait for dental treatment is observed. Some says that this long wait is due to shortage of NHS dentists. Despite of these challenges of overcrowded services, the majority of the elderly Punjabis are happy and satisfied with the existing healthcare services.

The respondents acknowledged the quality of healthcare services particularly for the older persons in the UK. For instance, 69 year -old female from Southall told her own experience in this way that. "I appreciate the quality of healthcare services for the older people in this country. Sometimes, my children are on the job. They fix up an appointment with the hospital if I need medicine or regular check-up. The hospital will send a vehicle and a nurse on duty to pick and drop me from my residence. It can never happen in India. Last time, I went to India to attend a marriage of my sister`s daughter I observed that the elderly people are badly treated in the government hospitals". She compared health services in India and UK, which cannot be appropriate. Similarly, explaining the services of the health department, a 73 year-old male from Birmingham revealed, "I do not have any financial problem since the day I migrated to this country. In this country, the older people can enjoy all medical facilities free of charges. For Instance, hearing aids are costly. I got my hearing aids free of cost from the hospital".

In a similar vein, 82-year-old male from Birmingham applauded the healthcare services in this manner, I suffered from a heart attack last year. I was taken to the hospital. I stayed for fifteen days in the hospital. The medical staff in the hospital are so caring and loving that one cannot imagine. My children and grandchildren used to visit me once a week during the whole treatment period in the hospital. Moreover, I did not pay even a single pound to the hospital. This respondent was so much impressed and mesmerized by the healthcare services in this country that he claimed, "I want to live and die only in this country. Yet another 86 year-old female from Wolverhampton explained the helping nature of the medical staff in the government hospitals in UK. According to her, "I had my knee replaced in the government hospital. Nursing staff were so nice to me that I did not encounter any problem. I was meals by the hospital. Once in a month, doctor with a nurse visit me at my residence and do thorough medical check-up and prescribe medicine if required.

"Housing Benefit (HB) provides help with rent and some service charges and is administered by local authorities. Housing benefit is based on income and capital" (Age UK, 2018). The applicant has to apply to the local government. The inspector of the area would come to the applicant and ascertain and verify the reasons given in the application. The applicant has to fulfill some prescribed criteria before getting a council house. For instance, 80- year -old female living alone from Wolverhampton told that I live in a council house. I had a quarrel with my daughter-in-law because of which I left my son`s house. I approached the government and it gave me a one-bedroom set fitted with all essential electronic items that I can use easily. I am physically fit and can do a number of activities. Whenever there is any medical emergency I can call 911. Let me tell you, 911 is an emergency services available for 24 hours to respond to emergency situation".

## Need-based Support of Close Relatives and Friends in Punjab

People in Punjab enjoy the benefits of close-knit society. "The family network is fundamental in people`s lives, but when it is inefficient, friends play an essential role in providing physical and mental support" (Faquinello and Marcon, 2011:1347). Left behind elderly parents are taken care of by the close relatives and friends in case of emergency. In the absence of their children, they seek the assistance of their nephews or nieces or friends. Normally, this kind of assistance is need-based. Community network also plays a crucial role in supporting the elderly people. The probability of receiving family support is higher when older persons reside with their children or other relatives than when they live alone. "Co-residence is a more important determinant of the livelihood of older persons` receiving private transfers than the fact that they have children who are still living" (United Nations, 2005b).

## Need-based Support of Close Relatives and Friends in UK

Due to social and professional engagements, the elderly people in UK are not happily welcome by the friends and relatives. Sometimes also because of old age related ailments. The researcher has found that the people in the western countries are overly busy since extra help is very expensive. Only rich people can afford the services of a maid servant. Generally, people avoid any sort of liability. Older people need constant help at the home.

## Social Status of Elderly Parents Left Behind in Punjab

In old age, a variety of social problems and stresses emerge. Old age is viewed as a handicap. Negative attitude toward the elderly people prevails. Several studies asserts that social stigma in the old age generally distracts the tranquility of the minds of the elderly people. In the family, the majority of the elderly people experience social challenges due to loss of social roles, esteem. Limited economic resources and depleted social networks also cause depression and disturbance. The common social problem among the elderly people occur due to loss of confidence, exaggerated withdrawal from unusual activities, feelings of physical incompetence, depression, anxiety, sleep disturbances. The survey found that those elderly who actively participate in household tasks and social services feel less depressed and isolated.

## Social Status of the Elderly in UK

"The Indian community has interval divisions caused by issues such as origin, caste, religion, and politics.The Punjabi community is divided into a number of social classes encompassing upper class, middle class, working class, and the lower class. The Punjabi community is also a socially stratified community. He further wrote that 'Sikh communities are grouped and classified in complex ways" (Kiyotaka Sato, 2010: 12-13).

## Isolation and Loneliness among left behind Elderly in Punjab

"Loneliness occurs when there is discrepancy between one`s desired and one`s perceived or actual relationship" (Pepalu and Pertman, 1979:128). Loneliness is common among the older person. The pain of isolation and loneliness among the left behind elderly parents is more tormenting. A national level study conducted by Agewell Foundation, New Delhi, India reported: "the level of isolation in old age of older persons living in urban areas was quite higher up to 89.8 percent in comparison to older persons of rural areas, where 77.62 percent people reportedly feel isolated"[1]. "Due to isolation in their life, elderly were found affected with the following problems"[2]. Nervousness and anxiety; Panic and aggressive nature; Eating disorders leading to health disorders; Addictions and substance abuse; Feeling of insecurity; Financial imbalance". This study found that the majority of the elderly parents miss their children. They want them to call them every day. They want their children should them regularly.

The following narratives illustrate the nature of loneliness and isolation among the elderly in Punjab. The researcher has asked specific questions to understand the nature of isolation and loneliness of the respondents in Punjab. In this context, 74 year-old-male from district Jalandhar responded, "In the absence of our son we feel lonely. Since the day he migrated to UK, we could not live happily. His face is always in front of our eyes. However, he keeps on calling us yet we feel isolated. You know blood relative is a blood relative". In a similar vein, 83 year-old male from Kapurthala argued, "From our village, many of my friends and relatives were sponsored by their children. After migration, they did not come back to India. I have an ancestral property in this village and I do not want to sell it. This property belongs to our forefathers. Now, in my village, I do not have any friend to sit and talk. Earlier, we used to have sittings for '*Gupshap*' but nothing sort of that. Society has changed.Community feeling has declined sharply hence we feel isolated and lonely".

In yet another, 68 year-old- male from district Hoshiarpur told, "Since the day my son has migrated to UK he stopped communicating with us. His wife is quarrelsome. She does not want my son to talk us. This pain is enormous. When we do not get any call from our son we really feel upset. This leads to isolation and loneliness. It is difficult to spend time". A mentally upset 82 year-old female told me "My son died in an accident in UK. After his death, his wife and children do not keep any communication with us. It really hurts us. We wanted to see our grandchildren but this dream could not be fulfilled because of my daughter–in-law. Her negative attitude disturbs us deeply. We feel distressed and isolated".

## Isolation and Loneliness in UK

"Racism and racial harassment as a major cause of distress for Asian people'(Kai, 1998:12). "The oldest may be at a greater risk for memory problems due to decrements related to increasing age, thereby increasing the vulnerability to loneliness" (Peter, 1997; 203). A study carried out by Hansson et al. opine, "Loneliness was related to poor psychological adjustment, dissatisfaction with family and social relationships. Depression in South Asian women is associated with difficulties in coping, anxiety, stress, isolation, negative body image, low self-esteem and feelings of guilt, pressure and isolation" (Hasnsson et al. 1987:42). "Older Asian women are often isolated because they lack social networks; are less likely to speak English and likely to be financially and practically dependent because they are not entitled to claim benefits" (Jagannathan, 1996). "A recent study conducted in UK shows that more than 9 million people in UK always or often feel lonely, while around 200,000 older people have not had a conversation with a friend or relative in more than a month" (Sonwalker, 2018).

This study found that the majority of the elderly people are victims of isolation and loneliness. There are several factors behind it including pressure to live alone when the children are on the job and grandchildren are in the school. Language barriers restrict their movement. They feel immeasurably isolated in the four walls of the house. Mental stress aggravates due to harsh weather conditions in UK. Hence, the health and well-being of the Punjabi elderly deteriorate physically and emotionally. The respondents during the interview revealed that life is tough in UK since they cannot move outside without the assistance of children and grandchildren. In this context, 84 year-old- male from Southall told, "Weather in England is really depressing. I cannot go out without the help of my children and grandchildren. They are so busy in their own day to day affairs. I spend my time in the four walls of the house. I do not know how to dial therefore it makes difficult for me to speak to a friend or relative unless somebody helps me to make a call. It makes me depressed and isolated".

In a similar vein, 74 year-old–male from Birmingham narrated, "I am a sick man. My son has given me a separate room in the house. Half of the day I am alone in the room because grandchildren come from school in the afternoon. They lock the main gate of the house since I cannot close and open the door because of pain in my knee. In England, most of the time it is dark outside. Do you know about three 'Ws' in UK? I mean to say Weather, Work and Women. All three are not dependable, in a jovial mood, he explained. It is depressing for me. Before death my wife it was not like that. However, children and grandchildren are there to look after me yet I always miss the company of my deceased wife. She used to sit and talk with me. Now, hardly anybody sit more than 10 minutes with me. It makes more sick and dejected". In a similar vein, 86 year-old-female from Wolverhampton explained that, "My son and daughter-in-law have no child. They both are working. They go to the job early in the morning and come late by evening. Most of the time, I am all-alone in the house. My husband went back to Punjab and did not return back. I feel lonely and depressed". From the above discussion with the respondents, we can conclude that the elderly people in Punjab and UK feel lonely and isolated.

## Elderly Abuse in Punjab

"Elder abuse has been defined as a single, or repeated act, or lack of appropriate action occurring within any relationship where there is an expectation of trust which causes harm or distress to an older person" (Bhatia et al., 2008:169). Elderly abuse is common in all societies across the globe and Punjabi society is no exception. Elderly parents are commonly abused in the families. BKPAI (2011) "Elderly abuse is growing concern for the ageing population. Almost 11 percent of the elderly in Punjab have reported facing abuse after turning 60. With the proportion of abuse being slightly higher in rural areas as compared to urban areas'. There are various types of abuses that elderly parents face during their old age". According to Pyrek (2006:262) physical abuse can include hitting, beating, pushing, shoving, shaking, slapping, kicking, pinching and burning. In a similar vein, Kapur (1997:18) mentions incidences of elderly abuse by family members ranging from neglect to physically throwing them out of the house". This study found that the elderly who have savings and property in their name get love, respect, and care than those who do not have. This study also observed that in cases the children's behavior is negative toward those elderly who do not have any source of income.

The following narrative illustrates the nature and dynamic of elderly abuse existing in Punjabi families in Punjab. In this context, 78 year-old-male from district Jalandhar argued, "the time has changed so the children. My elder son came from UK. He has been telling me to sell ancestral property and give his share so that he can repay the loan in UK. After consistent refusal, he started quarrelling with his mother and me. One day, under the influence of liquor he pushed me to the wall consequently my writs bone broke. I told him, come what may, I shall never sell my ancestral property". In a similar vein, 83 year-old- female narrated that, my son and daughter-in-law came from UK to visit us. My daughter-in-law is quite quarrelsome. She gets upset over trifle matters. One day, she was insisting to sell a piece of land. I refused. She did not like it. She went back to UK with my son. Because of her ferocious behavior I do not want to go to UK.".

## Elderly Abuse in UK

The elderly people try to force the youngsters to learn but the grandchildren do not believe in traditional norms and values hence there is sometimes tension and unhappiness in the family. Abuse of older people is a hidden, and often ignored problem in society. More than 6 million older people in England are being abused at any one time[3]. Elderly abuse is common in the Asian communities in the United Kingdom. Physical abuse includes hitting, striking, beating, pushing, shaking, pinching, kicking, slapping.

Emotional and psychological abuse includes verbal assaults, intimidation, humiliation, threats, insults, harassment. Due to the intergenerational gap, the elderly people are subject to various types of tortures and humiliations at the hands of the children and grandchildren. This study found that elderly women are more prone to physical and emotional abuse than elderly men in the Punjabi families. The respondents during the interview revealed that the family dispute involving women of the house often leads to abandonment and divorce. This dispute is common in the Punjabi families when a son from Punjab marries a Punjabi British girl or vice-versa. The prime cause of the elderly abuse usually occurs due to western culture. Children and grandchildren are imbued with the style of the west. Among the Punjabi families, social differences between the elderly parents and the children and grandchildren occur due to cultural differences. The migrated elderly parents want their children, grandchildren, and daughter-in-law to emulate Punjabi culture and practice Punjabi traditional values and customs. When there is resistance by grandchildren, differences usually occur among the members of the family.

The researcher has also tried to understand the nature and dynamics of elderly abuse among Punjabi families in UK hence conducted in depth interviews with the respondents. In this context, 79 year old male from Southall revealed that, "In England, the family dispute is common sometimes due to daughter-in-law or grandchildren. There is lot of cultural difference between India and Britain. We are old people and subscribe to religious customs, beliefs and rituals but this younger generation do not like at all. For instance, one day, I asked my grandson to touch feet of my friend but flatly refused to do so. I felt insulted. Rather, he called me 'punky oldy'. He abused me in presence of his parents. In England like India we cannot beat or scold children. In many cases, I have seen that children born and brought in England call the police and get their parents arrested for beating or scolding. It is not India where we can slap our son or daughter publicly".

## Social Exclusion in Punjab

"The caste system is an indispensable component of the Indian social fabric and it is stated and practiced among diaspora communities all over the world. In fact, there are caste specific associations among the diaspora. Family and kinship network too, operate on the basis of caste affiliation" (Puri, 2007). Indian society is divided into castes and sub-castes. The dominant Sikh Jats who constitute a majority in the state of Punjab practice caste discrimination against the members of the Scheduled Castes. Establishment of separate Sikh temples after the brutal murder of Sant Ramanand of Dera Sach Khand at Ravidass temple in Vienna by the Sikh militants emboldened the sectarian divide. This study found that the elderly members of the Scheduled Castes are subject to social exclusion. Ronki "Despite improvement in economic position over the years, there has not been a commensurate improvement in the social status of Dalits even after their conversion to Sikhism as caste iniquities, in the form of dominant cultural patterns, still persist in Punjab. The respondents revealed that the businesses of the Scheduled Castes particularly in the villages of Punjab are affected due to the prevalence of the caste system. Inter-caste marriage is subject to social resentment and sometimes social segregation" (Ram (2007:4070).

In the backdrop of discussion on caste, the researcher has tried to understand the prevalence of social exclusion in Punjab. In this context, 74 year-old male from village Talan in district Jalandhar told, "I belong to a Scheduled Caste (SC) community. There are three Sikh temples in the village. The Sikh temple is occupied by the Sikhs and they do not allow any other caste man or woman to occupy a position in the management of the temple. The caste system is prevailing till date. Sikh and Hindus practice caste and generally do not marry their boy or girl outside their caste. Hindus indulge in caste atrocities. The Scheduled Castes (SCs) are subjected to various kinds of humiliations and abuses at public places".

In a similar vein, 81 year-old-male from Nurpur in district Kapurthala revealed in anguish that, "In what kind of society we live today. The SCs have been suffering due to the caste system since centuries. Nothing has changed. Everyone talks about casteless society but it is nothing but hollow rhetoric. I do not know when it will disappear".

Discussing existence of discrimination in the educational institutions of Punjab, 68 year-old teacher, now retired argued, "I was a teacher in a Government Senior Secondary School in Hoshiarpur. The upper caste teachers in the school discriminated with me because I belong to Scheduled Caste community. For Instance, my colleagues used to tell the parents of the students that I belong to a lower caste. I found that the majority of the upper caste people in Punjab do not want to see a Scheduled Caste (SC) man or woman to rise up socially and economically in life. I cannot change their mentality since it is embedded in in their mind. I also noticed during my service that the upper caste teachers discriminate with the students belonging to the marginalized sections of the society. Now I am retired but still I face caste discrimination."

Similarly, 73 year-old male running a shop in the main bazaar of Jalandhar district narrated that "I run a cloth shop in the main bazaar. My clients are from different religion and castes. In the market, the upper caste people always speaks bad about the lower caste people. Reservation is always a topic over which they shout and abuse openly. We have a shopkeeper Association. The association is managed by the upper caste people. My name was proposed by like-minded shopkeeper for the post of Secretary General but there was strong opposition by the upper caste people just because of my caste. I strongly believe the caste system will never die in India". Now people are carrying this cancer to the Western countries and to some extent the upper caste people have succeeded in spreading this cancer in the world.

## Social Exclusion in UK

"Caste is a mark of identity and, through it, individual are assigned high or low status primary through the kinship group. The Punjabi word *zat* equated with the concept of caste and is defined as 'non-localized endogamous unit" (Kessinger, 1974:35). "Endogamy maintains the inextricable connection between kinship and caste. Significant caste inequalities and distinctions exist in Punjab. Despite an explicit opposition to caste differentiations within the scriptures and spiritual teaching of Sikhism, caste inequalities and discrimination are a significant feature of the lived reality of contemporary Indian Punjab" (Taylor et al., 2007:338).

The Indian community has interval divisions caused by issues such as origin, caste, religion, and politics. The Punjabi community is divided into a number of social classes encompassing Upper class, middle class, working class, and the lower class. The Punjabi community is also a socially stratified community. "Sikh communities are grouped and classified in complex ways" (Kiyotaka Sato, 2010). "Caste has moved beyond India with India diaspora as the latter does not move as individuals, but takes its cultural baggage along". The caste system is prevalent in the United Kingdom. Caste-based temples in almost in the whole of the United Kingdom indicate that the caste system is quite prominent among the Punjabis" (Kumar, 2004:115).

A study conducted by Equality and Human Rights Commission demonstrates that "inequalities experienced by ethnic communities across many areas of life in modern Britain, including education, employment, and the criminal justice system. Race remains the most commonly recorded motivation for hate crime in England and Wales at 82 percent[4]. "In 1997, a social exclusion unit was set up with the remit to implement local initiatives to target socially excluded groups, and inclusion agenda has never really evolved. Social exclusion in Britain has become the marker against which success or failure of the welfare system is judged, rather than the distribution of wealth and income across society as social transfers". "In 1999 the British Government set up units for neighborhood renewal, rough sleepers, teenage pregnancy, children and young people in designated areas of poverty and disadvantage. However, the Social Exclusion Report released in 2014 admitted that identified unskilled, unqualified adults, people with chronic illness or disabilities and poor ethnic minority com munities were helped little by these measures, and it is only very recently that social policy for inclusion has moved more towards whole community participation and consultation. Tolerance of migrants in Britain is low because of perceived lack of control of immigration". (Lin and Hermann, 2015:117).

The respondents during the interview revealed that the Jat Sikhs and Brahmins practice discrimination on the basis of social background in UK against the people of the lower castes. When inter-caste marriages take place it is subject to social resentment and social segregation. Civil society organizations such as caste Watch UK, the Dalit Network, and the National Secular Society have advocated for the legislation against the offense of the caste discrimination and it forced the UK government to pass a legislation. As a result, the Equality Act 2010 was passed by the British Parliament which treats caste equivalent to the race. The respondents from the members of the lower caste are skeptical about the annihilation of the caste system through the law. Many of them asserted that caste is going to stay because it is religiously and culturally embedded into the minds and hearts of the upper caste people.

A study conducted by Sharma in UK states, "a large number of marriages among the Indian diaspora are still arranged within the confines of caste, and the rules of 'purity' and 'pollution' associated with caste are also strictly adhered to. They claim that caste consciousness and associated notions of superiority and inferiority are passed on to successive generations. Furthermore, is claimed that there are instances that point to a growth of pride of Jats/Punjabi (as seen in popular music video and lyrics) amongst the Sikh community that reinforces caste and or community consciousness" (Sharma, 2012:32).

The researcher also conducted in depth interviews with the respondents in UK and collected empirical data to substantiate the universe of the study. In this context, 84 years-old male from Southall argued, "I came to England 50 years back. Upper caste people talk about the caste system. In Sikhism, there is no place for the caste discrimination but the Jat Sikhs practices caste in England. Similarly, Hindus do not mix up with the people of the lower caste in UK. The attitude of the upper caste people did not change even in the advanced countries toward the people of the lower castes. One can see separate Sikh, Ravidassi or Buddhist, Valmik temples in UK. Jat Sikhs running Sikh temples do not allow any Dalit caste member to become a trustee of the temple. Caste has never died and will never die in this world unless or until the practitioners stop practicing".

In a similar vein, 83 year-old male from Birmingham told that, "Caste is prevalent in UK. People bring caste with them. Hindus or Sikhs all are the same in matters of caste discrimination. I belong to Ravidassi community. Inter-caste marriage does not take place. If at all it happens, there is violent reaction by the upper caste people. Let me give you an example. My elder son was in love with a Jat Sikh girl and wanted to marry her. I went to the parents of the girl who happened to be a Jat Sikh from Punjab but currently the whole family lives in Southall. The Jat Sikh father of the girl simply refused to marry because of the caste. This is the situation. Indians will never learn from the developed countries". In yet another 86 year-old female met the researcher in the Valmiki temple, Wolverhampton revealed that, "I come daily to this temple. I clean the floor and statue, portraits etc. I belong to a Valmiki community from Ali Mohalla in district Jalandhar. For the last 35 years I have not seen even a single Hindu or Sikh visiting this temple. Caste is no doubt very much in their blood". From the above discussion with the respondents in UK, we can surmise that the caste is prevalent in UK and members of the marginalized communities are socially excluded.

## Conclusion

This chapter has tried to understand the socio-economic status of the elderly living in Punjab and England. This chapter has also analyzed the nature and dynamics of social exclusion, remittances, loneliness, isolation, elderly abuse and priorities of healthcare services available to the elderly from the lived experience of elderly Punjabis living in Punjab and UK in a comparative perspective. Further, this chapter is based on primary and secondary data. The primary data was collected by the researcher by conducting in-depth interviews with the respondents in Punjabi as the respondents lacked fluency in English language.

The primary data collected from 50 families from Punjab and 25 families living in three districts of UK. The difference is because of population size in both the countries. In Punjab, the researcher has found that the left behind elderly depend on remittances sent by their children from UK. Some of the elderly draw pension from their respective departments or companies in India but that is meagre hence they need extra financial help to meet their day to day expenses. Some are satisfied and some are not because their children stopped sending money to them from abroad.

The researcher has also found that in Punjab, the elderly people feel isolated and lonely because their children have migrated to UK. Due to poor health services particularly in the government hospitals, the health of the elderly people is always at risk in Punjab. On the other hand, the elderly are happy with the comprehensive and quality healthcare services in UK. The elderly feel isolated and lonely in UK. The elderly Punjabis feel isolated and lonely because of the language barriers, different culture, and aggressive and disrespectful behaviors of the grandchildren. It has been observed that intergenerational strife is prominent among the Punjabis living in UK.

The researcher has also recorded that in Punjab and UK, the elderly people are subject to various types of abuse such as disrespect, humiliation by their own children and grand-children. The perpetrators of abuse are mostly family members. This study has also found that due to prevailing isolation and loneliness, the resourceful elderly do not prefer to stay permanently in UK.

This study also found that there are similarities and differences in economic status, abuse, isolation, loneliness, social exclusion and healthcare services in both the societies. However, it is evident from the discussion that caste is prevalent Punjab and UK. The Dalit assert that they are victims of the caste system. They further emphasize that the caste system is a reality of Punjabi diaspora and elderly face exclusion on the basis of caste outside their homes. Though generalization are not possible as this study was very narrow data base and is based on purposive sampling. However, we can draw few inferences from this.

## References

*Agewell Study on Isolation in old age*. (2010). Agewell Foundation, New Delhi, available at https://www.ifa-fiv.org/wp-content/uploads/2012/12/Jan2010-Study-Isolation-Old-Agė.pdf, retrieved 20 Jan 2016.

Bhatia, V.K. (2008). Towards critical genre analysis. In V.K. Bhatia, J. Flowerdew and R. H. Jones (Eds) *Advances in Discourse Studies* London: Routledge, 166-177. BKPAI. (2011).The status of elderly in Punjab, 2011, available at http://www.isec.ac.in/BKPAI_Punjab State%20report.pdf, retrieved on Jan 2017.

Butt and A O'Neil. (2014).'Let's Move On': *Black and minority ethnic older people's views on research findings.* Joseph Rowntree Foundation, Retrieved from www.jrf.org.uk/publications/black-and-minority-ethnic-older-peoples-views-research-findings.

Chang, J., Peysakhovich, F., Wang, W and Zhu, J. (Undated).The UK Health Care System. Available at http://assets.ce.columbia.edu/pdf/actu/actu-uk.pdf.

CRRID Annual Report (2013-14), available at http://www.crrid.res.in/pdf/Annual Report.pdf, retrieved on 25 Feb 2016.

Dyson, Tim and Mick Moore. (1983). "On kinship structure, female autonomy, and demographic behavior in India", *Population and Development*, 3(5): 3-18.

Evans, R. G. (2002) "Financing Health Care: Taxation and the Alternatives," In Mossialos, E., Dixon, A., Figueras, J., Kutzin, J., *Funding Health Care: Options for Europe.* Buckingham and Philadelphia: Open University Press, 31-58.

Faquinello, P and Marcon, S.S. (2011). Friends and Neighbors: An active social network for adult and elderly hypertensive individuals, NCBI.45 (6), 1345-52. Available at https:// www. ncbi. nlm. nih. gov/ pubmed /22241191.

Ghuman, Ranjit Singh. (2012). The Sikh Community in Indian Punjab: Some Socio-Economic Challenges, *Journal of Punjab Studies*. 19(1):87-109.

Hansson R. O, Jones W. H, Carpenter B. N, Remondet J. H. (1987). Loneliness and adjustment to old age, *International Journal of Human Development*. 27 (1), 41–5.

House of Commons Health Committee report (2017), available at https://publications. parliament. uk /pa/ cm 200304 /cmselect/ cmhealth / 111/111.pdf, retrieved on 15 October 2017.

Husain, M. I., Waheed, W. and Husain, N. (2006). Self -harm in British South Asian women: psychosocial correlates and strategies for prevention. *Annals of General Psychiatry*, 5. 7.

Jagannathan, P. (1996). *National Asian Womens health organization*: Caring for the caregivers India Currents. www. sawnet.org /health / sahealth. html.

Kai, J and Hedges, C. (1998).*Minority ethnic community participation in needs assessment and service development in primary care*: perceptions of Pakistani and Bangladeshi people about psychological distress. Health Expectations, 2, 7-20.

Kapur, Promilla. (1977). Elderly Abuse Some Counselling Tips, *Research and DevelopmentJournal,* 3(3): 13-23.

Kessinger, T.G. (1974). Vilayatpur 1848-1968: *Social and Economic Change in a North Indian Village*, Berkley: University of California Press.

Kiyotaka Sato. (2010). Division among Sikh Communities in Britain and the Role of Caste System: A Case Study of Four Gurdwara in Multi-Ethnic -Leicester, *Journal of Punjabi Studies,* pp.1-26.

Kumar,Vivek.(2004).Understanding Dalit Diaspora, *Economic and Polticial Weekly*, 39.(1):114-116.

Lin, Kai and Hermann, Peter.(2015). Social Quality Theory:*A New Perspective on Social Development*, Berghahn Books.

Levitt, P. (1998).Social remittances: Migration driven local-level forms of cultural diffusion. *International Migration Review,* 32 (4):926–948.

Litwin, Howard. (1998). The Provision of Informal Support by Elderly People Residing in Assisted Living Facilities, *The Gerontologist*. 38(2): 239-246.

Nangia, Ethel Ngere. (2015). Energizing the Elderly through Remittances: Opportunities for Active Ageing in Cameroon, *International Journal of Innovative Research and Development*. 4(1): 197-203.

Peplau, L. A., and Perlman, D. (1982b). Theoretical Approaches to Loneliness. In L. A. Peplau and D. Perlman (Eds.), *Loneliness: A sourcebook of current theory, research, and therapy* New York: Wiley, pp. 123-134.

Peter Martin, Bo Hagberg, Leonard Wi Poon. (1997). Predictions of Loneliness in Centenarians: A Parallel Study, *Journal of Cross-cultural Gerontology*, 12(3): 203-204.

Puri, N. (2007).*British Hindus Divided by Caste*, BBC News, available at http://news. bbc. co. uk /2 /hi /uk news/7156139. stm, retrieved on 15 August 2017.

Pyrek, Kelly M. (2006). *Forensic Nursing*, New York, Taylor and Francis.

Ram, Ronki. (2007). Social Exclusion, Resistance, and Deras: Exploring the myth of Casteless Society in Punjab, *Economic and Political Weekly*, 42(40), 4066-4074.

Seema, G. (2005). Remittance Debate Revisited: New Evidence from Indian Migrant Labor in Lebanon. International Union for Scientific Study XXV International Population Conference Tours, France July 18-23.

Sharma, Sheetal. (2012). Immigrants in Britain: A Study of the Indian Diaspora, *Diaspora Studies*.5 (1), 14-43.

Singh, Lakhwinder.(2005). 'Deceleration and Industrial Growth and Rural Industrialization Strategy for Rural Punjab,' *Journal of Punjab Studies*, 12(2):271-284.

Sonwalker, Prasun.(2018).British PM appoints A Minister for Loneliness, New Delhi, *The* Hindustan Times.

Spitze, G., and Logan, J. (1990).Sons, daughters, and intergenerational support. Journal of Marriage and the Family, 52, 420-430.

Taylor, Steve; Singh Manjit and Booth Deborah.(2007). Migrtaion, development, and inequality: Estern Punjbai transnationalism, *Global Netrworks*,7(3):328-347.

## Notes

1. Ref: Agewell Foundation, New Delhi, Agewell Study on Isolation in old age (2010), available at https://www.ifa-fiv.org/wp-content/uploads/2012/12/Jan2010-Study-Isolation-Old-Age.pdf, retrieved 20 Jan 2016.
2. Ibid.13.
3. House of Commons Health Committee report, available at https://publications. parliament. uk/ pa /cm 200304 /cmselect /cmhealth / 111 / 111. pdf, retrieved 15 October 2017.
4. Healing a Divided Britain: the need for a comprehensive race equality strategy, Equality and Human Rights Commission, UK. Available at www. equality human rights. com /sites /default/ files / healing a divided britain the need for a comprehensive race equality strategy final. pdf, retrieved on 15 August 2017.

# VIII

# Conclusion

Chapter I gave a brief introduction of the study. We have looked into migration and ageing in Punjab and England (UK). This chapter has also discussed the patterns of migration of elderly Punjabis from Punjab to England (UK). The Punjabis have been migrating to England (UK) since colonial times. During pre-colonial period, migration was driven by Europe's mercantile needs and centered on the establishment of plantations for the large-scale cultivation of sugar, cotton, coffee, and tobacco. British abolished slavery in 1833 (Slavery Abolition Act, 1833, British Parliament, UK) and subsequently turned to indentured labor to respond to labor demands in the empire colonies. Punjabis also migrated when Punjab was experiencing drought and famines and the employment opportunities consequently declined. Punjabis were taken as indentured labor to work in British colonies particularly in British African colonies. It was the handy work of the British government. Some of the Punjabis were recruited by the British Army and sent to different parts of the world. We have found that a majority of the Punjabis migrated during colonial times did not return back to the homeland. Many of them settled permanently in British colonies and formed families. Therefore, today we have members of extended family out of these Punjabi families.

Different patterns of migrations during post-colonial period took place. Migration during this time was not out of financial requirement but it became a culture among the Punjabis (Singh and Tatla, 2008). After the liberation of immigration policies by the developed nations, immigration was made easy and simple. While taking advantages of the liberalized immigration policies, the majority of the Punjabis applied for immigrant as well family visa. Immigrated daughters or sons after obtaining British citizenship started sponsoring their older parents. Similarly, older parents who were already settled in England (UK) started sponsoring their left behind children. Last but not the least, a regular streams of students also went to UK. This study has observed that many students who came to UK, did not go back to India. It is these process of migration of Punjabis to UK in both during colonial and post- colonial period has formed a big diaspora in UK.

It is in this socio-economic background that we have located in this chapter the concept of ageing in India and England (UK). We have observed that older persons have been experiencing social and emotional problems in both the countries. In India, we have found that despite several welfare policies and schemes formulated for the older persons, the elderly people have been experiencing problems in availing the benefits of the policies and schemes on two accounts, one is because of inadequate awareness about the welfare policies and schemes and second is corrupt bureaucracy. In India, we have also found that the elderly people suffer more. Along with lack of awareness about welfare policies and schemes and corrupt bureaucracy there are inadequate healthcare services and shortage of doctors and nurses especially in government hospitals. In England (UK) we have observed that the older persons are treated carefully. The healthcare services are free of cost for the older citizens. We have found that doctors and nurses are very sensitive to the treatment of the elderly people. We have also found that the hospitals run by the government provide home delivery services to the older persons in England (UK).

It also includes statement of problem. Here we have argued that, migration has been taking place from Punjab since time immemorial. However, it picked up during and after the colonial period. Some migrants from Doaba region of Punjabi also took their elderly parents along with them and some left of them behind. Migrated as well left behind parents face physical, psychological, emotional and health challenges. We have found that although there have been a number of studies which have studied the status of migrant Punjabis, there have been studies which have given account of elderly within in India and Punjab. However, there have not been studies which compare the elderly in India and UK.

In this background It has undertaken review of literature related to the subject, Accordingly, we have found that Darshan Singh Tatla (2008), Verne. A Dusenbery (1989), Paramjit Singh Judge(1994), Manjit Singh(2013), Swarn Singh Kalhon (2016), Steve Taylor (2015) have conducted studies on Sikh Migration, Sikh Diaspora, and Sikh Diaspora Philanthropy, Sikh Diaspora Politics. Oberio (1980), Waltron-Roberts(2004), Supriya Singh(2016) have conducted studies regarding Indian diaspora. Further, we have also found that, Satwanti Kapoor(2004) and BKPAI(2011) have done study on the Elderly in Punjab. Similarly, in England a few studies by

Amarjit Singh (2014) and Sarah Lamb (2009) have been conducted but they are few.

It also includes the objectives of the study. The specific objectives of the study includes the followings: To assess patterns of migration of Punjabis from Doaba to England; To analyze the socioeconomic condition of elderly Punjabis migrant families in Doaba and England; To examine the family structure of Punjabi migrants in Doaba and England; To inquire into ageing conditions of elderly Punjabis left behind in Doaba and those who have migrated from Doaba and settled in England. Along with this, this chapter also includes research questions. Next we have discussed the methodology of this study. To begin with we have tried to give a rational of choice of the universe. As far as, universe is concerned. Punjab state of India and UK are the two places where this study has been conducted. Within Punjab we have selected Jalandhar, Hoshiarpur and Kapurthala in Doaba. In England (UK) we have selected Southall, Wolverhampton and Birmingham as the universe of this study of area. The rationale of the choice of the universe was that through the secondary sources, we have come to know that a substantial number of people have migrated from these districts of Punjab to England (UK). As far as the rational of choice of the universe of the study in the UK is concerned we have come to know that most of the migrated Punjabis live in three areas viz Southall, Birmingham and Wolverhampton of England (UK).

It also includes the methods of selections of respondents. Therefore, the researcher tried to have an assessment of the density of the population of migrant and immigrant population in Punjab and England (UK) respectively. The researcher has found that there exists a big population of the elderly people in both the places. In such circumstances, in-depth interviews from selected cases of elderly people were considerd to be the best way to select a respresentative sampling for this study. Accordingly, the researcher has applied purposive and snow ball sampling technique. On the basis of this, 50 elderly Punjabi families respondents were selected in three district of Doaba region of Punjab. In Jalandhar 20, Hoshiarpur 20 and Kapurthala 10 respondent families were selected respectively. Similarly, In England(UK) 25 elderly respondent families were selected. In Southall 15, Wolverhampton 05 and Birmingham 05 respectively. For the information of the readers, it is informed that Google shows these places in England(UK) as districts but the natives call it province. Most of the respondents were head of the family beloging to 60-80 years of age.

It also includes Tools of Data Collection, the primary data was collected through mixed methods. The data was extracted in an infromal interview with the help of interview guide. The first part of the interview guide included the information about the demograhic information. Second part included the health status of the respondents and third and the last inculded in-depth anlayse of socio-economic, family and health status of the elderly Punjabis. The interviews guide is attached in Annexure-I. Most of the conversations with the elderly Punjabis at the both the places were held in Punjabi language as the elderly Punjabis were not conversant with English. In addition to this, discussions were held with the younger population in both the destination of the universe and relevant data was collected. Last but not the least, this chapter has also included chapterisation of the study. Accordingly, this study has been divided into eight chapters including introduction and conclusion.

Chapter II is 'Research Settings'. After giving a brief historical background of Punjab. It has very briefly explored the socio-economic profile of Punjab and England (UK). In Punjab, we have discussed three districts Jalandhar, Hoshiarpur and Kapurthala. We have seen population and literacy rate in Punjab. We have observed that Punjab has a high literacy rate of 75.84, which is above the national level. Moreover, a high percentage of population is graduate and above. It is also interesting to note from Table 2.2 that a high percentage of population in Jalandhar and Hoshiarpur belongs to Scheduled Castes (SCs) that is 37 percent. Similarly, we have seen three districts in England (UK) Southall, Birmingham and Wolverhampton. In England (UK) we have explored the demographic profile of these places of the universe of the study. We have also discussed the causes of migration from Punjab to England (UK). Further, this chapter II has also discussed the caste system which is part of the social structure among Punjabis of both the countries.

We have tried to understand how the caste system is working in both the countries and how the people belonging to the marginalized sections of the society are excluded from the mainstream society.

Chapter III is 'Conceptual Clarifications and Literature Survey'.As the health and well-being and other concepts have general meaning however we have tried to give their specific meanings in which they have been used in this chapter. Indian and Punjabi diaspora in European, American and African countries, in particular have drawn attention of the scholars of history, sociology, demography, economics, and of course, literature. Their attention towards Indians settled in European countries, America and Africa is understandable as they remit a great amount of foreign exchange and wield considerable influence in shaping policies of the governments of the countries of their domicile and India and vice versa.

This study has examined the elderly Punjabi migrants and left behind in a comparative perspective between two diverse geographical regions that is Doaba (Punjab) and England (UK). Since the 19th century, the members of Punjabi families have been migrating to the developed countries. Our findings demonstrate that during the First World War, young, single and poor tend to migrate to the British colonies to pay off agricultural debt. Some young Punjabis joined British Indian army and migrated to several British Colonies to assist the British Army. The majority of the members of such Punjabi families belonged to the Sikh community. However, Dalits (Ad-Dharmi) also migrated to various western countries. In the early phase of migration, the push factor such as poverty, political persecution and riots pushed the Punjabis to migrate but later on pull factors such as individual choice have become the norm of the day. In this context, we can safely say that economically well-off families started migrating to the Western world to set up business. The Punjabis who went on Immigration Visa become citizen legally in UK hence they started the process to invite their left behind members such as spouse, children and elderly parents. This study found that the migration of Punjabis followed different trajectories. Some Punjabis arrived in the United Kingdom from African British colonies after expulsion from Uganda in 1972 and some directly migrated from India. This migration resulted in building the extended family. Family reunification under the liberal immigration policies of the United Kingdom gave impetus to bulk migration of Punjabis. In recent times, a lot of students from Punjab took admission in various UK universities to study. The Punjabi Diaspora in the United Kingdom is dynamic and vibrant.

Chapter IV is 'Policies, legislations and Institution for Older persons in India and UK'. This chapter began with depiction of older age and ageing. It defined that there are three interrelated processes of ageing: physical, psychological and social. The aspect of ageing also includes internal differentiation of class, gender, region, religion, educational background has been analyzes these factors in the field. We have found that these factors are prevailing in the universe of our study. Further, this chapter has revealed how United Nations defines ageing. We have found that the United Nation defines a country as ageing where the proportion of the people over 60 years. United Nation has also estimated that there 10.3 Crores of population which is 60 years and above in the world. Therefore United Nation has revealed number of policies so that older people can live dignified life.

Apart from UN, this chapter has also recorded the national policies and programs for elderly in India. Apart from the general articles of the constitution which upholds the rights of individuals, we have mapped the legislations for the elderly in India. For instance, Hindu adoption and Maintenance Act 1956 envisages that a Hindu child (male/female) will take care of his aged and infirm parents. In the same vein, along with sons and daughters, there are obligations on the State to take care of elderly in India. The state has entitled old age pension schemes which provide Rs200 per month per person. However, it can be argued that in today's time it is not a sufficient amount to survive. Moreover, there is a National Pension System as well which depends on how much a person has contributed while he was young. There are also health related policies by the state and private sector both. Above all, the Government of India has brought 'Senior citizen Act 2007' which provides number of privileges to the senior citizens. For instance it has made maintenance of parents and senior citizens by children and relatives obligatory, establishment of Old age home for senior citizens. Ministry of Social Justice and Empowerment is a nodal ministry which looks after the specific problems of the elderly. Different other ministries like, Health and Family Welfare, Railways, Ministry of Civil Aviation, Telecommunications etc. have been asked to provide their facilities and privileges to the senior citizens.

Further, this chapter has also analyzed the programs and policies available for the senior citizens in Punjab. For instance there exists, 'Old age allowance' scheme for older persons who attain the age of 65 years. In Punjab along with this there are many other policies and programs for the elderly women also, like for instance elderly woman above 60 years enjoy free travel in Punjab.

Along with these programs and policies at the national and state level we have mapped the programs and policies that prevail in the UK as well. At the outset, we have recorded what are the ways in which senior citizens can migrate to UK? What is the specific policy in this regard? It is interested to note that UK allows senior citizen visas who can demonstrate that they need long term personal care because of their illness. Apart from these there are number of legislations and constitutional provisions to safeguard the rights of the elderly in UK. Free passes for buses, discounts in trains and trams, free passport, free gas safety checks, state pensions, funeral payments, winter fuel payment etc. are few facilities available to the elderly in UK. There is also a facility of old age homes, free home checkups and medical facilities in UK. Last but not the least, this chapter has also recorded the roles of NGOs for the welfare of the elderly in UK and India. In the light of this review of programs and policies for the elderly in UK and India, it would be interesting to find out in the field whether these programs and policies are being implemented or they are only on paper. It would also be interesting to check whether the respondents are aware of these programs and policies for their welfare. And lastly what do they feel about these programs and policies. Are the satisfied or not?

This chapter further informed us that the population of elderly/senior citizens is increasing day by day. This trend is seen in every part of the world. According to the UN approximately 20.7 per cent of the world's population would be elderly by 2050. On the other hand World Health Organization (WHO) has argued that the Southeast Asian regions would have increased life expectancy and hence by 2050 SEAR will have 21.4 per cent of its population above 60 years. Hence, this analysis also suggests that as the ageing population would increase in future, it would become necessary to have effective programs and policies for the senior citizens in place or they will be left out to suffer. In this light this chapter has made the researcher to analyze the need for future preparation for our ageing population.

Chapter V is 'Family structure and socio-economic status of Elderly Punjabis in Punjab' This chapter has explored the family structure and socioeconomic status of elderly Punjabis in Punjab. We have tried to understand various forms of family including joint, nuclear and extended family. We have looked into isolation and loneliness among the Punjabi elderly. We have also examined social exclusion and elderly abuse in Punjab. We have discussed about the engagements of the elderly Punjabis in Punjab. We have examined the healthcare system in Punjab. We have tried to examine the impact of migration of children on the left behind elderly Punjabis. We have examined the role of remittance in the life of the left behind parents in the state of Punjab. This chapter has tried to understand and analyze the socio-economic status of the elderly Punjabis in three districts of Doaba region of Punjab namely Jalandhar, Hoshiarpur and Kapurthala. This chapter is constructed on primary and secondary data. The primary data was extracted from the respondents with the help of preformulated interview schedule. The researcher conducted in depth interviews in the local language as the respondents lacked fluency in English language. Later on, the narratives were translated into English by the researcher himself. The secondary data was collected to substantiate our arguments and findings from the field. A number of health reports and government documents were consulted for the same.

First and foremost, we have discussed theoretical dimensions of the family. After this, the chapter has dealt empirically the issues of family structure in three districts of the universe of the study. Through observation and general conversation, we have found that joint families are still prevalent in big way in Punjab. The data reveals that because emotional support and social security, Punjabis choose living in a joint family system. Due to industrialization, urbanization, and migration, however, the joint family system has been breaking. The researcher has found the members of joint family have migrated because number of reasons. Such as in search of occupation, education or lack of adjustment. Migration abroad is also major cause of disintegration of joint family. However, we have found in our studies that elderly prefer joint families with their immediate sons and grandchildren.

The next aspect of analysis was the financial status of the elderly in the universe of the study. We have found that most of the elderly in Punjab who are receiving help from their children or who are settled abroad are very satisfied with their economic condition. In these cases, the respondents were having double income one from their retired job and second from their sons, daughters or other relatives.

Secondly, most of the houses who have their sons or daughters living abroad they have well-furnished houses with all electronic goods. However the respondents revealed that these electronic items are not bought specifically for the elderly rather it is bought for their sons, daughters or other relatives living abroad. It is so because they will need when they come back to India. Thirdly, we have found that the economic condition of those people are very bad who survive only on their pension. It is difficult for them to live happily.

We have also tried to understand the experience and perception of elderly about the health services in three districts of Punjab where this study is conducted. The researcher has found that in spite of number of health schemes for elderly and general people in Punjab, the citizens do not get any satisfaction from public health department, doctors, and nurses. The respondents, the elderly men, and women have revealed the pathetic condition of the health services available in Punjab. The behavior of doctors and nurses are worse. There is lack of security about the suffering of the elderly patients. There is rampant corruption in the government hospitals. The medicines are not available. Even most essential facilities for elderly such as ambulances and wheel chairs are missing. Asked if they would like to visit the government hospital if private hospitals are available and affordable. The elderly replied that "they would never like to visit a government hospital again".

In this context, most of the elderly those who can afford go to a private hospital and are happy. However, those who survive on their meager pensions have to visit government hospitals are very unhappy and feel lots of stress and strain. Some elderly were found to be in strain because their sons and daughters stopped sending remittances to their old parents. The elderly have also revealed existing caste based exclusion in the Punjabi society. The elderly feel unhappy when they are alone in the absence of their loved ones hence they feel isolated and lonely.

Chapter VI is 'Family structure and socio-economic status of elderly Punjabis in UK' This chapter has explored the family structure and socioeconomic status of elderly Punjabis in England (UK). We have tried to understand various forms of family including joint, nuclear and extended family. We have attempted to look into isolation and loneliness among the Punjabi elderly in England (UK). We have looked into social exclusion and elderly abuse in England (UK). We have discussed about the engagements of the elderly Punjabis in England (UK). This chapter also examine the healthcare system in England (UK).

This chapter has tried to anlayse the family structure of the Punjabi families, However, due to industrialization, capitalism, and migration, the young people are drifting towards nuclear families. The inter-generational gap is prevalent in a cosmopolitan society of Britain. The family conflict arises when the older people stick to traditional norms and values and the young one defies traditional norms and values. Elderly who are currently living with their children depend on children for financial matters. Hence, most of the daily needs of the elderly parents are taken care of by the children.

Socially, they feel alienated and depressed because of English language barrier. The elderly parents living with the children have to depend on them for going to the market or to the place of relatives and friends. Cold weather is also one of the factors due to which these elderly Punjabi parents remain, most of the time, within the four walls of the house. Sometimes, these elderly parents get worried about their left-behind children in Punjab. The loss of close relatives and friends back in the homeland also disturbs them emotionally. Sometimes, it can also cause mental depression.

So far household engagements of the elderly Punjabi parents are concerned, the field survey found that the majority of the elderly Punjabi parents finds themselves engaged in the care of the grandchildren. Women remain busy in performing household chores. Despite social and economic disadvantages in an alien society, the elderly Punjabis feel satisfied with the quality and timely services provided by the healthcare centers run by the UK government. For older Britain citizens free medical services are an added advantages. From regular medical check-up to hospitalization, all the medical services in the UK for the older citizens are free. "The United Kingdom provides public healthcare to all permanent residents, about 58 million people Healthcare coverage is free at the point of need, and is paid for by general taxation" (Josh Chang et al., 2009). The respondents during the field survey informed that they are quite satisfied with the medical services in UK. "More than two thirds of people over the age of 65 say they are satisfied with the NHS, compared to just over half of 25-34 year olds.

91percent of people over the age of 65 are satisfied with their Gross Product (GP), compared to 74percent of 25-34 year olds. The same pattern is repeated for inpatient and outpatient care. For social care services, Social Services Inspectorate inspections of services for older people regularly show user satisfaction rates of around 80percent" (UK Government Report, 2011). Despite all excellent healthcare facilities available for the older people in UK, they still feel lonely and isolated. Sometimes, they encounter humiliations and abuses at the hand of the grand-children.

Chapter VII is, 'Elderly Punjabis in Punjab and England (UK): A Comparison'. This chapter has discussed about socio economic status, social exclusion, elderly abuse, isolation and loneliness of the elderly Punjabis in a comparative perspective. We have discussed social cultural and economic challenges experienced by the elderly Punjabis in Punjab and England (UK) with or without children. We have examined the integration experiences of the elderly in a British society in UK. This chapter has tried to understand the socio-economic status of the elderly living in Punjab and England. This chapter has also analyzed the nature and dynamics of social exclusion, remittances, elderly abuse and healthcare services from the lived experience of elderly Punjabis living in Punjab and UK in a comparative perspective.

This chapter is based on primary and secondary data. The researcher conducted in-depth interviews with the respondents in the local language Punjabi as the respondents lacked fluency in English language. The primary data collected from 50 families from Punjab and 25 families in UK. The difference is because of population size in both the countries. In Punjab, the researcher has found that the elderly left behind depend on remittances sent by their children from UK. Some of the elderly draw pension but that is meagre hence they need extra financial help to meet their day to day expenses. Some are satisfied and some are not because their children stopped sending money to them.

The researcher has found that in Punjab, the elderly people feel isolated and lonely because their children have migrated to the United Kingdom. Due to poor health services particularly in the government hospitals, the health of the elderly people is always at risk. On the other hand, the elderly are happy with the comprehensive and quality healthcare services in UK. The elderly feel isolated and lonely the United Kingdom, the elderly Punjabis feel isolated and lonely because of language barriers, different culture, and aggressive and disrespectful behaviors of the grandchildren. In this context, one can observe that intergenerational strife is prominent among the Punjabis living in UK. In Punjab and UK, the elderly people are subject to various types of abuse such as disrespect, humiliation, and abuse in the public places.

The perpetrators of abuse are mostly family members. This study has also found that due to prevailing isolation and loneliness, the resourceful elderly do not prefer to stay permanently in the United Kingdom. From this study, we can safely conclude that there are similarities and differences in economic status, abuse, isolation and loneliness, social exclusion and healthcare services in both the societies. However, it is evident from the discussion that caste is prevalent in Punjabi communities. The Dalits assert that they are victims of the caste system. They further emphasize that the caste system is a reality of Punjabi diaspora.

# Bibliography


Action on Elderly Abuse (AEA). Bulletin, May-June 1995, No 11, Astral house, London, UK. Agnew, Vijay, (Eds) (2004). Diaspora, Memory and Identity: A Search for home Toronto: University of Toronto.

Agnihotri, Rama Kanta. (1987*). Crisis of Identity: The Sikhs in England.* New Delhi: Bahri Publications.

Agnihotri, H.K. (1976). Problems of the old age. *Journal of Psychological Researchers*, 22, 1, 17-29.

Alam, Moneer and Anup Karan. (2013). "Health Status of Elderly in India: Trends and Differentials", in G. Gridhar, K.M. Sathyanarayana, S. Kumar, K.S. James and Moneer Alam (eds), Population Ageing in India, New York, Cambridge University Press.

Alam, Moneer, James K.S., Gridhar G., Sathyanarayana K.M., et al. (2012 ). "Report on the Status of Elderly in Select States of India, 2011", United Nations Population Fund (India), http:// india. unfpa. org / drive/Ageing Report 2012 F. pdf.

Alder, Leonore Laoeb and Uwe P. Gielen (Eds). ( 2003). *Migration: Immigration and Emigration in International Perspective,* Westport, CT: Praeger.

Ambedkar. B. R. (1944) *Annihilation of Caste*.Dept.of Education. Government of Maharashtra.

Anderson, Joan M. (1987). "Migration and Health: Perspective on Immigrant Women". *Sociology of Health and Illness*.9 (4):410-438.

Anetzberger, G.J; J.E. Korbin and C. Austin. (1994). Alcoholism and elder abuse, *Journal of Interpersonal Violence*, 9 (2), 184-193.

Andrade-Eekhoff, Katharine (Undated). "The Untapped Riches of Remittances? *NACLA Report on the America.* 38(4):42.

Angelo, Michael. (1997*). The Sikh Diaspora: Tradition and Change in an Immigrant Community.* New York: Garland Publishing Inc.

Arun, P. Bali. (1999). (Eds.) Understanding Graying – people of India. New Delhi: Inter India Publications.

Baker A.A. (1975). Granny battering.*Modern Geriatrics*, 5(8), 20–24.

Ballantyne, Tony. (2006). Between Colonialism and Diaspora: Sikh Cultural Formations in an Imperial World, USA: Duke University Press.

Ballard, Roger.(1994) *DeshPradesh. The South Asian Presence in Britain,* London: Hurst.

Banerjee, Biswajit and J B Knight. (1985). 'Caste Discrimination in Indian Urban Labour Market', *Journal of Developing Economics.*

Basu, A.M. (1988). "How economic development can overcome culture: demographic change in Punjab, India", *Population Research and Policy Review*, 7: 29-48.

Baubock, Rainer.(1994). *Transnational Citizenship: Membership and Rights in International Migration,* Aldershot: Edward Elgar Publishing.

Bennett GCJ. (1990).Getting through to the abused elderly.*Geriatric Medicine*.20 (8), 255.

Bhachu, Parminder. (1999). Multiple migrants and cultural reproduction and transformations among British Punjabi Women. In Carla Petievich, (ed.) *The Expanding Landscape: South Asians and the Diaspora.* New Delhi: Manohar Publication.

Bhardwaj, P.A. Khwaja, and A Mian.(2008). "The Big March: Migratory Flows after Partition of British India".*Economic and Political Weekly* 43(35):39-49.

Bischoft, Henry.(200). *Immigration Issues*. Westport, CT: Greenwood Press.

Bose, A.B and K.D. Gangrade, (Eds.), (1988). *Ageing in India: problems and potentialities, Citizenship Development Society*, Abhinav Publications, New Delhi.

Brah, Avtar. (2001). Women of South Asian Origin in Britain: Issues and Concern. *Journal of South Asian Studies,* Cambridge University Press.

Bridge, Carl and Kent Fedorowich (Eds) (2003) *The British world: diaspora, culture, and Identity,* London: Frank Cass.

Brown, Stuart S.(2006). "Can Remittances spur development? A Crittical Survey. *International Studies Review.8(1):55-75.*

Buchbinder E. and Winterstein T. (2003) "Like a wounded bird": Older battered women's life experiences with intimate violence. *Journal of Elder Abuse and Neglect*, 15 (2), 23–44.

Castles, Stepher, and Mark J. Miller.(2003). *The Age of Migration:International Population Movement Modern World.* New York: Guilford Press.

Chandan, Amarjit. (1986*). Indians in Britain*, New Delhi: Sterling Publishers.

Chokkanathan S Lee, Alex EY. (2006*). Elder mistreatment in urban India:* A Community based Study. J Elder Abuse Neglect. 17:45-61.

Clarke, Colin G. (1986). *East Indians in a West Indian Town. San Fernando, Trinidad, 1930-70*, London, Allen and Unwin.

Cohen, Robin. (1994). *Frontiers of identity: the British and the Others,* London: Longman.

Cooper C, Selwood A, Livingston G. (2008). The prevalence of elder abuse and neglect: a systematic review. *Age and Ageing*. 37, 151-160.

Coward, Harold; Hinnells, John; Williams, Raymond Brady (eds.) (2000) *The South Asian Religious Diaspora in Britain, Canada, and the United States*, New York, p.301.

Cumming, E., and Harry, S. (1960). Disengagement: A Tentative theory of ageing. *Sociometry,* 23, 23 – 35.

Cumming, E., and Henry, W.F. (1961).*Growing old.* New York: Basic Books.

De Haas, Hein.(2005). "International Migration, Remittances and Development: Myth and Facts". *Third World Quarterly.*26(8):1269-1284.

Dhaliwal, A. K. (1994). "Introduction: The Traveling Nation: India and its Diaspora", in: *Socialist Review*, 24, (40), 1-11.

Dhindsa, K.S. (1998). *Indian Immigrants in United Kingdom: A Socio-Economic Analysis*. Concept Publishing Company, New Delhi.

Dirk, N.B. (1989a). The invention of caste.Civil Society in colonial India, *Special Issue Series.*

Dumont, L.(1998). *Homo Hierarchicus: The Caste System and Its Implications*. Translated by Mark Sainsury, Louis Dumont, and Basia Gulati. Delhi: Oxford University Press.

Dusenbery, Verne A. (1995). 'A Sikh diaspora' in Peter van der Veer (Eds.) Nation and migration: the politics of space in the South Asian diaspora, Philadelphia: University of Pennsylvania Press, 17–42.

Dutta, E. (1989). Growing old in young India. Sunday Review, *The Times of India*, Sept 17.

Dyson, T. and Moore, M. (1983)."On Kinship Structure, Female Autonomy and Demographic Behavior in India", *Population and Development Review*, Vol 9: 35-60.

Ebrahim, Shah(2002). Ageing, health and Society,*International Journal of Epidemiology*, 31 (4): 715-718.

Engelhardt, Gary, V; and Jonathan Gruber.(2004). Social Security and the evolution of elderly poverty. NBER working Paper, No. 10466. Cambridge Massachusetts: National Bureau of Economic Research. May.

Erikson, E.H. (1982). *The life cycle completed*: A Review. New York: Norton Press.

Frmby,W.A.(1992). "Should elder abuse be decriminalized? A Justice System perspective". *Journal of Elder Abuse and Neglect,* 4(4):121-30.

Gibson, Margaret A. (1988). Accommodation without Assimilation: Sikh Immigrants in an American High School, Ithaca. London: Cornell University Press.

Gill, S.S., Singh, S. and Brar, S. (2012).*Social Security Schemes in Punjab*: A Blend of State and Central Schemes, Hivios Knowledge Programme, Centre for Development Studies, Trivandrum, and University of Amsterdam, Amsterdam.

Gillion, K. L. (1962).*Fiji's Indian Migrants. A History to the End of Indenture in 1920,* Melbourne: Oxford University Press.

Ghosh, Amitav (1989)."*The Diaspora in Indian Culture*", in: Public Culture.2 (1), 73-78.

Goldberg, D.P., B. Blackwell. (1970). Psychiatric illness in general practice. A detailed study using a new method of case identification, *British Medical Journal*, 1(1), 439-443.

Gonzales Jr., Juan L. (1990). The Settlement of Sikh Farmers in the Sacramento Valley of California: 1904-1964. In Mahine Gosine (Eds.) Dot-Headed Americans: The Silent Minority in the United States. New York: Windsor Press.

Government of India (GoI). (2009). Citizen Centric Administration: 12th Report, Department of Administrative Reforms and Publications, Ministry of Personnel, PG and Pensions, New Delhi.

Government of India (GoI).(2013). Report of the Committee for Evolving A Composite Development Index of States, September, Ministry of Finance, New Delhi.

Government of Punjab.(2013). Punjab Health System Corporation.

Grover, I., and Grover, D.K. (1987).Aged in comparative global perspective. In M.K. Sharma and T.M Dak (Eds.*). Ageing in India*: Challenge to the society. New Delhi: Ajantha Publications.

Gupta, D.(2004). *Caste in Question; Identify or Hierarchy*? Delhi: Sage.

Haberman, Clyde. (2006). "But in London the Foreigners Are US". *New York Time* (9 May): A 23.

Hagen, Jonas. (2005). "Migration *and Remittances*". UN Chronicle 42(4):12.

Hall, K.D. (2002). Lives in translation: Sikh youth as British citizens. Philadelphia: University of Pennsylvania Press.

Hall, K.D. (2004). The ethnography of imagined communities: The cultural production of Sikh ethnicity in Britain. The annals of the American Academy of Political and Social Science, 595: 108-120.

Harding, T. (Eds). (2004). *Hidden Voices: Older people's experience of abuse*. London, Action on Elder Abuse and Help the Aged.

Havighurst, R.J. (1961). Successful ageing. *The Gerontologist*, 1, 8-13.

Helweg, Arthur W. (1979).*Sikhs in England: the development of a migrant community,* Delhi: Oxford University Press.

Hindustan Times. (2013). Old age pension: HC Gives Punjab 3 months to probe anomalies. July 4, Chandigarh Edition.

Hindustan Times. (2013a). Police fail to act rapidly on rapid response system. October 15, Jalandhar Edition.

Hou, Xiaohui, and Palacios, Robert. (2010). "Hospitalization Pattern in RSBY: Preliminary Evidences from MIS", Working Paper No-6, October, South Asia Development Department, the World Bank.

Jacobsen, Knut A., Kumar, Pratap. (Eds.) (2004). *South Asians in the Diaspora.Histories and Religious Traditions*, Leiden, Brill.

Jain, Ravindra K. (1997). "A Civilizational Theory of Indian Diaspora and its Global Implications".*The Eastern Anthropologist*, 50, 3-4, 347-355.

Jodhka, Surinder S. (2001). 'Caste in the Periphery' Seminar, No. 508, special issue on Exclusion, symposium on caste race and dalit question, pp. 41-46.

____________ (2002).'Caste and Untouchability in Rural Punjab', *Economic and Political Weekly*, 37(19), 1813- 1823.

____________ (2004). 'Dissociation, Distancing and Autonomy: Caste and Untouchability in Rural Punjab' in Harish K Puri (Eds), Dalits in Regional Context, New Delhi, Rawat Publications.

____________ (2004) 'Sikhism and the caste question: Dalits and their politics in contemporary Punjab' in Jodhka S.S and P. Louis (2003) 'Caste Tensions in Punjab: Talhan and Beyond' *Economic and Political Weekly*, 38(28), 2923-2926.

Jodhka, Surinder, and Kumar Avinash, (2007) 'Internal Classification of the Scheduled Castes: The Punjab Story', *Economic and Political Weekly*, 42(43), 20-23.

Judge, P.S., (1997) *'Emerging trends in the Caste Structure of Punjab'*, The Administrator, Vol. 42, January-March, pp. 55-65.

Johnston, Hugh. (1989). *The Voyage of Komagata Maru: The Sikh Challenge to Canada's Colour Bar.* London: Oxford University Press.

Jones, Catherine. (1977). *Immigration and Social Policy in Britain. London*: Tavistock Publications.

Kalsi,S.S.(1989). "The Sikhs and Caste: A Study of Sikh Community in Leeds and Bradford". Unpublished Doctoral dissertation, University of Leeds.

Khatri.(2008, December).Elderly Abuse, In Info change human right news and analysis a social justice and development issues in India, www.Infochangeindia.org.

Kidwell, I.J; and Booth, a (1977). Social distance and international relations, *Gerontologists,* 17(5):412-420.

Kolker, Carlyn.(2004). "Touching the Untouchables". *American Lawyers,* 26(12):26-29.

Koser, Khalid. (2007*). International Migration: A Very Short Introduction*, Oxford: Oxford University Press.

Knott, Kim (1988). "Strategies for Survival among South Asian Religions in Britain: Parallel Developments, Conflict, and Cooperation", In: Conflict and Cooperation between Contemporary Religious Groups, hg. Von Chuo Academic Research Institute, International Symposium Proceedings, Tokyo.

Lal, Brij V. (2006).*The Encyclopedia of the Indian Diaspora, Singapore, Kuala Lumpur*, Paris: Editions Didier Millet.

Lawton, M.P. and Brody, E.M. (1969)."Assessment of older people: Self-maintaining and instrumental activities of daily living," *The Gerontologist*, 9(3), 179-186.

Lawton, U., and Gottesman, M. (1974).Ageing Successfully, New York: Columbia University Press.

Leung, A; Y.H. Lui and I. Chi.(2005). Later life learning experience among Chinese elderly in Hong Kong, *Gerontology and Geriatrics Education*, 26(2):1-15.

Llyod-Sherlock, Peter.(2006). Identifying vulnerable older people: Insights from Thailand, *Ageing and Society*, 26(1):81-103.

Mahal, Ajay. (2006). Health expenditures on the elderly in India and their financial future prospects.May.Unpublished.

Martin P., Hagberg B. and Poon L.W. (1997). Predictors of loneliness in centenarians: A parallel study. *Journal of Cross Cultural Gerontology*, 12, 203–224.

Mehta, Rajput. (2000). "Exploitation and neglect are indicators of abuse". *The Times of India*, Jan15.

Mitra, Sumit.(1998). "Old Parents unlovingly yours". *India Today,* July 13.

McGreevey J.F. (2004) Elder abuse: The physician's perspective. *Clinical Gerontologist*, 28(1), 83–103.

Mishra, S. (1987).*Social Adjustment in Old Age*. Delhi: B.R. Publishing Corporation.

Mohan Pai, (2002). *The Elderly,* Bangalore: Om Ashram trust Publications.

Montminy L. (2005). Older women's experiences of psychological violence in their marital relationships. *Journal of Gerontological Social Work*, 46(2), 3–21.

Nanda, A. K., Bansal, S. and Singh, M.M. (2011). "*Evaluation of Selected Social Security Schemes in Punjab*," Unpublished Report, Centre for Research in Rural and Industrial Development, Chandigarh.

Office of Registrar General and Census Commissioner, India. (ORGI). (2006). Report of the Technical Group on Population Projection India and States 2001-2021, New Delhi.

Ogg, J. (1993). Researching elder abuse in Britain, *Journal of Elder Abuse and Neglect*, 5(2):37-54.

O'Keeffe M, Hills A, Doyle M et al. (2007) *UK Study of Abuse and Neglect of Older People: Prevalence Study Report*. National Centre for Social Research.

Oonk, G. (Eds.) (2007). *Global Indian Diasporas.Exploring Trajectories of Migration and Theory*, Amsterdam: Amsterdam University Press for IJAS.

Orozco, Manuel.(2002). "Globalisation and Migration: The Impact of Family Remittances in Latin America".*Latin American Politics and Society*, 44(2):41.

Palmore, E. (1969). Sociological aspect of ageing; In E.W. Busse and, E. Pfeiffer (Eds.). Behaviour and adaptation in later life.Boston: Little Brown and Comp.

Paul, Sumita. (1998). "With a little help from friends "*The Sunday Times of India*, April 5.

Phillips, L.R.(1983). Abuse and neglect of the frail elderly at home: An exploration of theoretical relationships, *Journal of Advanced Nursing*, 8(5):379-392.

Rajan, I.S., and Mishra, U.S. (1995).Defining old age: An Indian Assessment. Bold, 5, 4, 31- 35.

Peter Vander Veer. (1995). "Introduction: The Diasporic Imagination," in Peter Vander Veer (Eds), *Nation and Migration: The politics of Space in the South Asian Diaspora*, Philadelphia: University of Pennsylvania.

Rajan, I. S., U. S. Mishra, and P. S. Sarma.(1999).*India's Elderly: burden or challenge*? Sage Publications, New Delhi.

Ram, Sodhi. (1986). *Indian Immigrants in Great Britain*. New Delhi: D.K. Publication.

Ram, Ronki. (2007) 'Social Catastrophe in the Making: Religion, Deras, and Dalits in Punjab, available at http: // www. ambedkartimes. com / ronkiram % 20page % 201. htm # social.

____________(2007). 'Social Exclusion, Resistance, and Deras: exploring myth of casteless society in Punjab', *Economic and Political Weekly*, 42(40), 4066-74.

Robin Cohen.(1997). *Global Diaspora:* An Introduction, Seattle: University of Washington Press.

Ruth, J. E., Obergi, P., Mattlar, C. E. Sandahl, C. (1990). Old age and loneliness illustrated by the Zulliger, *British Journal of Projective Psychology*.35, 61–73.

Ryan, M. C. and Patterson, J. (1987). Loneliness in the elderly, *Journal of Gerontological Nursing* 13: 6–12.

Sadananda, Sahoo, Pattanaik, B.K.(2013). *Global Diaspora and Development: Socioeconomic, cultural, and Policy Perspective,* Springer.

Schofield MJ, Reynolds R, Mishra GD, et al.(2002)Screening for vulnerability to abuse among older women: Women's Health Australia Study. *Gerontology*.21, 24-25. Sahoo, Ajaya Kumar and C.S. Bhat.(2003). Transnational Network among Punjabi and Gujarati Diasporas in the USA.In R. Gopa Kumar (ed.) Indian Diaspora and Giving Patterns of Indian Americans in USA. New Delhi: CAF India.

Schmidt, J.F. (1951). Patterns of Poor adjustment in old age.*The American Journal of Sociology*, 17, 33–42.

Schieber, George and Akiko Maeda.(1999). Health care financing and delivery in developing countries, *Health Affairs* 8(3):193-205.

Sell, H. and Nagpal, R. (1992). *"Assessment of Subjective Well-Being:* The Subjective Well-Being Inventory", Regional Health Paper, SEARO, No. 24, World Health Organization, Regional Office for South-East Asia, New Delhi.

Shah, Ghanshyam (1998): 'Caste and Untouchability: Theory and Practice', paper presented at seminar' Ambedkar in Retrospect', Jawaharlal Nehru University, Delhi.

Sharma, Neeru. (2012). "Caste in Punjab: Political Marginalization and Cultural Assertion of Scheduled Castes in Punjab". *Journal of Asian Studies* 67:1341-1364.

Shields; L.B., Hunsaker, D.M. and Hunsaker, J.C. (2004). Abuse and neglect: a ten-year review of mortality and morbidity in our elders in a large metropolitan area, *Journal of Forensic Science*, 49 (1) 122-7.

Shuval, J.T.(2010). Diaspora Migration: Definitional ambiguities and a theoretical Paradigm. *International Migration*. 38(5):41-56.

Singh, Pashaura and N. Gerald Barrier (Eds.) (1996).*The Transmission of Sikh identity in the Diaspora.* New Delhi: Manohar Publication.

Singh, Pashaura and N. Gerald Barrier. (1999). *Sikh Identity: Continuity and Change*. New Delhi: Manohar Publications.

Singh, Pritam, and Shinder Singh Thandi.(1999). *Punjabi Identity in a Global Context*. New Delhi: Oxford University Press.

Singh, Kesar, and Paramvir Singh. (2011). "Impact Assessment of MGNREGA in Punjab", Unpublished Report. Centre for Research in Rural and Industrial Development, Chandigarh.

Tatla, Darshan Singh. (1999). The Sikh diaspora: the search for statehood. UCL Press, London.

Tatla, Darshna Singh. (1995). Sikh Free and Military Migration During the Colonial Period. In Robin Cohen (Eds). *The Cambridge Survey of World Migration*. Cambridge: Cambridge University Press.

Tinker, Hugh (1974).*A New System of Slavery. The Export of Indian Labour Overseas 1830-1920*, London: Oxford University Press.

__________(1977). *The Banyan Tree: Overseas Emigrants from India, Pakistan, and Bangladesh*, Oxford: Oxford University Press.

United Kingdom. (1999). *With respect to old age long term care – Rights and Responsibilities*: A Report by the Royal Commission long term, Chairman Professor Sir Stewart Sutherland. Cm 4192-1 March London: The Stationary Office.

United Nations (1997b). Report on the world social situations. Sales no.E.96.IV 1 and corrigenda.

United Nations. (1999). Living conditions of low-income older persons in human settlements. HS/758/O5E.

United Nations (2002). Elder abuse widespread and unprotected – says New Report by Secretary General. Report presented at the Second World Assembly on Ageing. Madrid, Spain.

United Nations.(2005b). Living Arrangements of Older Persons around the World.Sales No.E.0.5.XII.9.

United Nations.(2009).Population Ageing and Development, 2009, Datasheet, United Nations, Department of Economic and Social Affairs, Population Division.

United Nations (2010). World Population Prospects, 2010 Revision, United Nations, Department of Economic and Social Affairs, Population Division, Population Estimates and Projections Section, accessed on 28 October 2011: http://esa.un.org/unpd/wpp/unpp/panel indicators. htm.

United Nations. (2013). "*World Population Prospects*: The 2012 Revision", Population Division of the Department of Economic and Social Affairs of the United Nations Secretariat, New York http://esa. un.org/unpd/wpp/index.htm.

Ushasree, S and S. Azmal Basha.(1999). Domestic abuse among the elderly,*Indian Journal of Gerontology*,13(3 and 4):99-104.

Vedgama, Kusoom. (1984). *Indians in Britain: The Indian Contribution to British Way of Life*. London: Robert Royce Ltd.

Verma, C.D. (1996). " Unwanted both by Kin and Society, *The Hindustan Times*, June 9.

Vertovec, Steven (Eds.) (1991). *Aspects of South Asian Diaspora*, Delhi: Oxford University Press, Papers on India, 2(2).

__________ (Eds.) (1991).*Aspects of South Asian Diaspora*, Delhi: Oxford University Press.

Kumar, Vivek.(2004). Understanding Dalit Diaspora.*Economic and Political Weekly*,39 (1): 114-116.

Walton-Roberts, M. (2003). "Transnational geographies: Indian immigration to Canada." *The Canadian Geographer,* 47(3), 235-250.

Weil, David N. (1994). The saving of the elderly in micro and macro data, *Quarterly Journal of Economics*, 109 (1):523-552.

Weiss, R. S. (1973). *Loneliness: The experience of emotional and social isolation*. Cambridge, MA: The MIT Press.

William Safran. (1991). "Diasporas in Modern Societies: Myths of Homeland and Return", *A Journal of Transnational Studies*, 1(1), 83-99.

William, Safran. (2009). The Diaspora and the Homelands, Reciprocities, Transformations and Role Reversals, in Eliezer Ben-Rafael et.al (eds.) *Transnationalism: Diasporas and the advent of a new* (dis)order (Series editor-Mehdi P Aminesh), Netherlands: Brill.

Young Robert, J.C.(2001). Postcolonialism: am Introduction. Oxford Blackwell.

_______________.(2005). Colonial Desire: Hybridity in Theory,Culture and Race, New York: Routledge.

Zepelin, H; Sills, R.A; and Health, M.W.(1986). Is age becoming irrelevant? An exploratory study of perceived age norm, *International Journal of ageing and Human Development*, 24 (4):241-256.

# Index